THE POWER of ONE

Printed in Victoria, Canada

Note for Librarians: a cataloguing record for this book that includes Dewey Classification and US Library of Congress numbers is available from the National Library of Canada. The complete cataloguing record can be obtained from the National Library's online database at: www.nlc-bnc.ca/amicus/index-e.html
ISBN 1-4120-1121-3

TRAFFORD

This book was published *on-demand* in cooperation with Trafford Publishing.
On-demand publishing is a unique process and service of making a book available for retail sale to the public taking advantage of on-demand manufacturing and Internet marketing. **On-demand publishing** includes promotions, retail sales, manufacturing, order fulfilment, accounting and collecting royalties on behalf of the author.

Suite 6E, 2333 Government St., Victoria, B.C. V8T 4P4, CANADA

Phone	250-383-6864	Toll-free	1-888-232-4444 (Canada & US)
Fax	250-383-6804	E-mail	sales@trafford.com
Web site	www.trafford.com	TRAFFORD PUBLISHING IS A DIVISION OF TRAFFORD HOLDINGS LTD.	
Trafford Catalogue #03-1500		www.trafford.com/robots/03-1500.html	

10   9   8   7   6   5   4   3   2   1

The Penn State eBusiness Research Center

THE POWER
of ONE
Gaining Business Value
from Personalization
Technologies

Nirmal Pal and Arvind Rangaswamy

From the eBRC Press at Penn State University

To our eBRC corporate sponsors for their financial and non-financial support – IBM, Unisys, Xerox, AT&T Wireless, SAP AG, Delphi Ventures, Cigna, Tyco, and HP.

- Nirmal Pal and
Arvind Rangaswamy

To the girls in our lives:

My wife, Mitra, my daughters, Neela and Nupur, and my grand daughter, Nina.

- Nirmal Pal

My wife, Ann, and daughter Cara.

- Arvind Rangaswamy

Table of Contents

Acknowledgments

Two years ago, our research center hosted a think-tank type workshop on Personalization, to which we invited thought leaders in academia and industry to share their experiences and insights on this important and growing area of e-Business. What resulted was a workshop that every participant felt was a truly rewarding experience. People came to the workshop with very different perspectives, but left with an emergent and coherent picture of the opportunities and challenges of conceiving and implementing technology-enabled personalization initiatives within organizations. In some sense, each participant brought a bucket of paint of one color, and left with a multi-colored canvas that had the beginnings of a great painting.

As the presentations and discussions unfolded at the workshop, we realized that it would be useful to capture the lessons and insights in the form of a book that could benefit many others who were not present at the workshop. We produced this book with contributions from the presenters at the workshop. We are grateful to them for agreeing to contribute chapters to this book – without too much arm-twisting!

Convincing our contributing authors was the easy part. Convincing book publishers was much harder. The past two years have been rough for most sectors of the economy, and they have been particularly harsh for books on e-Business. The publishers kept telling us there is no market for another book on e-Business, even though we tried our best to convince them that the Internet, e-Business, and Personalization will continue to profoundly transform the business landscape for years to come, and that our book provides the first detailed exploration of the personalization topic. Eventually, we decided to publish the book ourselves, with the expectation that our readers will prove the publishers wrong. Our authors deserve another round of thanks – this time for their patience during the long and tedious process of negotiating with publishers. We hope that they, and you the reader, will find this book well worth this struggle and wait.

We thank Ray Liddick and Danielle Wolfe for preparing the print-ready version of the manuscript and for the cover design, and Tim Holsopple for copy editing and indexing.

Finally, we thank all our colleagues at the Penn State eBusiness Research Center (visit us at www.ebrc.org), including our student interns, graduate research assistants, and our support staff for their help, support, and enthusiasm.

Nirmal Pal and Arvind Rangaswamy
University Park, July 2003

Introduction

Gaining Business Value from Personalization Technologies

Arvind Rangaswamy, Jonas H. Anchel Professor of Marketing and
    Research Director, eBusiness Research Center, Penn State
    University

Nirmal Pal, Executive Director, eBusiness Research Center, Penn
    State University

The engines of the industrial revolution were factories
that used mass production technologies to dramatically
increase efficiency in the production of goods. Over time,
mass production was combined with mass marketing
using mass media, starting with newspapers, then radio,
followed by television, direct mail, and telemarketing.
The resulting economic system relied heavily on
forecasting aggregate needs and then using factories to
produce large quantities of items for inventory based on
those forecasts. While this system has evolved to deliver
many varieties of products (for example, over 150 models
of cars and over 100 varieties of detergents), it is not
really designed to satisfy the needs of any individual

fully, because there is a fundamental asymmetry between production and consumption: production efficiency is maximized through economies of scale, i.e., producing large quantities of single items; on the other hand, consumption value is maximized by catering to individual needs, one customer at a time.

In recent years, technologies such as mass customization and personalization have emerged to provide firms with the ability to alter this asymmetry. In particular, personalization technologies enable firms to treat each customer as a unique person and serve their possibly unique needs. Customers are no longer anonymous members of some hypothetical groups that marketers term market segments. Today, many customers already benefit from various personalization initiatives that firms have undertaken. Consider the following:

- Women, or for that matter, men, can create their own signature lipstick and eye shadow at www.reflect.com, choosing from several product options and colors provided at the site.
- When you call Fidelity Investments, your call is routed to the most appropriate service representative based on your customer status (e.g., level or type of investments you have with the company) and the kinds of questions/issues you may have.
- At eBay.com, you can set up your own page, my eBay, where you can track the items on which you are bidding, the items you have won or lost in the past month, and access the complete history of your transactions as an eBay seller.
- You can set up your travel preferences at travelocity.com (e.g., preferred departure city, seat and meal preference, frequent flier numbers, etc.) so that when you book an airline ticket, those preferences are automatically applied to a reservation when applicable.
- When you visit the Lands' End Web site, the company extrapolates, based on what you do at the site, the colors you are unlikely to choose at all. When you then shop for other items of clothing, the colors that will appeal to you the most are shown first.

These are examples of personalization programs that have become economically feasible because of recent developments in e-business technologies. All indications are that new personalization initiatives will continue to be developed and deployed even during the current economic downturn. It is just a matter of time before Web sites become smart enough to adapt to your needs by presenting the information and navigation paths most relevant to you. Likewise, it is only a matter of time before Web sites are used more extensively to help you create food products designed just for you (both in terms of taste and nutritional content) and personalized medications (e.g., vitamins).

In this book, we have brought together thought leaders in academia and practice who have had considerable experience in thinking about, and implementing, various personalization programs. The result is a book that gives you a panoramic view of the continuing developments in this area. The various chapters in the book cover the "what," the "why," and the "how," as well as potential impact of personalization on business performance. By reading this book carefully, the reader should benefit in the following ways:

- Understand the role of personalization in differentiating the company from competitors by better serving existing and potential customers.
- Recognize the hidden dangers of personalization – avoiding those programs that serve customers well, but put the company out of business.
- Learn about the key opportunities and challenges in developing and implementing a strategy for personalization for your organization.
- Identify ways to measure the impact of personalization programs and articulate the value of the program to employees and management.

Our hope is that you, the reader, will have a feast of ideas to digest, as well as a long list of action items for implementing personalization initiatives within your organization.

True personalization is more than skin deep. It is more than just recognizing customers and greeting them by their names. It is more than just identifying and rewarding loyal customers. It involves rethinking the very basis of how organizational resources, processes, and customer offerings are configured to best cater to the needs of customers, one at a time. In some sense, if a firm is fully personalized, it "rents" out to customers just the right set of its assets for just the right amount to serve their individual needs. Personalization is really a way of co-creating, with your customers, a highly rewarding experience for them in purchasing and using a product or a service.

Benefits of Personalization

It is clear that good personalization programs can benefit customers. But how do these programs benefit companies? There are at least three major ways that companies benefit:

1. *Integrating customer and company systems:* Personalization provides the rationale for integrating e-business initiatives across

the Internet, Intranet, and Extranet as shown in Figure 1. With personalization, customer choices made at a Web site (Internet) trigger internal activities on the Intranet (e.g., inventory coordination across various divisions of the company), which in turn can trigger additional processes on the Extranet (e.g., order placement with suppliers). Likewise, ability to individually recognize the customer who makes a support request at a Web site, or at a call center, can trigger activities within an organization to send a replacement part, which in turn can trigger a product review with a supplier. Such market-facing integration of activities across various e-business systems within an organization provides the basis for developing a tightly knit, high-performance, real-time business. In our view, any other rationale for integration (e.g., process efficiencies) is a weaker basis than using personalization because the other rationales are not directly driven by customer demand.

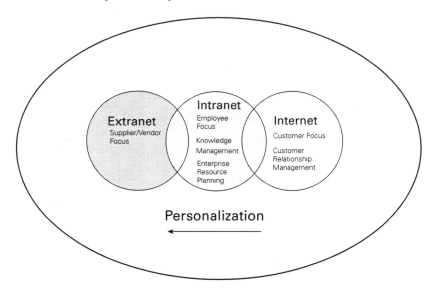

Figure 1. Personalization offers a strategic basis for the firm to integrate its Internet, Intranet, and Extranet.

2. *Meeting customer needs more effectively:* Personalization initiatives improve the effectiveness of the company in meeting customer needs uniquely. Just as Dell is able to custom-configure commodity components into a high-quality computer, other companies can also use personalization strategies to create competitively inimitable offerings from imitable commodities. Thus, personalization strategies offer the potential to differentiate the company from competitors.

3. *Improving efficiency:* Finally, personalization can improve the efficiency of company operations. When products are made to order, or when customer queries are directed to the right person, or when the customer can be offered a self-service environment for routine service issues, or when employees are better able to access organizational resources based on their "role-defined" needs, there is less wasted effort within the organization. For example, made-to-order products require lower inventory, have lower levels of accounts receivables, and generate higher return on invested capital (ROIC), all of which contribute to creating a highly efficient organization.

Personalizing Your Reading Experience

We have organized the chapters in the book to cover strategic issues first, before moving on to tactical issues. The first five chapters address strategic aspects of personalization, i.e., the "what" and the "why" of personalization. The remaining six chapters address the "how" of personalization, including the associated challenges of maintaining privacy and security in personalization efforts. The last four chapters (Chapters 7 – 11) explore important technical considerations in implementing personalization strategies. Each chapter is self-contained, so they can be read in any sequence:

Chapter 1: Business Imperatives of Personalization

Kirk Rothrock and Nirmal Pal present a set of frameworks for senior managers to help determine personalization opportunities and initiatives to pursue that will generate high levels of customer acceptance and maximize the financial returns for the organization. They use examples of personalization from many industries to illustrate possibilities for personalization in products, services, advertising, business-to-business interactions, and other areas.

Chapter 2: From Many to One: Personalized Product Fulfillment Systems

The potential for personalization is much deeper than Web site design. Arvind Rangaswamy and Anant Balakrishnan examine how product fulfillment systems have to be redesigned to deliver personalized products to customers, especially in the case of non-digital products. They contend that firms must use personalization as a business strategy for matching their resources and capabilities to the specific needs of each of their customers. The authors address various issues that companies must address in developing such product fulfillment systems, which are already emerging in many economic sectors. The authors conclude that eventually the World Wide Web will transform into a personal medium through which customers will obtain personalized access to the vast productive resources of the global economy.

Chapter 3: Personalization in the Wireless World

With wireless technology that allows firms and companies to know where their customers are and communicate with them anywhere, managers can tailor offerings not only to customer preferences but also to their geography. Bruce D. Weinberg, Judy Cavalieri, and Terry Madonia point out the wireless world offers customers greater and faster access to need-satisfying solutions and offers providers more touchpoints to deliver highly valued personalized solutions. To effectively implement personalization with wireless technologies, firms must have the capabilities to recognize a customer's situation-specific needs and preferences, and have processes in place for satisfying these needs, including treating the customer as he or she would like to be treated through pre-defined preferences.

Chapter 4: Beyond Personalization: Experience Architecture

John Adcox and Mike Wittenstein bemoan how traditional personalization strategies and tactics such as junk mail have become tools for marketers to find customers that fit the needs of the enterprise, rather than tools for shaping the enterprise to fit the needs of the customers. The authors urge companies to view personalization in terms of what firms can do for customers, not what they can do to them. They propose the concept of "experience architecture" to realize this new vision for personalization. Using many examples, they describe how experience architects working in marketing, operations, technology, research, human resources, and at the executive levels can craft meaningful and unique experiences for customers to enjoy and appreciate. Experience architecture isn't about a quick fix; it's about creating true and lasting value for customers, a more inspiring environment for employees, and in the end, greater returns for the shareholder.

Chapter 5: Personalization of Global Sales and Marketing Activities in the Digital Economy: A Strategic Perspective

Venkatesh Shankar and Mary P. Donato bring both academic and industry perspectives to the issue of developing strategies for personalization of global sales and marketing initiatives. They focus on sales and marketing actions that tailor a company's Web site to the different needs of users or groups of users around the world, and develop a strategic framework to guide the formulation of personalization strategies in global sales and marketing organizations. To help managers apply this framework, they develop a checklist of questions to explore, ranging from understanding the value added through personalization to the metrics used to monitor and evaluate personalization initiatives.

Chapter 6: Learning About Customers Without Asking

Customers don't always want to have to tell you their life stories or fill out extensive questionnaires to get more personalized services. How can you find out about your customers without being so intrusive? Alan L. Montgomery and Kannan Srinivasan describe the innumerable opportunities available online for companies to learn about their customers. The authors explore the potential of passive learning, whereby companies can learn by directly observing the online activities and choices of consumers. The authors examine techniques such as user profiling, collaborative filtering, path analysis, and conjoint analysis that can be used to extract knowledge from clickstream data, cookies, and e-mail responses. With such knowledge, companies can direct their valuable resources to creating more personalized environments for consumers, which results in higher value for customers, and more loyal and profitable customers for the companies.

Chapter 7: Personalized Product Presentation: The Influence of Electronic Recommendation Agents on Consumer Choice

How do online recommendations by electronic agents or personalized product offerings on Web sites affect consumer purchase decisions? Gerald Häubl, Kyle Murray, and Valerie Trifts explore the consequences of online stores being able to configure the products they present to suit each customer's preferences. Without the constraints on space and organization faced by bricks-and-mortar stores, online stores can endlessly rearrange the way they present their products, but they need to be aware of the cognitive limitations of their customers. The authors report on their empirical studies, which show that online stores could use electronic recommendation agents to help their customers make good decisions with low effort. The authors also discuss how configuring the choice environment can influence the choices that customers make.

Chapter 8: Personalizing Your Web Site: A How-to Guide

Personalizing Web sites is not a simple matter. Anindya Datta, Helen Thomas, and Debra VanderMeer examine the complex interplay between available technologies and business needs that firms should take into account in thinking about the architecture and design of Web sites for personalization. Web designers typically adopt a layered design, which has at its core a set of dynamic scripting technologies that generate HTML pages in response to user requests. Personalization schemes based on collaborative and rule-based filtering are sophisticated, but require specialized and costly software. The authors also describe new technologies such as content caching and dynamic page-assembly, and offer some guidelines for managers to choose the most effective solutions.

Chapter 9: Modeling and Personalization of Users

Companies use models of users to personalize their online offerings, but they face the challenge of selecting appropriate models and then fitting specific customers to them. Eren Manavoglu, Lee Giles, Amanda Spink, and James Z. Wang examine strategies for these models, which are representations of all the properties of a user that may be relevant to his or her behavior in the system. This chapter offers different implementations of user modeling systems in different applications. The right model and inference methodologies depends on the nature of the application.

Chapter 10: Technological Aspects of Privacy and Security for Personalization

Privacy is a central challenge in personalization. Ingemar J. Cox, David M. Pennock, and Eric J. Glover note that the relationship between a Web site and its users is fragile, and can be easily damaged through privacy or security infringements. They examine the advantages and disadvantages of different identification technologies from a business perspective. The appropriateness of these technologies depends on what implicit information is available to the server and the consequences of incorrect identification.

Chapter 11: The Role of Privacy in the New Reality

In the concluding chapter, Thomas Summerlin and John W. Bagby offer broader perspectives on strategies for addressing privacy concerns. Balancing the customer need for privacy with the business need for information is critical to successful personalization. As the authors write, "On the continuum between personalization and privacy, where one stops and the other begins will vary by individual. If it's information that I want tailored to me, it's personalization, but if it's something I don't want tailored to me, it's a privacy problem." The privacy balance must be addressed by society as a whole because privacy for some, and not for all, is untenable. Also, the events of September 11, 2001 could alter the balance inexorably, because they have brought the privacy issue into public debate.

The chapters in this book offer multiple perspectives on the opportunities and challenges of personalization – from broad strategic and policy issues down to the brass tacks of Web site design and software architecture. It is clear that personalization has already had a big impact on business and promises to have an even greater impact in the future. Yet we are still in the very early stages of this revolution in personalization, and the preliminary experiments discussed in this volume probably represent the equivalent of Henry Ford's first assembly line in the evolution of mass production. There will be many opportunities for innovations and enhancements to personalization processes and strategies in the years ahead. We hope that the foundation offered in the following chapters will help readers and researchers in making these next-generation innovations.

1 Business Imperatives of Personalization

Kirk Rothrock, President, Intracorp, CIGNA Corporation

Nirmal Pal, Executive Director, eBusiness Research Center, Penn
State University

Since the emergence of mass production and mass markets,
companies have had to make tradeoffs between reaching
large markets with standard offerings at reasonable prices
and providing individualized products and services. While
Henry Ford put the automobile in the reach of the common
man, his idea of personalization was any color you want as
long as it is black. New technologies for personalization offer
the possibility of serving mass markets while efficiently
catering to individuals one at a time. The rapid growth of
e-business and related technologies are creating significant
opportunities for providers of goods and services to cater
to personal preferences, sometimes at a premium that
consumers are willing to pay, and for which consumers are

ready to part with personal information. As a result, we are witnessing a movement from mass marketing to micro marketing or one-to-one marketing.

In the wake of the dot-com debacle, it is fair to ask whether this move toward increased personalization is a fad propelled by the new technology that supports it, or a business shift driven by real value creation. What are the benefits of personalization for companies? In this chapter, we explore some of these benefits that make personalization an imperative for business.

What is Personalization and Why is it Important to Businesses?

The Personalization Consortium, an international advocacy group formed to promote the development and use of responsible one-to-one marketing technology and practices on the World Wide Web, uses the following definition that we can use as a reference.

> Personalization is the combined use of technology and customer information to tailor interactions between a business and each individual customer. Using information either previously obtained or provided in real time about the customer and other customers, the exchange between the parties is altered to fit that customer's stated needs so that the transaction requires less time and delivers a product best suited to that customer.

To include all aspects of the business impact of personalization, we extend the definition beyond the traditional business-to-individual-customer interaction. In any interaction between a business and individuals, the business has the opportunity to use the tools and technology available to tailor that interaction to best meet the needs of the individuals. Thus, the scope of personalization goes beyond the narrow definition of the consumer to all interactions between a business and its

- customers,
- suppliers,
- distributors,
- business partners,
- stockholders and other stakeholders, and
- employees.

Personalization can be defined as providing the right information to the right person at the right time. By using personalization, the firm can make efficient use of the time of its employees, partners, or customers to understand the value equation of each interaction and then cater to that mutually understood and agreed-upon value and thus significantly increase individuals' acceptance of the firm's products and services and satisfaction. An increase in product acceptance and customer satisfaction will directly contribute to increased sales, and using appropriate e-business processes and tools efficiently contributes to increased profit margins. Thus, business leaders are keenly interested in pursuing personalized relationships with all of their stakeholders as the tools for personalization become more prevalent in all aspects of the business.

In the past, firms gained efficiencies through mass production, in manufacturing or in communicating of information. The move to personalization implies greater customization, which translates to lower efficiency and potentially increased costs. These are issues of price elasticity: customers and stakeholders generally place a higher value on products and services that anticipate and meet their needs, but at some price level the cost of providing personalization exceeds their willingness to pay.

The challenge for the business leaders, then, is to determine when to use personalization and with what level of specificity, in order to determine a balance between value to the consumer and the cost of providing it, and between consumers' acceptance of personalized products and services and consumers' reluctance to share private information.

Industry Practices and Anecdotes

The Web and related technologies have brought about a revolution in the understanding of personal needs and wants, and then in the delivery of personalized information, products, and services to their customers. The frontier of this digital world is changing constantly. There is no best practices database to refer to, because best practices are just emerging.

In order to better understand the opportunities to increase the breadth and depth of personalization in business and to begin to understand the factors that determine its effectiveness, we can look at successful implementations of personalization in various industries.

We will then analyze these emerging best practices and build a management framework that business leaders can use in developing and prioritizing their personalization plans and initiatives. The basic premise of this framework will be as in Figure 1. Those initiatives that have high customer acceptance and return high business value are more desirable. We will have a detailed look into what constitutes high customer acceptance and high business value.

In the following discussions, we have given many and different examples of what we consider effective and successful implementations of

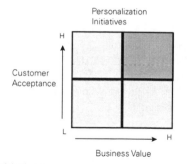

Figure 1. Personalization Initiatives

personalized products and services. We tried to capture many and varied examples from different industries as many of these best practices are applicable across industries.

Services

While discussing personalization in services, supermarket chains and airline companies come to mind right away. Supermarket chains created loyalty cards which are presented when shoppers pay for their goods. The cards allow the supermarkets to understand their individual customer's buying patterns and needs, and can use this information in many different ways to their advantage and offer personalized services to their customers. In return, customers can enjoy varying levels of automated discounts without suffering through the tedium of clipping out store coupons as in the past.

In the October, 2001 issue, *Business 2.0* talks about how technology advances have allowed coupon-king Valassis to quickly access and analyze loyalty card statistics it collects from supermarkets. It allows them to track the shopping preferences of 38 million households in 120,000 zones across the United States. They can perform pinpoint-targeted marketing of hot items to specific households in specific communities. What about the business benefits? Valassis increased its revenue 5.2 percent in the first three quarters of 2001 to $445 million, and its stock price went up to $35 in late August, 2001 from $20 in the fall of 2000.

Airlines, in a much similar way, started offering frequent-flyer mileage to their customers. They collect a lot of information about their customers and use this information to provide highly personalized services to their customers. Such programs are becoming more and more sophisticated with the passage of time and improvements in technology. American Airlines has over 40 million AAdvantage members from whom it constantly collects information through member profiles and click-stream data, and use these to tailor its offerings.

When one of us lived in Japan, I used United Airlines' Tokyo hub for all my trips to the USA and to other Asian countries. Obviously, United knew my seat and food preferences, and would often upgrade me to first class without even asking. But, what I liked most was that on almost in every flight the chief steward would come to my seat to greet me and ask me if I needed any services to make my flight more comfortable. United could do all that because of the knowledge it collected about me through its frequent-flyer program. I became so loyal to United Airlines that I rarely travelled by any other airline.

Hotel chains soon caught on to this scheme, and they were followed almost immediately by car rental companies. Those with gold card status at Hertz or similar status with other rental companies enjoy special privileges, such as having their preferred automobile waiting with the engine running and being dropped off by the courtesy van driver at exactly the right spot.

Many hotel chains started frequent-stayers programs to increase customer loyalty and satisfaction. The Hilton chain with its HHonors program is among the successful leaders for this program. While some hotel chains offer either air miles or hotel points, Hilton offers both. This also improves its partnership with the airlines, allowing for cooperative marketing programs. Hilton is also making good uses of technology to provide its guests with personalized experiences, so they will visit their property again and again. Its investments are paying off. Between October, 2000 and October, 2001, it has increased the size of participating hotels from 500 to over 2100. While more details of the return on its technology investments are not readily available, the payback is understood to be large.

Again, when one of us lived in Japan, I became a loyal customer of the Marriott Hotel in Hong Kong and the Sheraton Hotel in New Delhi. At both hotels, I could go straight to my hotel room without having to wait in the registration line, which is always a nuisance after a long flight, and someone would bring the registration form to my room. In New Delhi, the hotel provided free airport pick-up and drop-off service. It is not just discounts or free trips that win customers, it was this extra personalized service that made me visit these hotels repeatedly.

No discussions of personalized services would be complete without mention of Amazon.com. Amazon's much-publicized personalization scheme, in which it offers customers individualized book recommendations, is all about distribution. The manufacture of the product — the book or CD — is not altered. What is personalized is the manner in which customers search for, compare, and ultimately buy products.

Amazon is successful for two main reasons. First, you don't have to set up anything. The system keeps track of your buying records and thus learns about your preferences. Second, by analyzing the buyer's purchases the system learns which books are similar in content and then uses this information to make personalized recommendations. In addition, Amazon also uses the similarity data to provide hypertext links between related books.

One criticism of the current U.S. health care system is its fragmented approach to individual patient care, exacerbated by fragmented patient information. Treating physicians and admitting hospitals do not always have access to complete medical histories or accurate information on the medications the patient is taking. The result is medical care that is less than optimal from the standpoint of effectiveness (will the treatment help the patient to recover fully?) or efficiency (how much does it ultimately cost to make the patient well?).

Metrikus and other technology companies like it are establishing secure Web sites on which to maintain individual-patient medical information and records. The patient, the treating physicians (generalists and specialists), hospitals, and pharmacists will all contribute information to this Web site and access information from it. The result should be much more personalized and much more effective management of each individual patients' overall health than the current system provides.

The online brokerage business is a prime example of how personalized services can be keys to survival and success. This business has gone from spectacular growth in mid-2000 to almost no growth in mid-2001. A shakeout in this industry seems imminent. A new battlefront is emerging from online brokerage to unified online financial services, where personalization features will be central. Today consumers have multiple financial relationships with, for example, a bank around the corner, a mortgage lender located in the same state, and many credit-card issuers throughout the country. Consumers have to spend time and energy to put together a complete picture of their investment portfolio and other financial dealings. Wouldn't it be nice if a financial services organization were to create a portal where all these details were available at one window, along with personalized recommendations for tax angles and investments? Several brokerage houses are building such services to provide personalized relationships and to increase their share of financial investments of individual customers.

RealAge.com's medical and lifestyle age assessment on their Web site is yet another example of personalization. With a prompted questionnaire that asks about your lifestyle, family, and medical history, they will tell you the difference between your chronological age and biological age. And then they will follow up with a highly personalized newsletter about how to grow younger biologically. You can also use its Myplan facility to create your own personalized plan for lifestyle choices and decisions. RealAge supplies data to pharmaceutical companies, who in turn will use this data to improve their product offerings.

Products

Dell is perhaps the most well-known example on personalized products for both corporate and individual customers. The way they offer options to configure systems fits the definition of personalization very well and puts Dell ahead of its competition.

Dell has an interactive service for its key business customers called Premier pages which streamlines the purchasing process. This service reduces the cost of the purchasing process and helps business customers to manage the total cost of computing. Dell, on the other hand, gets to build an understanding of the needs and wants of the end users of their business customers as well as build a closer relationship with the purchasing people in their client organizations. According to *Business Week*, since 1997, Dell has created 65,000 custom Dell stores on the Web for its largest buyers. With that data streaming in, the company stays in constant touch with the needs and wants of these customers. Over 50 percent of Dell's sales are placed online through these custom Web sites and through its consumer Web sites. This allows Dell to handle the work of hundreds of call-center telephone operators with only a handful of online staff.

IBM's Microelectronics division is making significant inroads in the computer-chip market. Instead of competing with such established players as Intel and AMD in the microprocessor market, IBM's Microelectronics division caters to niche demands by providing custom-built chips that handle specific tasks, such as routing data and manipulating video images. Nintendo is so enthusiastic about this technology, which it strongly believes will give it an edge, that it is putting IBM's logo on its packaging, almost like an Intel-Inside scheme.

One way to learn about customers and their preferences and then to personalize products is come right out and ask them online. Last year, Lands' End introduced a new service called My Personal Shopper, which helps to guide buyers to items that they might like. Lands' End presents a shopper with six pairs of outfits, asking which one he or she prefers. Based on the answer, the software recommends several items that theoretically match his or her tastes and style. According to an *Internet Week* study, users of My Personal Shopper buy on site 80 percent more often than users who do not use this facility, and the average order value is 10 percent greater.

BrooksBrothers.com is testing a tool that is intended to attract shoppers through a specially targeted home page. When a shopper accesses the Brooks Brothers site, software scans the shopper's computer for its Internet address and the "cookies," a list of previously visited Web sites stored in the shopper's machine. The software develops a profile of the shopper based on matching the information with others in an externally managed 100-million-member database. The site then sorts the shopper based on its best guess regarding the shopper's gender, marital status, and geography, and shows one of four different home pages designed for that profile.

Pricing

A persistent question is whether different levels of personalization will always require different levels of pricing. In other words, do the costs of developing personalization tools get passed on to customers? Do higher levels of personalization of products and service translate to higher prices?

It depends. In the mid-90s, beginning with FedEx and then followed by the rest of the package-delivery industry, individual package tracking numbers were made available to customers. Customers could then go to the Web site of the company at any time and track the status of the packages they had shipped. Customers enthusiastically took on this job because it gave them accurate and timely information regarding the status of their packages.

As this work was previously performed by the call-center operators of FedEx and others, these companies were able to eliminate hundreds of call center operators with significant amount of savings to the package delivery companies, and it did not cost their customers any more money. The same amount of time they would have taken calling the 1-800 numbers can now be utilized to look up the Web site.

Soon thereafter, the package delivery companies followed up with other personalized services for their customers such as getting customers to print their own package labels. Personalization improved customer satisfaction and at the same time lowered the companies' cost of doing business.

When Dell sells computers to its corporate customers, they often offer to personalize each machine by either putting a inventory sticker or preloading corporate-specific software before shipment. While Dell charges for this service, Dell's economies of scale translate to a cost for personalizing of each machine that is much less than the cost customers would have incurred performing these activities internally.

Catalog company Lands' End sells button-down Oxford white cotton shirts for business attire. Let's assume it costs $40 for each shirt. For an additional $2 per shirt, Lands' End can personalize the shirt by monogramming it on the cuff or on the breast pocket. Many people spend the additional $2, seeing value in adding the initials to the shirt.

So, as we have seen from the above three examples, personalization does not always have to be at a premium price. It depends! It depends on the cost of creating the personalization and the customer's perception of value.

Advertising

In advertising, personalization means providing specific content to targeted buyers: in other words providing the right information to the right person at the right time. Now, how can you make it work? Let us look at several examples.

Athletic shoe retailer Road Runner Sports in San Diego wants to give its online customers the same personalized service it gives customers who visit one of its stores or call on the phone. So, it created a special and tiered Web site for its special customers, who are club members. The system knows the purchasing history of club members and presents them with more informative articles and special offers than it shows to nonmembers. Club members represent 10 to 15 percent more lifetime value than nonmembers. VIP club members, who have greater lifetime value than ordinary club members, get even more in-depth content and special deep discounts.

The system also keeps track of customer data and presents specific and relevant data to each customer. For example, a customer that recorded a knee injury might get recommendations and a special offer of a book on physical therapy for knee injuries.

In a recent report in *Information Week*, it appears that the investments are paying off handsomely to Road Runner Sports. Average online orders have gone up from $5 to $7 and the conversion rate from visitor to buyer has doubled from 3 percent to 6 percent.

Terms and Conditions

The extranet e-sites IBM created for its key corporate customers are good examples of providing personalized terms and conditions at a business to business level. A few hundred corporate customers around the world contribute the bulk of IBM's total revenue. The terms and conditions for procuring IBM products and services are unique for each of these key clients and are represented in the extranet sites specially created for them. Client buyers no longer need to fill out IBM's lengthy machine order forms but simply log on to their own procurement systems and order online. These orders are transmitted to IBM's fulfillment and production scheduling systems, and the customers can check the status of the orders and their shipment status online at any time.

Relationships

Is your organization product focused or customer focused? There is an easy way to find out: by examining your organization. Are you organized around product lines, as most organizations used to be and many are even today?

A good example would be IBM, which had at one time 19 product divisions, with each having their own routes to market, causing multiple and independent relationships with customers. Today, all IBM organizations are customer facing with one team representing all of IBM to a global customer. Also, IBM recently created a new position called managing director. These are senior executives each responsible for relationship management of one key corporate customer, and focus on the needs and wants of only their corporate customers. They each have the power to leverage the entire IBM company's resources to personalize their products and services offered to his or her single corporate customer.

Obviously, a firm can go to such a length for relationship management only for large and very large corporate customers, who collectively and individually represent large chunks of revenue and profit. Therefore, personalized relationships will vary from large to small customers with high levels for large to low or none for small customers.

Print Media

The National Football League (NFL) created a personalized newsletter that has over 1.5 million subscribers. Subscriptions have grown from 50,000 to over 1.5 million in just over two and a half years. Fans can subscribe by clicking on the newsletter icon on the NFL page, supplying their names, e-mail addresses, and the names of their favorite teams. Over time the system gets smarter by asking subscribers for more details, for example their favorite players, and their second favorite team, and by tracking online purchasing from the NFL Web site. The program basically mines data and matches it to available information.

The 1.5 million subscribers get 1.5 million versions of content. A subscriber's favorite team might be the New York Giants, but his favorite player might be on another team. So his newsletter will display the Giants header, graphics, and logo in the background, and run a story with a photo of the favorite player from another team.

The system gets smarter all the time, and the level of personalization grows. In the future it will be able to notify Giant's season ticket holders in the greater New York area of special rates offered by the nearby hotels, restaurants, and shops. The possibilities are limitless.

Intranet

The Ford Motor company, even though it is reeling under severe expense control measures, is going forward to extend its My Roadmap system to all its employees around the world. Ford beta-tested this internally developed tool with its sales and marketing staff and is now going to make it available to those in the human resources, supply-chain management, purchasing-and-logistics, and materials-planning departments, and eventually to all 350,000 employees worldwide. Using this system, employees can make annual self-assessments to ascertain their strengths and weaknesses.

Using this data, they can build individualized plans for developing skills and competency to further their careers in the company. Employees can seek training through a combination of classroom and online learning courses.

Role-based Personalization

Personalization can greatly help firms to improve their employees' job satisfaction and productivity.

IBM's My News service, for example, provides IBM employees role-based, industry-specific, individualized information. Employees can obtain information based on their job roles and interests from a variety of news channels, such as the financial market, the semiconductor industry, the telecommunication industry, e-business, and the public services industry. Each of these channels has several links from which to choose. Employees can also decide the mode of communication, by e-mail or on a Web page. After employees input their preferences, My News automatically accesses information from various locations; adds value through analysis, through evaluation, or through some combination of related information; and displays the resulting content where and when it is needed.

In a further step, such vendors as IBM and SAP provide enterprise portals for employees that give them personalized, fast, and convenient Web-based access to all internal and external information, business contents, software applications, and services they need to do their jobs. By providing role-based, personalized information and services, these tools enhance employees' efficiency and enable them to perform effectively in current dynamic, market-driven business environment.

These tools work because they are role-based and personalized. People planning different roles in a company have different job responsibilities. Technically, a role is a container for business transactions, applications, reports, Web links, and links to all the related information. A person's role in the company determines the transactions, information, and services that he or she needs to perform his or her tasks.

If you work in the customer-fulfillment department in your company, for example, when you turn on your laptop in the morning, the personalized, integrated user interface, which contains role-based activities, will allow you to pull up the applications, services, and information specifically designed for you. You will automatically get up-to-date, role-based information and applications, such as e-mail, order status, company news, and a Web browser. You can create production orders, access inventory and backlog information, search FedEx's Web site to track shipments, and run weekly reports. You can easily configure the interface by adding links to applications you often use and delete others.

By providing the right information, applications, and services to the right person at the right time, personalization can help organizations to improve their employee's productivity and morale. A study conducted by PricewaterhouseCoopers shows that employees who use Web portals for personalized work functions produce 2.7 times more revenue than those who do not.

My Everything

The portal market for personalized information delivery is becoming ripe with competition, as this is seen as providing competitive positioning for the provider of services. In the past, personalization within the portals meant an ability to rearrange the data on the screen to create a preferred work environment for an individual.

Customers are now demanding rule-based personalization, in which customer's or employee's access to tiered information is based on their status within an organization. User profiles are created that represent their interests and behaviors. Content is also profiled based on a set of attributes that are assigned specific values. Business context has certain rules that determine which content to display and how to present it by matching the user profile with the matching attributes of the content.

Further refinements are being sought where users want their click stream data analysis to produce real-time recommendations about where they can find information they are looking for.

The next generation of personalization applications will cater to location-based services for wireless users and include some artificial intelligence. Such systems will know who you are, what you are doing, where you should be, and apply this information to the current environment and provide appropriate recommendations. So, if your flight leaves in half an hour and you are an hour away from the airport, the system will tell you what other flights are available, help you to reschedule your flights, and it will inform the car-rental company and hotel on the other end accordingly.

If you are walking along 42nd Street in New York City in the late afternoon, you might get a wireless invitation from a bar in the next block to come to its happy hour.

Opportunities

Segmentation

Almost all organizations segment their customer bases in many different ways. A common method is to segment by the amount of business from each customer. Quite often firms use the 80/20 rule: 20 percent of the firm's customer base may be driving 80 percent of its revenue and perhaps 80 percent or more of its profit. A key question for the senior executives is how much it is worth to lock up the loyalty of these most valuable customers. The answer is it is worth a lot. And if the firm can get even more business from its existing valuable customers it is worth even more. This is where personalized services can be important.

Don Peppers and Martha Rogers coined the term, learning relationship. The context for this is that if you encourage your customers to teach you how to tailor your services to meet their needs, you become more adept at understanding their changing needs and wants and at providing personalized services. Your customers become increasingly loyal to you. Once a firm has built such a relationship, competitors cannot easily steal that customer. Bank customers who have been introduced to PC banking services seldom switch to other banks. If you can constantly personalize your products and services to meet individual needs, you will gain customer's loyalty and retain them forever.

You can easily justify a high level of personalization for your most valuable customers. You can then decrease the level of personalization as you move down the scale to lower value customers.

In "A Measure of Success," Larry Selden and Geoff Colvin (November, 2001) successfully argue that strategic planning should be built around customer segmentation and a cultural belief that not all customers should be treated equally.

They use Fidelity Investments to drive home their point. Fidelity long held the belief that treating all customers equally was almost a moral obligation. However, since 1999, it has made significant progress in creating and acting on multiple customer segments. This has resulted in higher customer loyalty, which then resulted in higher shares of customers total spending ("wallet share") on their financial services.

Many such studies show that retaining customers is much more profitable than acquiring new customers.

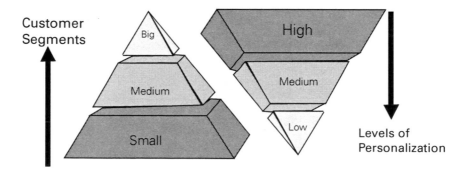

Figure 2. Segmentation and Prioritization

To figure out which are your most valuable customers, you should consider both current revenue and lifetime revenue. Other ways of segmenting customers are by geographic location, by language, by culture, and by legislative differences. You can then vary the personalized products and services you offer to customers in the various segments.

Sales

A firm's sales may increase because it sells more in existing markets and because it may start selling in new markets. Increased sales in existing markets will come from gaining a greater share of the expenditures of existing customers (more wallet share) and from acquiring new customers in the existing market. It can penetrate markets by selling in new geographic areas and by serving market segments it had previously ignored.

In their study, Selden and Colvin (2001) refer to a major global retailer who found that the top 1 percent of its customers accounted for about 25 percent of its total credit card sales. The executives found it difficult to believe and called for a second study. Retailers run big sales and discount their merchandise, but they seldom differentiate between their big and loyal customers and casual buyers. Doesn't it make sense to do something special for this valued 1 percent?

Instead of asking whether it generated more revenue this year than last year, retailers should ask whether they generated more revenue from their most valuable customers this year than last.

Profit

Many opportunities exist for using personalization to increase profits.

One way to increase profits is to reduce the costs of goods sold (COGS) and operating expenses. Organizations must clearly understand the economics associated with personalization and customization. Not all personalized offerings can be produced efficiently. They must understand what aspects of personalization they can deliver in a cost-effective manner.

Developing learning relationships, in which customers teach the organization how to personalize its products and services, in general, reduces marketing expenses.

Customers have shown that they are willing to pay extra for products and services that are more personalized and have a higher degree of fit with their specific needs. As a result, there is an opportunity to charge prices that are higher than the costs to deliver the personalization.

Another aspect is to understand the impact on profitability if an organization can increase each customer's wallet share by providing personalized products and services. No organization has a better opportunity to anticipate a customer's specific needs than the existing supplier to that customer. A study by Harvard Business School (2001) found that reducing customer defections by 5 percent can increase bottom line profits by as much as 25 percent.

It is important to understand the organization goals and define the scope of personalization they will attempt to offer. Then they need to focus on execution and monitor the results of each initiative to ensure they are keeping an eye on the ball at all times.

Issues

User Acceptance

Usefulness and usability are two key ingredients for user acceptance. When they are online, after dealing with their e-mail, people spend most of their time searching for things of their choice. Most popular Web sites, such as Amazon.com and eBay.com, have provided prominently displayed search windows in each Web page, thus making it easier to search. Many Web sites ignore the powerful influence of search tools by keeping the search window at the bottom with small size and failing to keep up to date with search technology. The other aspects of usability is making choices available within a navigable and well-designed content space so that average people can easily get around the sites.

For more sophisticated users, provisions for levels of personalization, to be defined by the user, would be most appropriate. Since the personal information users are willing to share varies, except for a minimal set of mandatory information needed for the minimal level of personalization, all other fields could be left optional. Also, a disclaimer about not sharing the personal information with other organizations will make the initial acceptance that much more easy. Then as the user becomes familiar with the site from repeated visits and realizes benefits of personalized features, we can ask for further personal information and gather intelligence from the user's click-stream data.

Also, usage patterns can be studied to learn more about how the personalization features are used, which will give insights into customer acceptance for further enhancements.

Privacy

Respect of user privacy and protection of personal information supplied by the user are key considerations for personalization. To receive benefits from personalization features, users must be willing to part with key and personal information. They may be more willing if they are assured how this information is going to be used. Users, also, may not be fully aware of their click-stream data that is being gathered. A privacy statement, of exactly what information is gathered and the policies of how this information will be protected and used, is highly recommended.

Legal

There are basically no laws to protect privacy, nothing that guarantees a citizen the right to privacy. Governments traditionally have far greater access to personal information than the average citizen realizes. The Social Security Act specifies that the social security number cannot be used for any other purpose. But, we have already seen widespread abuse and misuse. The Health-Care Privacy Act is the first real attempt at privacy legislation. For the first time, health services will be permitted to use and sell consumers' personal health records to reasonable third parties   as long as they let the patients see their own records. The industry tells the consumers, don't worry, we are only analyzing your records to understand what drugs you will need to live a better life. No one expects these to be the last words.

As a business executive, you need to attend to the legal aspects of personalization, and most importantly you should be aware of changes in legislation across the USA and other countries.

Trade-offs

Value vs. Risk

The risk of not providing personalized products and services needs to be analyzed. What is your competition doing? Is your wallet share declining? Can you maintain your current customer base and acquire new customers without providing differentiated levels of products and services?

Value vs. Cost

What is the cost of providing personalized products and services? Should the level of personalization be the same for all customers and other stakeholders?

These are some of the serious business issues that need to be dealt with through proper business disciplines. Otherwise, personalization will only be for the sake of providing it, and not for sustained business operations and profits.

Successful Planning and
Execution of Personalization

Many business gurus have written about the shift from a design-make-sell model to a sell-design-make model, or in other words a shift from build-to-plan to build-to-order. Dell is the best example of building-to-order that we have discussed elsewhere in this chapter and will discuss in other chapters. It requires a constant and deep focus on your customer and a very efficient and highly modular production process for both products and services.

Any change in the organization must be supported by changes in the management and measurement systems. The way you provide incentive to your people must change. In EDS, they provide incentive to their people by the success they bring to their customer's organizations through EDS's services. To make a new incentive system work, you must change the measurement system it uses.

We present some frameworks for thinking through the personalization proposition in a systematic way to assure sustained performance and success.

Vision and Goals

To begin with we must first understand the overall vision of the organization for personalized products and services. The value proposition must be thought through. The vision must be seen as delivering new values to the recipients. Creating a powerful and compelling vision is the intellectual task of the leadership team. While creating a vision, it is most important to keep in mind who the organization's customers and other stakeholders are, and the priority to be given to each and segments within each for personalized products and services.

After the vision is established, the next thing to do is to establish goals for personalization. Goals will allow us to measure our progress towards the vision. Goals will also allow us to create focus and provide specific directions for initiatives and clearly define the scope of these initiatives. Please refer to our Leadership Pyramid in Figure 3.

Governance

After the vision is created and goals have been established, the leadership team should think through the governance aspects before execution can begin. The two most important elements are marketing strategy and organization focus.

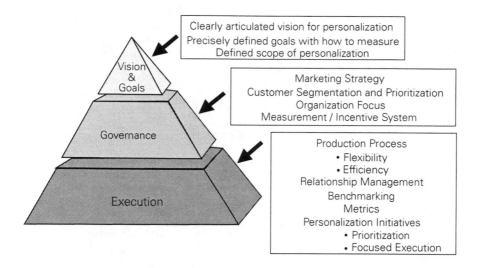

Figure 3. Leadership Pyramid

For developing an effective marketing strategy, it is necessary to conduct a segmentation of the customers and other stakeholders to be served with personalization initiatives. This new segmentation process should include the criteria currently used by the organization, such as size, industry, geography, language, culture, and legislation. The resulting stratification of customers and stakeholders may look very different from the organization's historical segmentation, but it will provide greater insight into the purchasing habits, information demands, and expectations of the customers and stakeholders, and it will help the leaders to establish different levels of products and services for each of the various segments.

It is also important to look at the organization structure. The success of personalization will be based, neither in providing the customer or stakeholder the vehicle with which to communicate his/her needs, nor in analyzing this information in order to conclude the best configuration of product or service for them. The success of personalization will be in effectively acting on those findings, from manufacturing to individual specifications to delivering unique information in a custom format. Thus, the impact of personalization is far reaching in an organization and may require changes in structure. For example, if the organization is product line based then serious consideration should be given to whether a customer facing organization might be more appropriate.

Lastly, within the governance layer, measurement and incentive systems will play a key role in ensuring the appropriate behavior and results. Changes in organizational focus, segmentation of customers, and response times to customers cannot effectively be implemented without related changes in job roles and objectives, measurement criteria, and reward systems. As such, all of these need to be revisited before execution of a personalization-focused agenda can begin.

Prioritization and Execution

It is very important to have an effective structure for decision making and execution that reinforces and complements the governance framework.

With a series of interconnected two-by-two matrixes, we present personalization initiatives frameworks (Figures 4, 5, and 6) to systematically think through the issues and variables to derive the most appropriate initiatives. This is an expansion and further elaboration of our basic matrix shown earlier in Figure 1 that business leaders can use in developing and prioritizing their personalization plans and initiatives.

As shown previously in Figure 1, the key to decision making regarding personalization initiatives lies in balancing customer acceptance and value to the business. (Please note that the premise of the chapter is to expand the definition of personalization beyond customer to include all stakeholders. However, for this description of the personalization initiatives frameworks, we use the term customer acceptance. The following terms can be used interchangeably with customer acceptance, depending on the situation: supplier acceptance, distributor acceptance, stockholder/stakeholder acceptance, employee acceptance, etc.)

Figure 4 focuses on the customer acceptance component of the personalization initiatives framework. It illustrates that the concept of

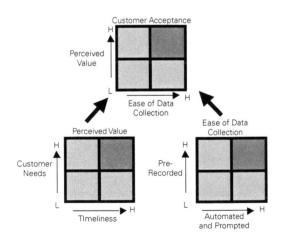

Figure 4. Personalization Initiatives – Customer Acceptance Framework

personalization requires the collection of data about a specific customer in order to tailor an interaction between the organization and that customer. It would follow, then, that the more data that can be obtained about each customer or customer segment, the greater the level of personalization that can be achieved.

However, from the customer's standpoint, the ability of the organization to gather the information, and the time and effort required by that customer to supply the information must be considered. Clearly, if a customer perceives that value is created by supplying this information, they will be willing to spend the time and resources required to supply it. At some point, the concept of diminishing returns begins to impact the customer's decision to provide that information, as the effort to supply the information generates less and less perceived value.

The bottom-level matrixes help to further define and clarify the organization's thinking about customer acceptance by expanding on the axis of perceived value and ease of data collection.

Perceived value must be defined and stratified by the customer according to their business priorities. However, given increased competition, the rate of change in needs and wants, and the shortening of product lifecycles, the relative timeliness of the organization's response to its customers is a critical component of determining which personalization initiatives to pursue.

Ease of data collection will also be determined by the customer. As described in earlier examples of existing business practice, data can be gathered by saving information about historical interaction to build a profile of the customer and augmenting it with data supplied by the customer on a real-time basis through specific requests initiated by the organization. While virtually all personalization initiatives require the customer to provide some level of input, the organization must consider the customer's willingness to invest the time and energy required/requested. The bottom line: the easier and more efficient for the customer, the better.

Figure 5 focuses on the internal analysis and decisions an organization must make regarding resources and time to commit to various personalization initiatives. The top-level matrix illustrates that, similar to virtually every business and investment decision made by an organization, the issue relates to the effort required to increase sales and revenues, or customer's wallet share. The goal is to get more business from customers, to sell more of the same products and services and sell new products and services.

Theoretically, it is possible to gather significant amounts of information about each customer and to build a product or deliver a service that is highly specific and unique to that individual customer.

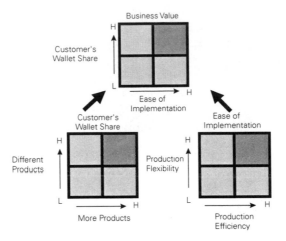

Figure 5. Personalization Initiatives – Business Value Framework

However, practically, the expense to do so becomes significant and the resulting price that would have to be charged for the product or service could be so high as to make it undesirable for the customer to purchase. This manufacturing or delivery cost must be taken into account when determining the nature and scope of personalization.

The bottom-level matrixes help to further define and clarify the organization's thinking about the value to the business by expanding on the axis of ease of implementation and customer's wallet share.

Ease of implementation should be viewed as the time and resources both financial and operational necessary to deliver the personalized product or service. This analysis is a very traditional, very straightforward economic assessment of the tradeoffs between production efficiency and production flexibility. The key is optimizing the organization's resources for maximum impact.

Customer's wallet share can be thought of as maximizing revenues to the organization by selling more of the same products and more different products to the same customer. Again, this is a fairly traditional analysis that any organization must undertake in order to most efficiently allocate internal resources to build and deliver its products and services.

Figure 6 brings together both the customer and internal focus to provide inputs to the personalization initiatives framework. Optimization of the personalization opportunity lies in the pursuit of activities that generate the highest levels of customer acceptance while maximizing the financial return for the organization.

It is important to conduct periodic benchmarking to see how your competitors are doing, and use this data to position your organization appropriately. You should also look at the leaders in related industries

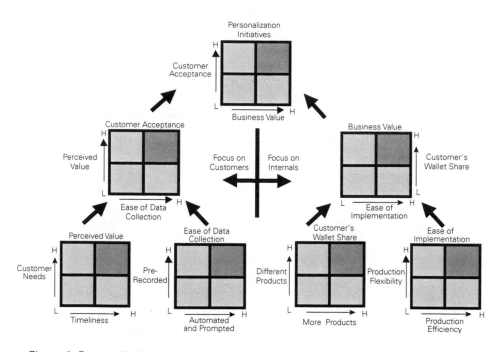

Figure 6. Personalization Initiatives Framework

and benchmark against them to see if any of their best practices are relevant to your organization.

Appropriate metrics need to be developed to measure progress against our goals. We are implementing new business models here, and old ways of evaluating and tracking organizational and marketing performances are no longer valid. A key management question to ask in designing new metrics is whether our new measurements allow us to provide incentive and reward appropriately and whether these are driving desired behavior to reach our goals and visions.

Conclusions

In closing, we quote from Venky Shankar's chapter in *Pushing the Digital Frontier*. The goal of personalization is to create customized value, not customer value. Customer value is about delivering value to a general customer. Customized value is about creating and delivering value solutions for each customer through the use of personalization. It is about increasing the wallet share of our existing customers and acquiring new customers, and keeping them satisfied and loyal. Thus, personalization is a key business imperative.

References

Bonnet, Monica, Personalization of Web Services: Opportunities and Services. Harvard Business School, 2001.

Information Week, August 27, 2001 and September 3, 2001.

Pal, Nirmal, and Judith Ray, Pushing the Digital Frontier. New York, AMACOM.

Peppers, Don, and Martha Rogers, The One to One Future, New York, Doubleday.

Personalization Consortium.

Personalization Issues in e-Business: The Penn State eBRC white paper, April, 2001.

RealAge.com

Selden, L., and G. Colvin, A Measure of Success, Business 2.0, November, 2001.

2 From Many to One

Personalized Product Fulfillment Systems

Arvind Rangaswamy, Jonas H. Anchel Professor of Marketing and
Research Director, eBusiness Research Center, Penn State
University

Anant Balakrishnan, Red McCombs Endowed Chair in Business,
University of Texas at Austin

The Web has made personalization a buzzword. Many companies see personalization as an antidote to the commoditization plaguing their industries and the magic formula that will reverse eroding customer loyalties. People have proposed various definitions for the personalization concept:

> "Personalization is the use of technology to tailor content to the needs of individual consumers," (Study conducted by Personalization Consortium and Cyber Dialogue, March 2001, www.personalization.org).
> "On a website, personalization is the process of tailoring pages to individual users' characteristics

or preferences. Commonly used to enhance customer service or e-commerce sales, personalization is sometimes referred to as one-to-one marketing, because the enterprise's webpage is tailored to specifically target each individual consumer. Personalization is a means of meeting the customer's needs more effectively and efficiently, making interactions faster and easier and, consequently, increasing customer satisfaction and the likelihood of repeat visits" (www.whatis.com — November 4, 2001).

These definitions present a limited view of the potential of personalization, particularly the potential value for customers and for businesses. Personalization may start with Web pages, but if it were only Web deep, we would miss out on much of its value. The Web site is the tip of the iceberg that hints at the fundamental changes that personalization can trigger in the deeper parts of supply chains. To succeed in personalization, companies must do more than customize the content of their Web sites or their products. They must change the way they are organized and how they relate to their suppliers and their customers. Personalization should become a business strategy for matching the firm's resources and capabilities (its people, technologies, and processes) to the specific needs of its individual stakeholders, including customers, employees and business partners. We will focus here on the needs of customers and not those of other stakeholders.

In what follows, we present three main themes:
1. In non-digital product categories, to fully benefit from personalization efforts, firms may have to redesign their product realization and fulfillment systems to have the capability for assembling or manufacturing personalized products. (Personalized products and customized products refer to the same thing — the former as viewed by customers and the latter as viewed by firms).
2. There are several enduring trends that are driving firms in many industries to experiment with, and deploy, systems capable of producing and delivering personalized products, with the expectation that this will offer them strategic advantages.
3. There are also many challenges that firms have to overcome to fully exploit the opportunities afforded by a personalized product fulfillment (PPF) capability. We offer a few high-level recommendations for developing such a capability.

Embracing and Extending Personalization

Defined narrowly, a firm's personalization strategy might focus on online content, such as targeting e-mail messages to individual customers, or

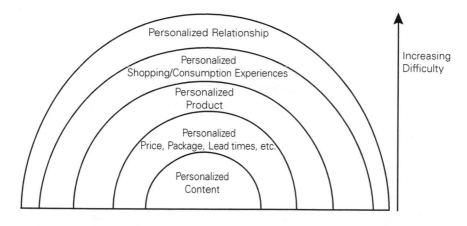

Figure 1. Layers of Personalization
Shows the range of personalization options available to firms. Personalized content
is the starting point, which could lead to personalized services, personalized
products, personalized customer experiences, and personalized relationship
between buyers and sellers.

presenting customers only with selected Web pages designed to meet their
needs. However, defined broadly, a firm's personalization strategy could
be the basis for its establishing long-term relationships with customers,
and it goes beyond personalized content to include personalized prices,
products (when we say products, we mean products and services),
shopping experiences, and overall relationships (Figure 1). A layer of
personalization can be seen as embedded within more general layers,
with personalized relationships being the most general:

> ***Personalized content:*** For pure digital products (for example, news or
> music) personalizing content is adequate in most cases (for example,
> customizing news based on zip codes). Digital content can be configured
> in innumerable ways in real time, and one can personalize content
> automatically to a large extent by asking visitors for some nonidentifying
> information, such as age, sex, and zip code. Roughly speaking, the cost
> of personalizing content at a Web site is about $1.5 million (Stefani Eads,
> BusinessWeek Online, August 4, 2000).
>
> Equally important, firms have many opportunities to add nondigital
> components to digital content (for example, music on a physical medium
> like a CD) or to add digital content to nondigital products (for example, a
> personalized ringtone to a cellphone). For example, Vacationcoach, Inc.
> offers extensive personalizable content — you can rate over 60 interests
> and activities that you like or dislike and then tweak your personal
> preferences as much or as little as you want to find a vacation package
> suited to you. However, is finding a preexisting vacation package that meets
> your stated preferences make you feel you got a personalized vacation?

Will the hotel room conform to your preferences? Will the concierge cater to your preferences? Will the airline automatically assign you the seat you prefer? A travel service can provide truly personalized vacations only by personalizing both the digital and non-digital components.

Personalizing prices, shipping methods, packaging, lead times, and support services: At the next level of personalization, firms can offer personalized prices (discounts), shipping methods, specialized packages, warranties and technical support. Products often have to adhere to tight specifications, but prices and services can vary to accommodate differing customer needs. However, unlike personalizing Web site content, personalizing prices or other marketing variables may have strategic consequences, disrupt operations, or have other impacts. For example, to make personalized pricing worthwhile, the firm should also make corresponding changes to the underlying products. Otherwise, it may just subsidize the customers that get lower prices.

Personalized products: Web-based personalization combined with mass customization production techniques make it possible for firms to offer products tailored to individual needs. Perhaps the best-known purveyor of this approach is Dell Computer Corporation. At its Web site, customers can custom-configure their own computers (from a large set of options), and Dell then builds the selected products using a network of suppliers tied to a real-time IT (Information Technology) system, who provide the parts and assemblies on demand. In 1999, Dell produced 25,000 different computer systems for its customers!

A number of recent developments make it feasible to personalize products. Firms use modular product designs and standardized interfaces to produce great product variety without incurring substantially higher costs, than they would with little variety. Information technologies, including Internet technologies, further limit the firm's costs of mass customization by improving communication and coordination within the firm and with outside stakeholders. Finally, competitive pressures have forced firms to form strategic alliances to expand their product offerings, and to save on costs by outsourcing. In personalizing products, firms also trim the inventory they make to forecasts and reduce their requirements for working capital, something particularly important in capital-intensive industries. For example, through a well-designed personalization strategy, carmakers could realize total capital savings of $65 billion to $80 billion a year. Nissan Motor Co. has estimated that this could amount to savings of up to $3,600 per vehicle (Agrawal, Kumaresh, and Mercer 2001, p. 67).

In spite of its allure, product personalization could lead to complexities in manufacture and fulfillment, that might make the whole enterprise unprofitable (Fisher and Ittner 1999). Also, customer needs may not vary enough on attributes that are most easily customized (Zipkin 2001), or customers may not value the attributes that are easiest to customize.

Personalized experiences: With online technologies, firms can guide customers individually during a shopping-and-purchase process, displaying only products and services of interest to that customer based on what information the Web site has about that person's characteristics and his or her site-related activities (the profile). For example, customers of peapod.com, an online grocery store, can set up various personal lists of products and shop only among products of interest to them. A typical supermarket stocks over 20,000 different items. However, most consumers choose from fewer than 200 items. The personal lists feature that Peapod offers greatly simplifies grocery shopping, especially for consumers in a hurry. Regular Peapod customers are able to shop for over $200 worth of groceries in 10 to 15 minutes. Peapod personalizes and enhances the shopping experience for its customers. In a similar vein, Dell has set up individualized Web sites (called Premier pages) for 65,000 of its largest customers, each with customized content drawn from the totality of Dell's total content base. The Web site also incorporates customized invoicing procedures, customized prices, and product upgrades (for example, updated drivers) conforming to the requirements of specific clients.

Business-to-business firms can customize consumption and re-ordering processes for their customers using Internet technologies. Air Products & Chemicals, for example, builds plants at client sites for storing, mixing, and supplying industrial gases. By using various Web technologies, the company helps its clients to manage their consumption of these gases through remote monitoring, inventory management, order tracking, and automatic replenishment. This type of personalization requires a lot more effort on the part of the firm than content personalization.

Personalized relationships: Personalization can offer several benefits to sellers. By using personalization strategies, they can expand their markets, increase sales per transaction, and most importantly, cement long-term relationships with their customers. One survey of retailers showed that only about 1.3 percent of purchasers at their sites returned to make repeat purchases. However, most of these retailers felt that some form of personalization could help them to build a more loyal following (Stefani Eads, BusinessWeek Online, August 4, 2001). In fact, it is the allure of developing and sustaining close long-term relationships with customers that largely drives personalization efforts. Personalized relationships have been around for a long time; just ask high net-worth clients of investment houses (if you know any) how the firms treat them, or ask regular high fliers (if you know any!) how the big casinos treat them. The Internet promises to help firms offer some of the same types of personalized treatment and relationships to the mass market.

If you are a frequent flier and a member of United's Mileage Plus program (or, a member of other airline frequent flier programs), you have seen several changes in how the airline personalizes some elements of its relationship with you. If you prefer a window seat or vegetarian food, it records those preferences and uses these with every reservation. The airline also provides a special telephone number for reservations, where presumably your wait will be shorter than at the regular reservation line; you will gain priority boarding status, get upgrades, can check your account online anytime, and find it easier to change flights. Providing these perks and services costs the airline more money and forces it to make more operational changes than it would to send you personalized e-mail promotions or customize its Web site for you. In some sense, the firm has configured its entire product to better meet your needs, combining both online and offline resources with a high-end IT infrastructure. The firm's potential benefit lies in developing a long-term relationship with you, and increasing its lifetime earnings from you. (Although the general comfort level of air travel has gone down over the past few years, it has gone down less for frequent fliers!).

Given the many layers of personalization that are possible, a firm has to develop a comprehensive strategy that determines the extent of personalization that it pursues and the resources it uses to meet each customer's needs. Wholesale personalization does not make sense, nor does it make sense for firms to ignore personalization as a fad. Instead, firms should tailor their personalization strategies to the characteristics of their products and the structure of the markets they serve. They should analyze and understand their opportunities for personalizing the product realization process – from helping customers to discover their needs to fulfilling those needs by configuring or manufacturing customized products. We call systems for personalizing product realization "personalized product fulfillment" (PPF) systems.

Personalized Web pages are a small part of a PPF system. More important, firms decide how to determine the resources they will use to configure and deliver the products that meet each customer's wants, while also making the whole effort worthwhile for the firm. PPF systems can be characterized as systems that enable firms to make the transition *from finding customers for their products to finding products for their customers.* In a sense, the firm "rents out" its assets to each of its customers. Wind and Rangaswamy (2001) call this notion of personalization as mass customerization. At first, the concept seems far-fetched, but digital technologies are making it possible to tailor products and services to customers — at least partially and in some sectors of the economy.

The Long Route from Pull to Push and Back to Pull

To understand the growing need for personalized products, it helps to first understand some fundamental transitions occurring in the economy.

Through much of human history, production and consumption took place in close physical proximity. Farmers sold their products to their neighbors and in the neighboring villages. The blacksmith sold to the farmer next door, and so on. Most of these exchanges, whether commercial or social, were personalized, with producers matching their goods to buyer's wants. In some sense, customer pull drove supply mechanisms. The personalized nature of such exchanges explains their high sales-completion ratios — the same reason why, even today, the sales-completion ratio is far higher in face-to-face selling efforts, than over the telephone, or over the Web.

In the past couple of centuries, the industrial revolution spawned a vast, impersonal, multi-layered infrastructure to push products from their sources of production to their points of consumption worldwide. In today's parlance, this infrastructure is composed of factories, logistics providers, marketing channels, and other elements of global supply chains. This infrastructure is also *supplier centric*, and it is driven by the logic of inventory smoothing, bulk breaking, and consolidated shipping. Central edifices of this infrastructure are the large and specialized production facilities that dot the economic landscape. For example, GM produces Oldsmobile cars at its Lansing plant, Buicks at its Flint plant, and Cadillacs at its Livonia plant. To support the push approach, firms deploy considerable resources to foretell customers' needs and wants and carry large inventories to satisfy the varying needs of their customers.

Over the past few years, the Internet has been transforming the infrastructures for matching production with consumption. The dot.coms led the way screaming, but many of them disappeared with a whimper. But in their passing, they exposed major weaknesses in the traditional product fulfillment infrastructure and left behind vastly altered systems and structures for matching supply and demand that have changed customer expectations and business processes. We are heading back to a pull-driven supply system. Instead of producing inventory to match their predictions of customer needs and wants, firms are deploying their resources to design flexible manufacturing and assembly systems that are linked to Web sites. Customer-friendly Web sites enable customers to discover their needs themselves and express those needs by selecting the products that best fit those needs. Customers do not necessarily predefine their wants — rather they shape and refine their wants in interacting with the marketplace in different ways, including visits to Web sites. The following scenario captures this vision for a car company:

The customer will go to a Web site (either the company's Web site or a third party site), configure the car of her dreams from hundreds of options, read testimonials from other customers, compare similar models, and with the click of a mouse, order the car, the financing, and the insurance. That click will set off a series of lightning-quick automated responses. The order will go to another site, where it will be inserted in the appropriate production-line schedule at a factory. Procurement orders will be aggregated and placed over a trading exchange to provide the needed parts. Space will be reserved on a train or truck out of the plant on the scheduled date. And the accounting and forecasting system at GM's headquarters will be updated. The entire flow of information will occur almost instantly, without human intervention. Ten days later, the car will arrive at the dealer closest to the customer (Adapted from an article in *Business 2.0*, July 2000).

This scenario is plausible, although its success in the market is yet to be determined. Internet technologies, however, have already changed product fulfillment strategies: (1) Product fulfillment is becoming *net centric*, that is, the players and the resources that anticipate, recognize, produce, and deliver products are progressively being linked together by a common digital backbone. Because they are connected in this way, the partners can communicate inexpensively, compress lead times, reduce physical movement of products, and experience enriched decision making. (2) The product-fulfillment infrastructure is also becoming *customer centric* – that is, it is increasingly able to read demand signals (often directly from customers) and detect and anticipate individual wants and needs through a Web presence, and then respond to those needs efficiently. These two trends create opportunities for firms to reduce demand-forecast errors and to ensure that the products they produce closely meet the needs of more customers.

Many companies are already creating some aspects of net-centric and customer-centric systems for product fulfillment. For example, Dell Computer Corporation is realigning its resource base toward a PPF system. In November 2001, Dell made over 50 percent of its sales online; it handled over 80 percent of its supply relationships online; and it had over 85 country-specific Web sites tailored for local conditions in local languages with prices in local currency. Its Web sites deliver unambiguous demand signals – the specific type of computer that each customer wants to buy. Dell then produces the product (or retrieves it from existing inventory) just for that customer and delivers it in a couple of weeks.

Taking this approach to its logical conclusion, one could envision fully configurable manufacturing systems that would create, on demand, the products that a particular customer wants. Consider, for example, G5 Technologies, a company that has developed technologies and services that can create and operate made-to-order systems for manufacturing capacity, using a network of collaborating firms. The company has implemented the concept of an agile virtual enterprise (AVE), a new organizational form consisting of a temporary structured alignment of geographically dispersed individuals and organizations linked by electronic communication who coordinate their manufacturing activities to exploit emerging market opportunities. On behalf of one customer who wanted to manufacture a waste treatment system to sanitize medical waste into something that could be disposed off by municipalities, G5 Technologies custom-designed a virtual company by leveraging excess manufacturing capacity at several partner firms located near each other. With its growing database of information about capacities on various pieces of equipment and assembly lines that its suppliers have available, G5 Technologies can opportunistically match available capacities with market needs. In some sense, we can view any type of capacity (or more generally, capability) as a set of resources that could be combined with other resources and opportunistically aligned to market needs. G5 Technologies and other firms like it that can virtually link capabilities across a network will become important components in efforts to personalize products.

Many other companies are making similar transformations, all attempting to develop product fulfillment systems that better match operations capabilities with market demand by deploying productive resources flexibly to produce products that customers want.

Mind over Matter

The traditional marketer often views the customer as a passive participant in the exchange process until the time of the sale. Firms typically decide the terms of exchange and develop a marketing plan (for example, a menu of product configuration and prices), and customers choose to accept or reject particular offerings. In today's market environment, customers' expectations and behavior are changing because of the growth of the Internet. Even if they don't buy anything online, customers are greatly influenced by the wealth of information and options available online. For example, according to a study by Cyber Dialogue, an Internet consulting company, 21 million people used the Internet in 1999 to get information about new vehicles. Of those, 8.4 million actually bought vehicles, but only 170,000 (2 percent) bought vehicles directly over the Internet.

  • Customers are increasingly aware of the spectrum of market
    offerings and fulfillment practices (e.g., online customization
    options and order-tracking services), and so their expectations

have increased on many dimensions: they expect a great variety of products, responsive firms, and Web sites that provide detailed information.

- Manufacturers and service providers can observe and monitor the preferences of individual customers and then tailor their outputs to finer-grained customer needs, using such technologies as recommender systems, reverse auctions, and exchanges.
- The Internet also enhances two-way communications between customers and firms — permitting customers to express their specific preferences and to participate in (and sometimes control) product design and fulfillment.

In the final reckoning, PPF systems will always be at the mercy of the vagaries of customers, who can change their minds unpredictably. The emerging demand-fulfillment systems, however, are customer centric in their design philosophies (Table 1).

Traditional Supply Chains	Personalized Product Fulfillment Systems
Supplier-driven	Customer-driven
Order-to-delivery (OTD)	Discovery-to-delivery (DTD)
Linear, sequential links between firms	Web of inter-related links between firms
Static	Dynamic, closer to real time
Products	Products + value-added services
Reactive	Opportunistic
Standardization of process	Integration across processes
Integrated decision making	Autonomous decision making
Rigid	Flexible

Table 1. Emerging pull-based product fulfillment systems differ on many dimensions from the push-based traditional supply chains.

In some sense, PPF systems have the characteristics of biological systems. Biological organisms have gradually evolved from simple single-cell structures into complex coordinated structures with trillions of interrelated cells. In much the same way, individual elements of supply chains across the economy are becoming part of a complex and organic economic system. The analogy to a biological system extends further. For example, demand-to-delivery (delivery of a product in response to a specific demand) is similar to a customized response of the immune system to a virus attack. A human being has over 75 trillion cells categorized into about 200 different types, which produce different proteins. In an immune response, the body dynamically configures the appropriate sets of proteins (antibodies) to destroy invading organisms. The body might activate some dormant cells that produce the right antibodies and replicate these cells as necessary to deliver a measured immune response calibrated to the specific threat. In some ways, the emerging PPF systems must exceed biological systems in their sophistication. They should also have the intelligence to anticipate, not just react to, opportunities. PPF systems should have the following capabilities:

- They should anticipate, recognize, and service a single customer's wants,
- They should engage customers in articulating their underlying needs,
- They should adapt quickly to changing demand, supply, and other environmental conditions,
- They should reduce inventories and wastes in "matching" supply with demand,
- They should improve customers' experiences in pre-purchase, consumption, and post-purchase activities.

Now, the Hard Part...

Are current methods of market segmentation adequate for supporting PPF systems? What pitfalls should firms avoid in developing PPF systems? How valuable are PPF systems across product categories? For example, do they apply equally well in the automobile industry and the computer industry? Are they useful in product categories with little or no digital content? Are there major privacy issues concerning personalized products? Next, we address these and related questions.

Forget macrosegmentation. It is time for adaptive microsegmentation.

Traditional fulfillment infrastructures depend on products having a high degree of sameness to enable firms to operate efficiently. To comply with this constraint, firms have pursued segmentation strategies that put them in the happy middle ground between making one product for all (Coca-Cola from 1886 to 1961) and making a personalized product for each customer. Today, the Coca-Cola Company offers over 230 different brands of products catering to different segments. Segmenting customers into groups of many who have similar needs is the accepted way to accommodate the heterogeneity in customer needs and wants. A firm then targets its products to selected segments that it can serve profitably. But, increasingly customers want to buy products that fit with their individual preferences exactly or very closely, and they want to be treated as individuals. Thus, current segmentation strategies are increasingly misaligned with the requirements of personalized product fulfillment systems (Table 2).

Traditional Segmentation	Segmentation for PPF Systems
Firm specifies segments: The firm decides on the segmentation strategy and the marketing programs to use to target selected segments.	Customers signal the segment to which they belong: Customers specify or signal their characteristics, and indicate the products, prices and other elements of the marketing mix they want.
Clear and stable boundaries between segments: The objective is to identify customer groupings that are stable and well separated.	Blurred boundaries: Acknowledges that segments are constantly in flux and develops flexible product assortments and marketing programs to cater to customer needs.
Static: Once designed, the segmentation strategy is static until it is redesigned.	Dynamic: Segmentation and targeting strategies are responsive to changing customer behavior, with the firm designing marketing programs to satisfy changing customer needs.
Firm centric: The firm's motive for segmentation is to allocate marketing resources efficiently and improve firm profits.	Customer centric: The firm's goal is to enable customers to discover their own needs, to facilitate their dealing with the firm, and to get what exactly they want, in the expectation that this approach will lead to sustained long-term profits.

Table 2. Segmentation methods have to be better aligned to a world in which customers specify the segment to which they belong (which can vary over occasions), and where the market environment and customer groupings are constantly changing.

Web environments enable customers to discover and articulate their needs and wants for themselves, that is, customers categorize themselves into appropriate segments. Even for seemingly straightforward products, such as windows or jeans, customers have difficulty explicating their needs clearly in market surveys. Many times they cannot say exactly what they want but know it when they see it. With Internet technologies, firms can provide customers' simulated experiences about a product's features and functions before producing the product. Andersen Windows uses a program called Window of Knowledge to enable customers to "see" how various Andersen windows would look in their homes. If a customer wants to install a bay window in her kitchen, the simulation shows her the options inside and outside, including the impact of sunlight in the kitchen. The ability to interact with customers in this way offers firms new ways to understand the different segments of customers in their markets.

In an online environment, asking customers about their wants directly provides firms with specific ways to segment customers. For example, in its segmentation scheme, priceline.com allows customers to quote their own prices for airline tickets and hotel rooms, but if priceline.com accepts the offers they make, they must buy. By coming to priceline.com and by accepting low flexibility to obtain low prices, these customers signal their approximate reservation price and that they are in a price-sensitive segment on that occasion. (Priceline.com actually accepts only about 30 percent of the customer bids submitted).

Using Internet technologies, we could segment people in many new ways that are infeasible or expensive in offline markets. These include segmentation based on: (1) Web search patterns (how they go about choosing products), (2) the complementary products they buy (revealing cross-selling and up-selling opportunities), (3) the problems they encounter using the product, and (4) the anticipated date when they will buy. For example, hotels typically segment customers as either business travelers or leisure travelers, and see each group as having a standard package of needs. In the online environment, hotels can dynamically determine the specific needs of each customer. Does this customer need accommodations for entertainment purposes? Does this customer need office-support services or a quiet work area or a nearby golf course? By understanding customer needs at this level of specificity, the hotel can provide products and services (from a list of available offerings) that best suit that customer. As an example, the Marriott chain can custom configure hotel options just for the golf enthusiast or a leisure traveler with a pet or travelers with other types of specific needs.

The Internet is also forcing firms to implement real-time segmentation strategies; otherwise they may lose potential prospects for good. Web sites attract broader and more diversified groups of customers than do firms in traditional offline settings. Although firms in traditional settings frequently use real-time segmentation (for example in face-to-face selling), online it is far more economical to segment customers on a broader scale. Customers looking only for special deals could be offered instantaneous unique promotions (for example, stay at the hotel for two days instead of one, and we will offer an additional 10 percent discount); customers who want other customers' views about a product could be offered testimonials from other customers or guided to a chat area of the Web site. Customers who do a search using specific keywords (e.g., HP Jornada 720) could be served customized content relevant to those keywords, including product reviews and descriptions of available accessories. These targeting methods can be employed with little or no prior knowledge about that customer.

Firms should increasingly base their segmentation schemes on their capabilities to put together product and service assortments that take advantage of their networks of partners. A firm that is part of a network could provide a single service (e.g., digicash for enabling online transactions) or function as an infomediary or metamediary (as does carpoint.com, which can orchestrate an entire fulfillment system to meet a customer's auto needs). Each firm in a network contributes to creating a unique partnership that can put together difficult-to-replicate assortments and to provide products and services that suit individual customers. This is the real promise that Internet technologies bring to segmentation: they offer firms the ability to characterize the needs and wants of customers even without knowing who they are, to do so in real time, and to link capabilities distributed across a network to satisfy those customers, one at a time.

The personalization of firms' interfaces to customers and the capabilities of online segmentation can enhance product fulfillment. Firms can use PPF systems to orchestrate and deliver a large variety of products, including individually customized products, and to customize the information they provide, the service levels, and their prices. However, PPF systems must be cost-effective. Even for build-to-order systems, firms must carefully forecast the demand for the components that go into their final products. For example, auto manufacturers must estimate the number of white cars and the number of silver cars they will produce, to economize on purchasing costs and the paint costs. Product configurators at Web sites are important sources of such preference information. Finally, PPF systems should be responsive to customers' changing preferences. They must recognize and articulate customers' preferences, and must respond to changing preferences, from, say, a high demand for white cars to a high demand for silver cars. To meet these requirements, firms must develop methods to segment their markets at regular intervals, or continuously, to identify emerging sales opportunities.

Beware of profitless personalization

Although customers may want personalized products, they may not be willing to pay a whole lot more for them. At the same time, customers expect customized products to perform better than standard products – customers who buy custom-tailored suits have higher expectations of performance than customers who buy suits off the rack. Customers who buy personalized products expect them to match their needs perfectly. If customized products fail to meet these higher expectations, customers will likely remain with standardized products. Competitors selling standard products are just a few clicks away.

To meet customers' expectations of better quality and better service firms may have to make substantial investments to create the appropriate PPF systems. To make such investments worthwhile, either customers should value the personalized products more than standard products and pay higher prices for them, or the firms should obtain some strategic benefits (e.g., increased loyalty) through their personalization efforts. Firms have two broad ways to produce personalized products, offering different mixes of costs and benefits: (1) customized assembly using primarily standard components, or (2) customized manufacture of the products (at least of critical components):

1. Custom assembly: Firms can assemble customized products from standard components, a strategy many firms increasingly adopt. Firms can realize such custom-assembled products in several ways. Perhaps the easiest way is to partner with other firms to put together service enhancements to a core product that the firm already manufactures. For example, a firm selling a car might offer customized insurance, finance, and warranty packages, all produced by partner firms. A firm selling computers could offer a selection of third-party software to be installed and tested on the computer. Firms are limited only by their imaginations in combining new features and services with their products because they can use various mechanisms available today to add services in cost-effectively. For example, firms can assemble customized products by merging them in transit. Dell, for example, fills orders for a computer and a monitor by shipping the computer itself and having the monitor manufacturer ship the monitor and having a logistics provider (e.g., FedEx) merge the two in transit so that both arrive at the same time.

   Firms can achieve remarkable levels of product personalization by grouping and assembling standard parts. Just as people combine mass-produced clothing in standard sizes to create their own outfits, firms can create customized products by combining mostly standardized components. Although Dell computers differ very little technologically from other computers, the company has developed a hard-to-imitate process for configuring customized products from standard components. This process is the strategic ingenuity of the Dell system – making customized products from commodities, an approach we might call *inimitable commoditization*.

Inimitable commodities do not necessarily lead to a successful business model as Garden.com found out (it shut down in October 2000). This company helped its customers configure and order garden plants and related items. Customers started with blank palettes or any number of starting designs, such as Japanese or English gardens, and designed their own gardens on their desktop computers, customizing their gardens to the configurations of their lots and local climates (at the level of zip code). Customers could choose from over 16,000 products and try out various landscaping options before deciding what they wanted their gardens to be like. The site also contained an encyclopedia of information related to gardening, helpful hints for both amateurs and experts, and editorials, all designed to help customers make decisions. Once customers designed their gardens, they could generate bills of goods for the items in the garden with a click of the mouse. Garden.com then coordinated the supply chain for these products from its set of over 100 supplier partners and orchestrated the delivery of the products through FedEx, so that it delivered all of the items in one shipment. A most remarkable aspect of garden.com was that it customized products without owning any production resources (nurseries)!

The failure of garden.com is a compelling reminder that product customization is not a sure route to business success – firms need to think hard about the business model that can justify product-personalization efforts. In the case of garden.com, customers did not buy enough to support the personalized fulfillment system. In many cases, firms must find a way to recover the costs of customization by generating more revenue.

2. Custom manufacturing: The most difficult and expensive way to personalize products is to build a flexible manufacturing system to build products to order. But some products, such as automobiles, may require firms to do some degree of custom manufacturing to create personalized products. According to auto industry surveys (reported in the June 2000 issue of *Business 2.0*), over 50 percent of car buyers do not find the model and options they really want and they settle for something less than their preferred car. To overcome this problem, car manufacturers are investing billions

of dollars to put together build-to-order systems. For example, BMW has implemented a customer-oriented sales and production process (its version of build-to-order), allowing its customers to modify product features until six days before production. BMW expects to shorten production times to 10 days by 2003. Eventually, by producing or assembling most of its models in most of its factories, BMW also hopes to reduce the times for production to delivery significantly.

The auto firms will incur substantial costs to reconfigure car manufacturing so that they can build to order. For example, Fisher and Ittner (1999) studied the impact of product variety on the performance of automobile-assembly plants. They concluded that the day-to-day variability in production caused by changing sets of options increased labor hours per car produced, the overhead hours per car, the assembly line downtime, the extent of minor and major repairs, and inventory levels, although it had no significant short-run impact on total direct labor hours. Further, to develop and maintain ERP (Enterprise Resource Planning) systems connected to those of suppliers and customers, firms have to enhance their organizational and information technology infrastructures. The challenges on the marketing side are also enormous – providing sales support and service support for each potential unique product could add to the expense. Firms would have to respond to more complicated after-sales queries from customers, suppliers, auto dealers, and mechanics. Already one in 23 workers in the economy are supporting call center operations!

In other product categories, custom manufacture is less complex. Consider for example, clothing. Through its Original Spin program, Levi's offers customers a choice of 1,485,000 different jeans based on size and styles (49,500 sizes in 30 styles). Customers go to an Original Levi's store in one of eight states where this program is available and are fitted by a sales associate using a proprietary technology. Levi's ships the jeans ordered within two to three weeks. The custom-fitted jeans cost about 25 percent more than the regularly priced jeans. Customers can assign names to their jeans, which they can use for re-ordering. Other companies, such as Lands' End and shirtcreations.com, are also trying to create business models for custom clothing.

Another well-known example is Reflect.com, which has developed a proprietary online customization process for beauty products, such as cosmetics, fragrances, skin care products, and hair care products. The company crafts its formulations to suit individual characteristics (for example, hair color and length) and preferences (for example, fullness, lift, or wave). Consumers can even specify the type of container, the packaging, and the name on the product. Reflect.com then produces and delivers its products by mail within 10 days.

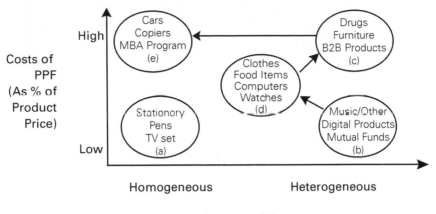

Figure 2 a-e. Potential for Personalized Product Fulfillment (PPF) in Various Product Categories
The attractiveness to firms of product personalization varies by product categories, being most attractive in area b, where customer wants are heterogeneous and personalization costs are low.   However, many firms are likely to compete in those categories to provide personalized products. The next most attractive categories are those with moderate levels of heterogeneity in customer wants and moderate costs of personalization (area d), followed by categories with high levels of heterogeneity but high costs of personalization (area c).   Product personalization will occur more gradually when customer needs don't vary that much and costs of personalization are high (area e). The arrows indicate the sequence of product categories by which product personalization efforts are likely to evolve.

Firms can classify their products to identify those categories in which personalized products could make business sense (Figure 2) and to identify contexts that favor custom assembly versus custom manufacturing. In some product categories (e.g., car batteries), customer preferences vary less than in other categories (e.g., clothing; carpets). Personalized products are generally more attractive for firms in categories with higher heterogeneity in customer wants. Product categories also vary in the costs of personalization, being high in such categories as drugs and cars, and low in such categories as music CDs and business cards. Personalized products are generally more attractive for firms when the costs of personalization are low compared to the product's price. When personalization costs are high, particularly for products for which customer tastes vary little, firms must carefully evaluate their personalization efforts in terms of the incremental value they provide to customers. Only attributes that customers value highly should be candidates for personalization. For example, to personalize cars, auto manufacturers might start by offering a large range of colors (e.g., on the Mercedes Smart car, customers can easily change several side panels to change the color of their cars, even after purchase). Categories with high heterogeneity in customer preferences are candidates for the strategy of custom assembly from standard components, whereas categories with low to moderate levels of heterogeneity are typically candidates for custom manufacturing.

Product categories in the middle offer intriguing opportunities (Figure 2, e). Such product categories include clothing, perfume, carpets, and computers. Customers do not have unique needs, nor does personalization cost too much (relative to product price). Firms may be able to standardize most product attributes, and customize a few attributes. Most people are happy with rectangular books (few would want or even imagine such shapes as pentagons or octagons) but they want wide choices in topic, author, and other aspects of content. Firms may gain some competitive advantages by offering personalized products in the middle area. Although it requires some effort and ingenuity to construct personalized fulfillment systems for these categories, companies can differentiate themselves by personalizing some products, and at the same time enjoy the economies of scale by also producing standard products on the same platform for sale to the mass market. We expect to see a lot of activity in the immediate future in this middle ground as personalization efforts migrate from product categories in the easiest area where personalization costs are low and customer needs vary a lot (Figure 2, b) to the middle ground (Figure 2, e) to the area where customer needs vary but costs are high (Figure 2, c), and then to the area where customer needs vary little and personalization costs are high (Figure 2, d). The rate at which customers adopt personalized products will also depend on whether they buy such products on impulse for instant gratification or are willing to wait for personalized products to be produced and shipped. In the past, customers were willing to wait two to three months for cars to be custom-built, but their patience is shrinking. Unless firms can personalize products quickly they cannot expect customers to adopt them widely.

Partner and flourish. Go it alone and perish.

An operating principle at BMW is, "He who works alone adds to his success. He who works together with others multiplies his success." This principle is equally important for personalized product fulfillment systems. No company today can hope to provide services at the levels customers expect by operating independently. The benefits of optimizing the processes that are directly under a firm's control, typically in the range between five and ten percent, pales compared to the gains a firm can realize by optimizing the processes across its partner firms. For example, by linking up with a third-party logistics provider, firms offer greater flexibility to their customers and reduce their own costs. Logistics providers, such as FedEx and USPS, are increasingly tied into firms' operations. They help firms to better manage small packages in production and in distribution, processes that could be very expensive if done by the firms themselves.

We all recognize that the Internet is blurring all kinds of boundaries – across time, geography, corporate functions, customers, and product categories. Perhaps the most important boundary it is blurring is the one between firms and markets. As transaction costs fall in online markets, the rationale for boundaries separating a firm from its suppliers and its markets weakens. As these boundaries blur, firms can seamlessly put together offerings that combine products and services from many different strategic partners. What we see emerging are extended enterprises, supply hubs, and resource networks, that combine the resources and products of multiple organizations to more fully satisfy customers.

Cisco tripled its sales without increasing its workforce by forming a network of partners and encouraging online sales, which now account for about 75 percent of its sales. By expanding the choices of product configurations it offered its customers to include modules offered by other manufacturers, Cisco improved the overall desirability of its offerings. Customers and resellers configure networking products online and arrange for appropriate financing online through Cisco Capital. (Eventually, Cisco could also include other services, such as maintenance and training.) Cisco shows buyers lead times instantly based on the availability of its own products and those of its supply partners. Seventy percent of the orders Cisco receives are filled directly by its strategic partners across a seamless digital boundary. To eliminate multiple shipments, these firms and third-party logistics firms merge the modules to form the products in transit. Also, the different partners serialize their component products with appropriate codes to enable customers to assemble or configure products.

In another example, Travelocity, the Web's biggest online travel site, took advantage of its data to put together a synergistic marketing program with TWA. In early 2000, TWA announced a special $360 round-trip fare between Los Angeles and San Juan, Puerto Rico. A traditional marketing pitch would have notified the whole Hispanic community in the L.A. area, including people who have no interest in Puerto Rico. Instead, Travelocity analyzed its data warehouse, and within a few hours, it identified 30,000 customers in L.A. who had inquired about fares to Puerto Rico within the past few days. It sent them an e-mail message the next morning, with an astounding 25 percent of the targeted segment either taking the TWA offer or booking another Caribbean flight (Forbes, July 9, 2001, p. 70).

The biggest merger yet – online + offline

The dividing line between dot coms and not coms is eroding rapidly. Firms are combining online and offline efforts to leverage the capabilities of each. We should be thinking about smart sales and not-so-smart sales, instead of thinking in terms of online versus offline sales. For example, Net Perceptions, a few years ago, sold most of its personalization software to dot coms. Today, most of its business comes from retailers who want to coordinate their online and offline efforts to sell to all of their customers across multiple channels. These multichannel retailers want to make it easy for customers to configure products online, then go and "test-drive" comparable products at a brick and mortar store, buy the product at the store, and later obtain customer support by telelphone, all the while being recognized as the same customer.

Another example is Levi's implementation of its Original Spin program for customized jeans. Customers go to a real store to be measured by a real person. After that, information technologies take over. The salesperson sends the customer's measurements, style, and color preferences to a factory – the automatic machines are configured at production time to make the jeans the customer ordered. The systems record the order – later on the customer can order jeans with the same measurements online, on the phone, or at the store. Levi's approach satisfies customer demand for high tech combined with high touch — customers expect online convenience in their offline interactions, and they want the depth of the offline experience in their online shopping.

Prepare for manufacturing as it will be in a few years

Firms face many challenges even in building a single product in a single factory. They must coordinate production with sales forecasts and make updates as the forecasts change. They must also coordinate production on the factory floor. They must organize inventory so that it comes just in time from many different suppliers and from assembly stations within the factory. When the same factory makes 1,000 variations of the same product, the complexities increase exponentially. Without elaborate information technology support, such variation would be difficult, if not impossible, to manage. But IT support is only necessary, not sufficient, for wider implementation of personalized product strategies. A more important driver is changed customer expectations. If cost and time were not factors, would any customer turn down personalized products?

To produce personalized products, factories must organize their operations differently than most do today. To satisfy the conflicting requirements of providing personalized products quickly and incurring minimal additional costs, manufacturing will undergo many fundamental transformations, albeit gradually. Firms will distribute production facilities and particularly their assembly operations more widely to put these closer to the locations of demand but will better integrate them through information technologies. To minimize inventories in process, firms will make their systems more transparent to strategic partners and customers alike. They will structure important data by the logic of internal operations, and also by customer-facing processes (e.g., order tracking), in much the same way that FedEx does package tracking. Thus ERP systems that used to treat manufacturing as a black box will start looking at it as if it were a fish tank visible to the whole world!

The evolution in manufacturing demands that we rethink, from the ground up, how to design and manage product fulfillment systems, and integrate them with other functions of a firm. Advances in information technologies, including enterprise integration technologies, distributed computing, electronic exchanges, intelligent agents, and advanced decision technologies, have created new organizational and coordination options that firms can exploit. In particular, firms can use information technologies to remove the walls separating their factories, which will result in new ways to communicate and collaborate within product fulfillment systems:

- As intra- and inter-organizational connectivity becomes easier and more standardized, firms can link seamlessly with other firms, both horizontally and vertically, to take advantage of market opportunities and to improve the efficiency of their fulfillment operations. These alliances can increase revenues (for example, two firms collaborate to supply different components of a bundled product) or reduce costs through specialization (for example, manufacturers using third-party logistics providers for warehousing and distribution) or by pooling activities (for example, two firms sharing a truck to carry products from their co-located plants to warehouses).
- With increasing integration of information across systems and the resulting visibility of transactions and plans (relating to demand, inventories, production, and shipping), firms can better coordinate their actions and achieve more efficient operations.
- With instant electronic exchange of information between product fulfillments systems and factories, firms can decrease costs by

reducing inventories and can do more product customization by
moving the make-to-order signaling point upstream.
- With real-time monitoring and control capabilities (including
location-awareness of wireless systems) firms can further increase
their factories' efficiency and responsiveness to fulfillment
operations.

When a customer places an order on a PPF system, the firm (or
its automated decision agent) will make several quick decisions, in
response to the following questions: (1) Can it produce this product
from inventory already available somewhere in the distributed system?
(2) How quickly can it satisfy this demand? (3) Should it offer additional
or alternative features to the customer to leverage existing resources
or to provide a better product? (4) Who should do what and when in
the fulfillment system to satisfy this demand? In some ways, such a
system already exists in the airline industry. Every time a traveler
tries to make a flight reservation, he or she triggers a complex decision
process to determine whether and how that request will be fulfilled.
What we see emerging are even more complicated systems that will
apply to a broader set of product categories. Such systems will be
capable of managing production in small lot sizes and sequencing
production resources and capabilities to improve use of those resources
and minimize downtime. Clearly, this will not be easy. Even seemingly
trivial types of product personalization are extremely hard to accomplish
in practice. For example, if customers choose car colors from a digital
palette at a Web site, transmitting that information to the shop floor is
easy. It may even be feasible to automate and optimize the mixing of
paints to get the selected colors. But paint shops currently run in batch
mode to cut costs and to minimize the emissions and waste produced
by flushing the paint guns between colors (Agrawal, Kumaresh, and
Mercer 2001, 67).

In spite of the many difficulties of implementing PPF systems, over
the next few years firms will try to find ways to produce personalized
products. Carpet mills, for example, can custom-produce carpets in lot
sizes as small as 25,000 square yards (Santilli 1999), a vast improvement
from minimum order sizes of 250,000 to 500,000 square yards just a few
years ago. However, carpet mills are still working to build the capabilities
to make carpets based on customers' designs.

Not every product attribute needs to be personalized. Indeed,
personalization on even a few attributes could create a tremendous
variety of alternatives because of combinatorial explosion. The trick is
to find product attributes and features that customers value highly *and*
for which they have heterogeneous preferences *and* the firm is able to
produce those personalized products efficiently.

Balakrishnan, Kumara, and Sundaresan (1999) describe in detail the emerging trends in organizational design and in information technologies, and discuss how these trends create opportunities for firms to design and improve their product realization systems. They conclude that product-realization-and-fulfillment systems are becoming more modular, increasing their flexibility and efficiency. At the same time, tighter integration of information is ensuring that these systems remain responsive to customer needs and wants. Unlike product fulfillment systems designed for static market segment(s), emerging PPF systems will be versatile. They will be capable of meeting the needs of multiple, dynamic market segments that might impose different priorities in terms of the extent of product personalization, response time, reliability, quality, and cost.

Personalization and privacy

Privacy issues have come to the forefront because of the wide use of the Internet. To personalize products, firms must have some knowledge about their customers, or customers must be willing to provide the information needed to personalize products. However, until the time of purchase when the customer actually pays for the product, firms do not need personal-identification information to personalize products in most categories. In some ways, firms can personalize online in exactly the same way good salespeople do it offline — by getting information about customer's needs without raising concerns about privacy. They know what to ask without appearing to be inquisitive. In a similar vein, firms can use PPF systems to ask generic questions to help them to customize their products to individual preferences: What options do you prefer? What shipping method do you prefer? What is your zip code? Are you male or female? Firms can glean additional information from what the customer does at a site. A customer looking for product information may not yet be ready to buy but needs help finding products that meet her needs. A customer who goes straight to the shopping cart may know exactly what she wants; the firm may have an opportunity to recommend accessories and companion products. In short, a well-designed PPF system does not raise any special issues about privacy that are not already well recognized. When privacy-protection measures are strengthened online, they will also apply to product fulfillment systems.

Conclusion

People often say that the customer is king and that customers vote in the marketplace with their dollars and they, ultimately, determine resource allocation in the economy. Until now, customers in the aggregate did determine resource allocation, at least imperfectly. In the emerging economy, customers could determine resource allocation, even at the level of individual customers. Someday, Ford Motor Co. may not manufacture a particular car unless a particular customer wants it.

It is getting hard to remember the world without e-mail, eBay, cell phones, or Web sites. In a few years, it is going to be hard to remember the world without ubiquitous personalized product fulfillment systems. Not everyone will use such systems, but they will be there for those who want to use them. These systems will transform the Web into a personal medium through which customers get personalized access to the vast productive resources of the global economy.

References

Agrawal, Mani, T. V. Kumaresh, and Glenn A. Mercer. 2001. "The false promise of mass customization," The McKinsey Quarterly 3:62-71.

Balakrishnan, Anantaram, Sounder R. T. Kumara, and Shankar Sundaresan. 1999. "Manufacturing in the digital age: Exploiting information technologies for product realization," Information Systems Frontiers 1(1):25-50.

Fisher, Marshall L., and Christopher D. Ittner. 1999. "The impact of product variety on automobile assembly operations: Empirical evidence and simulation analysis," Management Science 45(6):771-786.

Santilli, Chris. 1999. "Made to order," Architecture 88(3):88.

Wind, Jerry, and Arvind Rangaswamy. 2001. "Customerization: The next revolution in mass customization," Journal of Interactive Marketing 15(1):13-32.

Zipkin, Paul. 2001. "The limits of mass customization," Sloan Management Review 42(3):81-87.

3 Personalization in the Wireless World

Bruce D. Weinborg, Associate Professor of Marketing and E
commerce, Co-Director, Consumers and Technology Research
Center, Bentley College

Judy Cavalieri, Vice President of Emerging Products, AT&T
Wireless Services

Terry Madonia, Vice President, Business Marketing and E-Business
Strategy, AT&T Wireless Services

Imagine a world in which you know the location of your current and potential customers and you have the means to directly and knowingly reach them at any time via voice or Internet. This is the wireless world. Imagine a world in which, no matter the time and place, consumers want to be treated well and want access to solutions that will meet their specific needs, cater to their preferences, and solve their problems. This is the consumer-centric world. Put the two worlds together, and you have the makings for personalization in the wireless world; understand both worlds well and you have the makings for successful personalization in a wireless world.

Providers are excited about the marketing potential in the wireless world because wireless devices, such as Internet ready cell phones and personal digital assistants (PDA), offer another means for finding and reaching consumers, for acquiring new customers, and for building stronger relationships with existing customers. In wireless communications to people possessing portable wireless Internet ready devices, it is possible for firms to know the identity and location of users and to use this information when interacting with them. The potential benefits of wireless connectivity are distinct when contrasted with communication vehicles that neither allow the marketer to know precisely who is receiving a message, nor enable a direct interactive dialogue, for example, media such as billboards, radio, television and print advertisements, and closed stores.

Knowledge and understanding are power. Among marketers, the kings own segment-level information about consumers while the emperors own individual-level information about consumers. Wireless technology enhances marketers' ability to obtain individual-level information about consumers, and to better understand them. By better understanding consumers, marketers can increase their chances of establishing healthy long-lasting relationships with them.

Being in the right place at the right time creates opportunity. Providers aim to make their products and services accessible and at the top of consumers' minds wherever and whenever they are in need. For example, Coca-Cola wants its beverages to be available wherever and whenever people are thirsty or need refreshment, and it wants consumers to always think Coca-Cola and "drink Coca-Cola" when they want something to drink. Coca-Cola strives to achieve this ideal state through marketing activities such as intensive distribution, frequent and far reaching advertising and heavy promotion.

Wireless technology makes it possible for providers to be available and accessible to consumers in any place and at any time of need, that is, to be accessible in the right place at the right time. You might think that wireless technology would be useful only for marketing products that can be digitized, such as music. Not necessarily. We acknowledge that wireless technology does not change the nature of the physical world. Physical products cannot be beamed up as in Star Trek. A wireless world does, however, change people's perception of the physical world, and their interactions with it. Locating and interacting with people, places, and things becomes easier. Consumers in a wireless world have greater awareness of physical elements and greater access to them. For example, a consultant who realizes she needs 50 hard copies of a document while driving along in the middle of the night in an unfamiliar area could request GPS-guided directions to the nearest open copy center; further, with a wireless device, she could access a digital form of the document from a home or office computer and transmit it, along with payment authorization, to the copy center. Even further, if she were going to be staying at a nearby hotel, she could ask the copy center to deliver the order there.

The likelihood of being in the right place at the right time increases in a wireless world because the exchange space is not limited to a specific physical location such as a store. An exchange space may be constructed anywhere the consumer is located, by the provider or by the consumer — in a car, on a park bench, at a friend's house, in a backyard.

Consumers are excited about the possibilities of the wireless world because wireless technology can help them solve problems when they arise. No matter where they go, people carrying mobile devices have ready access to resources such as the Internet, friends, 9-1-1, and business associates.

Information is power. People are fortified by the ability to quickly summon their own or others' knowledge and expertise about any problem. This information provides consumers with convenience, saves their time, and puts them on an equal footing or gives them an advantage when dealing with providers, who traditionally have held the upper hand because of advantages in knowledge and experience.

Consumers are empowered by the control and immediate action they can take with mobile devices. Solutions to problems are at their fingertips. For example, a cell phone makes obtaining roadside assistance less of a hassle with AAA or OnStar just a button push away; traffic conditions or directions, email, stock trades, and product purchases are instantly available anywhere.

So, implementing successful personalization should be a no-brainer given providers' and consumers' excitement about wireless access, right? Well, not exactly. First, people have survived just fine without wireless technology – although, smoke signals and reflective devices were useful in some situations and periods. In general, consumers in a free society have exhibited a stable pattern of behavior, getting along well with the status quo when a new offering is devoid of compelling, worthwhile, and easy to realize benefits. The burden of proof is on providers, not consumers, to create valuable personalization.

Second, people see mobile devices as highly personal, to control as they choose. Individuals set them up to suit their own tastes, preferences and desires, for example, ring tone, volume, and password. Owners of cell phones, pagers, PDAs, and other wireless devices use them for their own reasons, for example, storing company contact information, chatting with someone, or buying a product. Mobile device operators expect incoming messages to be specifically for them. Mobile devices are typically associated with and controlled by a single individual, unlike communication technologies that are shared and used by a number of people, such as traditional land-based telephones or televisions. Therefore, consumers will likely reject personalization services that they do not perceive as tailored for them or for their own use.

Third, for personalization to be effective, consumers must participate in the process. They must be willing to reveal or authorize the release of important information about themselves and they must be willing to use personalization services. Though personalization services may be created and launched by manufacturers or other providers, consumers will ultimately decide whether they are valuable applications.

Given these three realities, we believe that successful implementation of personalization in a wireless world depends on taking a consumer-centric approach, which demands a strong understanding of consumer behavior, and of important marketing and wireless issues that influence consumer behavior.

The definition of personalization varies among scholars and practitioners. Our own working definition is that personalization is a process that facilitates recognizing a consumer's situation-specific needs and preferences and offering a tailored solution with respect to these needs and preferences. Informally, we consider personalization to be a set of procedures for helping consumers get precisely what they want in various situations and treating them as they would like to be treated. The two consumers in the following section had different experiences which reveal important lessons for personalization in the wireless world.

Ben's Baby Gift and Selina's Book

One Tuesday evening, Benjamin was in New York City to visit some friends who had recently had their first child. As he walked up Madison Avenue toward their apartment in the Upper East Side, he realized that he'd left his gift for their newborn at his hotel, which was across town. With neither the time nor the desire to head back to the hotel, he decided to find a baby store nearby and buy another gift. Ben was unfamiliar with the neighborhood, so he used his Internet and phone enabled PDA to call his personal service agent provider who could either direct him to a nearby store or find a merchant willing to deliver a gift to him quickly at some nearby location.

Ben's personal service agent provider had come to his rescue in situations such as this several times over the past few months. It was a buying service that could assist him in most buying situations and maintained a database containing information about his self-reported buying preferences and about his product purchase experiences in which it provided assistance or in which Ben provided information. Service agents with access to this database were available any time to Ben via email, chat or voice.

The agent responding to Ben's call identified a store that had the item he wanted and was located further up Madison Avenue toward his friends' apartment. Ben decided to walk to the store. The agent pushed a map with directions to the store, along with the store name and telephone number, onto Ben's PDA. After Ben ended the connection, the agent directed the retailer to pull the item off the shelf, wrap it in light blue paper – as Ben had requested during the phone call – and process the payment using Ben's preferred credit card account. When Ben walked into the store, his PDA transmitted a signal announcing his name and location within the store – as was his preference. A cash register, wirelessly enabled to receive such a signal, displayed Ben's name and identified him to the salesperson standing behind it. After Ben reached the sales counter, the salesperson smiled, greeted him by name, thanked him for his patronage, commended him on his fine gift, handed him the package, and wished him a pleasant evening. Ben thanked the salesperson and headed out the door.

At the same time that Benjamin was walking uptown in New York, Selina, who lives near Cooperstown, New York, was driving home from her office and listening to her favorite drive-time talk-radio show. The show's host was interviewing the author of a recently released book on picture framing titled *Frame Your Pictures Creatively*. Selina thought the book sounded appealing, and she considered buying it immediately through her mobile device. She decided, however, that she wanted to take a look at it and see whether she really wanted it. Selina said "store book, this Saturday ok, discount only, any merchant nearby." Selina's mobile device, outfitted with voice recognition software, proceeded to accept a transmission from the radio station that contained the book's ISBN and recorded this information as well as Selina's willingness to receive messages related to the book on Saturday while she was out and about from any nearby bookseller who would offer her a price discount. On Saturday, as she was strolling along in a shopping district, her mobile device alerted her to a transmitted message from a bookstore she was approaching. The message subject on the device screen was "Selina, *Frame Your Pictures Creatively* just released, in stock, 20 percent off. Come thumb through it." The detailed message provided four options for her to select: "Hold and I'll pick up later, Extend discount for next seven days, Deliver, Remind me again later." She entered the store without reading the detailed message. After thumbing through the book, she decided to buy it. After the sales assistant scanned the book at the checkout, the cash register, equipped to receive and transmit data wirelessly, recognized the 20 percent discount signal from Selina's wireless device, and displayed the discounted selling price on its monitor. She paid for the book with cash. The sales assistant thanked Selina for her purchase and then, as he handed her the book, asked her if she would like to extend the discount seven days for any other book. She agreed. The sales assistant then clicked a couple of buttons on the cash register and the details of the discount were transmitted to her Selina's device.

In their shopping experiences, Benjamin and Selina benefited from a variety of personalization services that were based on an understanding of what consumers do during the buying process and of what services the wireless Internet permits.

Consumer Buying Decision Process

The main requirement for success in personalization and also in marketing in general is an understanding of consumers' buying behavior. Weinberg (2000) shows that the consumer buying decision process model explains very well the pattern of consumer behaviors in online environments. From a managerial perspective with respect to strategy and tactics, the model provides an important framework for the following reasons:

- It has stood the test of time.
- It enables a systematic approach to attracting and satisfying customers, and maintaining healthy customer relationships in a wireless environment or an integrated-media environment.

The consumer buying decision process consists of five stages (see Figure 1): problem or need recognition, information search, alternative evaluation, purchase and post purchase. These stages characterize the general types and the sequence of behaviors that consumers exhibit when in the process of buying a good or service. Consumers do not, however, necessarily go through all the stages in each buying decision. For example, brand-loyal consumers may buy products without searching for information or evaluating alternatives, as in figure 1.

Figure 1. Consumer Buying Decision Process

Stage 1 - Recognizing the Problem or Need

The first stage consists of the processes through which a consumer realizes that he or she has a problem or need. For example, Benjamin's problem was that he had left his gift for his friends' baby at his hotel and did not want to show up empty-handed. He needed a replacement gift immediately. In Selina's case, a radio interview with the author of a book on picture framing prompted her to seek out the book and perhaps buy it — she had many pictures that needed framing.

Consumers realize needs because of either internal or external triggers. Benjamin's need was triggered internally; he realized he had left his gift behind, which motivated him to get another gift. Selina's felt need to consider buying a book was stimulated by an external trigger, the radio interview.

When consumers' needs arise internally, each marketer hopes that its solution to the problem is the most accessible, the most appealing and the most actionable among the solutions stored in consumers' memories. Alternatively, marketers send external messages to consumers hoping that they will prompt consumers to realize they need their products.

Even after consumers realize they have a need, however, they may fail to act on it or attempt to move on to the next stage of the buyer decision process because they may have insufficient motivation or access to tools that would support moving forward to satisfy a need. Both Benjamin and Selina were motivated enough to take action. Selina, however, was not initially ready to buy; she wanted to first see the book. Once she had inspected it and found it suitable, she bought it. Benjamin was ready to buy. Both consumers, however, were able to act on their felt needs promptly because they possessed mobile devices that provided instant access to resources which were useful in buying situations.

Implementing Wireless Personalization

- The instances in which a consumer need can be aroused internally are infinite. Opportunities to offer consumers personalized solutions to their internally triggered needs abound.
- Consumers connected wirelessly could be reached directly at any time and in any place. Therefore, the opportunities to externally stimulate consumers to realize their needs are endless. We do not advocate, however, that organizations send constant streams of messages to people; we recommend that firms send messages at the right time, at the right place, and in the right situation when consumers invite them to do so.
- Whether a need results from an internal or external trigger, marketers should carefully consider the problems for which they can provide viable wireless solutions. In many cases, offering a wireless solution or resource is like being on call. Firm's should consider very carefully the benefits they may gain by being on call and the resources they need to provide effective on-call service. Consumers will expect fast access to available wireless services and they will be disappointed if these services are ineffective.

Firms must make sure the costs of a personalization service or feature will not exceed the revenue it brings in, and they must clearly differentiate what they are and are not offering.

- A wireless connected environment provides opportunities to automatically detect consumer problems or needs. For example, after an accident in which an OnStar equipped motor vehicle deploys its airbags, an OnStar service advisor can detect theses emergency conditions and automatically summon help.
- When given access to tools, consumers figure out which needs they can satisfy with them and they identify various ways to use them effectively. For example, wireless consumers have shown enthusiasm for some location-related information, such as traffic conditions. Some experts doubt that wireless Internet service will offer anything significant to providers and consumers. We disagree because we remember a similarly dour sentiment expressed by banking professionals about automated teller machines when they first appeared and by telecommunication executives about mobile phones when they were introduced. Given consumers' interest in maintaining constant access to individuals, information, and resources, we believe that wireless Internet service has great potential and that consumers will identify the killer applications through their usage. Technological advances that will transform the market are already coming into view, for example, faster 2.5G technology became available in 2002. The time to start learning about this environment is now.
- When deciding how to satisfy or react to a felt need, consumers consider the availability, accessibility, and usefulness of potential solutions. The likelihood that a consumer seeks out and uses available solutions increases as access to them increases. The wireless world can increase access to solutions; and personalization can increase their usefulness.

To understand the latter point, consider how Benjamin and Selina might have behaved had neither wireless Internet access nor personalization services existed when they realized their needs. Benjamin might have (a) headed back to his hotel to retrieve the gift and arrived at his friends harried, exhausted and late with less time to visit his friends and to admire their newborn infant, (b) spent a lot of time searching for a store that sold baby gifts and for a gift that his friends might like, and as a result, arrived anxious and late and with less time to spend with his friends, (c) gone to the closest drug store and bought some ordinary baby toy and a gift bag to put it in and arrived on time, but embarrassed by the gift, or (d) showed up without a gift and felt terrible about it.

Selina might have (a) recalled the title and author incorrectly and purchased the wrong book and been unhappy with her purchase, (b) forgotten the title and author of the book and given up on finding it, or (c) forgotten all about the book.

Stage 2 - Searching for Information

Stage 2 consists of consumers seeking and gathering useful information for solving a problem or satisfying a need. After gathering information, consumers eventually do one of four things: seek additional information, advance to another stage in the buying process, drop an existing felt need, or realize a new need.

In searching for information, consumers
- Store information either internally in their memories, or externally using various mediums;
- Retain only a limited amount of information internally;
- Consider the source of the information when assessing its value and use;
- Use information to reduce uncertainty about a situation, product, person, or firm;
- Use information to support decision making; and
- Value the increased access to external information offered by the Internet.

Searching for information is an extremely important stage for personalization in a wireless environment. In deciding whether to buy something, consumers seek information to confirm whether they should buy. The type of information they seek may vary in unusual situations or it may be constant in routine situations. For example, an investor making buy, sell, and hold decisions for a financial portfolio may routinely search for price of held stocks, or may spontaneously search for the price of potential new purchases. In either case, personalization mechanisms should simplify the process of obtaining stock prices.

Selina, for example, heard enough information during the radio interview to interest her in the book; she did not, however, feel sure enough to buy the book without examining it. She stored information about the book on her mobile device so that she would not forget about it. Before deciding whether to buy the book, she wanted to look at it. She expressed her preferences clearly when she recalled and used this information when she was near a bookstore on a Saturday.

The retailer recognized and respected her preferences. The headline message and action alternatives that the store transmitted to her mobile device signaled its awareness of her current stage in the decision process

— information search — and attempted to ease her through this buying stage to the purchase stage.

Benjamin, on the other hand, was eager to make a purchase. He was seeking information from his personal service agent about the location of a nearby merchant who sold baby gifts so that he could move quickly to the purchase stage and get something he wanted. Without this information, he would have been hindered in making a purchase, perhaps prevented from making a purchase.

Implementing Wireless Personalization

- Consumers value information. To provide consumers with effective personalized experiences, anticipate, prioritize, and provide access to information that will reduce their uncertainty about their potential purchases or will advance them to the next stage in the buying decision process.
- Consumers know that information from marketers is different from that obtained from nonmarketer sources, for example, from their friends or Consumer Reports, and they process and use this information differently. We recommend that marketers provide information from a variety of sources. We understand that organizations may find it difficult providing information that is not under their control or that might reflect viewpoints different from their own. Realize, however, that personalization is in the eye of the beholder; the individual searching for information assesses the effectiveness of a personalization service.
- Personalizing information for consumers should enhance their abilities to find and process information and to record, store, and recall information. Consumers want to store potentially useful information beyond what their memories can handle. They use external depositories, such as paper, computer servers, or memory-equipped handheld devices.
- Consumers may want different levels of detail in information depending on the situation. In a wireless world, we believe that they tend to prefer information in a compact form because they will tend to use wireless devices while on the go and because of technology limitations such as small screens.

Stage 3 - Evaluating Alternatives

In the third stage, consumers analyze alternatives based on their strengths and weaknesses and apply choice decision rules, for example, buy the one with the lowest price. The two most prominent decisions that they make prior to purchase are which product or brand to select and from which merchant to purchase. When they are considering various alternatives, consumers want to draw on their preferences in making a decision. They must generally make trade-offs and apply choice decision rules in using relevant information.

Choice decision rules range from the rational and analytic to the emotional and holistic, for example, buy the one with the lowest price, or buy the one that feels right. Sometimes people use rules of thumb, for example, always buy the product that is most highly rated by Consumer Reports, or they may use ad hoc decision rules for novel situations.

During this stage, it is critical to be in the consumer's consideration set, that is, among the alternatives the consumer considers purchasing. Consumers rarely buy products or even shop in stores that are not in their consideration sets, though it can happen, because of stock-outs or other unexpected events. Marketing efforts for getting into the consideration set vary and include generating awareness or trial, modifying the positioning of a product, or changing consumer perceptions about which product attributes are most important.

Various factors influence consumers' evaluations of alternatives:
   • The consumer's makeup, knowledge, experiences, and preferences,
   • The context or situation defined by such issues as time pressure, resources, importance, and involvement,
   • The availability and format of information relevant to the choice,
   • The types of decision rules used, such as mathematical, analytical, or holistic,
   • The use of automatic or ad hoc decision rules.

In our example, Selina may have been heavily influenced by three elements when considering whether to buy the book: timing, price, and convenience. She recorded preferences of "Saturday, " "discount only," and "any merchant nearby" when storing information about the book on her mobile device. Benjamin considered two alternatives for making his purchase: going directly to a store or waiting for a direct delivery to some nearby location. His decision was largely based on time; he did not want to wait for delivery.

Implementing Wireless Personalization
   • Record and store choice decision rules used by consumers, and provide them with access to these rules and the ability to employ them automatically.
   • Provide one-click at a time interactive processes for ad hoc preference formation and decision making.
   • Locate and access the types of information consumers use regularly in employing choice rules. A road warrior who makes

air-travel decisions based on ticket price, number of connections, departure time, and total travel time should automatically receive this information every time he or she seeks to buy a ticket.

Stage 4 - Purchase

The purchase stage includes ordering or product selection, payment, delivery and acquisition of a good or service. An exchange agreement consists of a set of terms, for example, a product, a price, a form of payment, and a warranty. Purchasing is made up of sub-processes, for example, specifying the details of an order, indicating how payment is to be made, acknowledging payment, and delivering the item.

Each part of the process affects consumers' evaluations of their purchase experiences. The smoother each part of the process goes, the greater the likelihood that a purchase will be completed successfully. Online retailers curious about the cause of the wide spread abandoned-shopping-cart problem, would find much of it explained by inconveniences that consumers encounter when attempting to purchase a product online, for example, difficulty in identifying shipping costs or product availability.

Many aspects of Benjamin's and Selina's purchase processes were designed to keep their buying on track. Benjamin's personal service agent automatically provided payment with his preferred credit card. It was very easy for Selina to use her 20 percent off discount because it was automatically recognized once the book she was purchasing had been scanned. Similarly, the cash register display confirming the application of the discount assured Selina that this part of the purchase promise and terms were being kept. Had the 20 percent discount been overlooked and not processed at checkout, Selina may have abandoned the purchase and held ill-will toward the bookstore and the service enabling the personalization.

With respect to wireless commerce in general, many analysts believe that the design of purchase procedures deserves the greatest attention because purchase is likely to be the most frequently exercised stage of the buying decision process. They believe that mobile device users are on the go and are geared toward getting things done, taking action, and moving forward. In the buying decision process, purchase is the goal.

At present, technological limitations, such as the small monitors on handheld wireless devices, are affecting consumers' willingness to use wireless devices for working through the buying stages preceding purchase. In the long run, assuming that these limitations have been overcome, the incidence of consumer behaviors in each buyer decision stage in a wireless world may be similar to that in tethered-digital or face-to-face environments.

When the wireless world reaches maturity, the wireless buying experience may differ from the nonwireless experience, not in the frequency with which consumers exhibit each type of behavior, but in the speed with which consumers progress from the problem or need stage to the purchase stage. We base this on our assumptions that access to both digital and tangible resources will be greater in an environment providing access to a mature wireless world than in those without this access, and that increased access to resources accelerates the decision-making process. We also expect the number of habitual purchase processes that can be automated to increase.

The objectives of personalization to encourage purchase in a wireless environment are similar to those in other instances: make the process easy, clear, and fast and insure that the customer receives the product as promised.

Implementing Wireless Personalization

- Be ready to facilitate this stage of the buying process as purchase is what generates revenue.
- Record and recall customers' preferences in order to simplify and hasten their purchases.
- Minimize the number of purchase processes that consumers need to perform. The easier it is for consumers to carry out each purchase process, the more likely a purchase will result.
- Communicate upfront and clearly all exchange terms and processes; and make the overall process easy and quick. Uncertainty about critical exchange terms is a principal reason why consumers do not follow through on a purchase for which they are disposed, qualified and have an expressed interest.
- Confirm, confirm, confirm. Significant time periods may separate purchase sub-processes, for example, between payment and delivery. Consumers will perceive this time as a waiting period. Consumers dislike waiting as it can cause uncertainty and discomfort. Therefore, keep the consumer apprised of the purchase process from beginning to end, either wirelessly or through other reasonable means.

Stage 5 - Postpurchase

The postpurchase stage includes consumer satisfaction with the purchase experience and experiences with the purchased item: using it, being satisfied or dissatisfied with it, getting answers to questions about it, getting repairs or service, returning the item, contributing to word-of-mouth information on the item, buying its replacement, and so forth.

After purchase, trial can turn into loyalty, loyalty can turn into passion, and passion can turn into evangelism. Evolving from one of these states to the next takes time and reflects the rewards and intensity of the consumer's relationship with the product, brand, or provider. A firm's marketing activities during this stage are central to fostering and strengthening its long-term relationships with customers. Marketers should focus on identifying the type of relationship they want to build with each consumer and then take actions to achieve this objective.

From a consumer perspective, acquiring a product marks the beginning of the experience in using the product and satisfying the needs behind the purchase. For many reasons, consumers want access to resources, such as service and repair centers, as they use the product to solve problems. Access to resources is particularly important for services that people depend on constantly, for example, wireless phone or home electricity services.

The greater the variety of situations or ways in which a service may be used, the greater the value of personalization. For example, someone who travels frequently and relies on wireless technology to conduct business may find great value in personalization features that facilitate placing and receiving phone calls, maintaining a schedule, using email, and carrying out other business activities.

Organizations that recognize the endless process of satisfying consumers' needs and that provide increasing access to valuable resources, take care of their customers and strengthen their relationships with them. Their personalized care includes making sure the goods or services they sell perform as expected and selling related products and upgrades. The heart of personalization is taking care of each customer.

Consumers who perceive this intent are likely to reciprocate. Benjamin, realizing his problem, immediately contacted his personal service agent provider for help because of its track record in rescuing him from similar crises.

Provide consumers with opportunities and choices to advance and strengthen a relationship. The bookstore salesperson did this by offering a seven day extension of the 20 percent discount to Selina for any other book. Inherent in the effectiveness of this type of personalization is the ease in which a consumer can communicate her or his choice, that is, accept or reject an offer. Selina chose to accept the offer; the process for this response was easy as the discount details were automatically stored on her mobile device.

Implementing Wireless Personalization

- Customers assess their satisfaction with an exchange after the sale. Therefore, it is critical to provide personalization services during the postpurchase stage. Firms that value building relationships with customers will emphasize personalization during the postpurchase phase more than during any other stage in the buying process.

- Treat consumers well. Customers who are treated well will seek to continue a relationship.
- Give consumers opportunities to advance and strengthen the relationship.
- Make the most of being by your customers' sides. Consumers carrying mobile devices feel connected to those to whom they can reach out for contact or assistance.
- Work toward obtaining inner-circle or trusted-advisor status. This gives an organization opportunities to get to know better its customers, permission to monitor their behavior, and openings to send them information or provide services.
- Get to know your customers and give them information about you; relationships are two way. Provide customers with mechanisms for sharing information with you, and listen to them, for example, through e-mail, electronic newsletters, and online forums.
- Maintain digital records of consumers' contact, purchase and service information to enhance postpurchase interactions.

Consumer Buying Decision Process Summary

To provide effective personal service to consumers, you must first take a consumer-centric approach, understanding what consumers do to satisfy needs. The consumer buying decision details what consumers do when engaged in these processes.

Buying is a process made up of five stages: recognizing a problem or need, searching for information, evaluating the alternatives, purchasing, and conducting postpurchase behavior. To effectively personalize this process in the wireless world, marketers must understand it and create personalization experiences for each of its stages.

Marketing in the Wireless World

When assessing opportunities for personalization, it is important to understand the issues of the wireless world that are of greatest concern to consumers, for example, the ability to identify a person's physical location, privacy of personal or sensitive information, and security of wireless communication.

Location

Analysts and practitioners identify three differentiating characteristics of the wireless world: location, location, location. Wireless Internet technology enables marketers to identify the geographic location of a particular mobile device, and hence, the location of its user. Wireless devices extend the marketers' ability to interact directly with consumers from any time (24/7) to any time and anywhere (24/7/365).

One of the touted benefits of the online world has been its 24/7 nature; that is, the Internet and the information it provides are available any time. This characteristic permits marketers to practice consumer-centric principles of marketing exchange that were previously not pragmatic. For example, in a 24/7 environment, consumers shop, obtain product information, and seek customer service at times that fit their schedules. We have learned, perhaps harshly, that 24/7 online shopping is not a panacea. It does, however, give consumers better and quicker solutions in some problem situations.

With the emergence of wireless Internet connectivity, marketers have focused on devising broader solutions for consumer needs that concern not only time, but also space. Many marketers are excited about the potential for using Internet technology to interact directly with consumers any time and anywhere. For example, advertisers see great opportunities in ubiquitous access to mobile-device-carrying consumers and the potential for sending them more messages or for sending them messages dependent upon their location, for example, as they pass by a store which sells a particular brand.

Knowing the location of a customer indeed extends a firm's reach and makes it possible for it to initiate a meaningful exchange almost anywhere. We caution, however, against implementing communication tactics that focus predominantly on applying technologies simply because they exist and we advocate against push-oriented approaches to marketing. Don't push information to consumers unless they expressed or articulated an interest in receiving that information. One of the main lessons from the "dot com" era was to first recognize consumer needs and behaviors and then to identify how to use technology successfully and profitably to deliver more value to a consumers. We learned that permission is a central tenet for successful relationships with consumers in an online environment; consumers want to feel empowered and in control. Given the opportunities opened up by wireless devices to contact consumers anywhere, we recommend strategic thinking based on serving customers, enriching their lives, and respecting their privacy and security.

This means recognizing that location identification makes it possible for providers to more easily find individual consumers and for consumers to more easily contact providers. This makes any place, wherever a problem or need arises, a shopping environment. Consumers are likely to be active in seeking solutions in untraditional or unexpected problem situations.

Consumers will increasingly use wireless Internet connections to fill local needs. Both Benjamin and Selina sought out nearby merchants. Automobile drivers in emergencies need help where they are located. Consumers are likely to use wireless devices to search for information they can use to satisfy an immediate need where they are located. Therefore, it will be critical to provide information resources that are local in nature or that can be used locally.

Identifying Customer Preferences

Marketers use two general approaches to identifying consumers' preferences. One approach is to get consumers to indicate explicitly their preferences, sometimes in response to a marketers direct request. For example, with MyYahoo!, a Yahoo! member can create a page that will present specific types of information based on the member's explicit requests, for example, up-to-date data on a particular sports league or prices of selected stocks. In Selina's case, she specified her willingness to receive communications related to her book interest with respect to time (Saturday), price (discount), entity (any relevant merchant), and space (nearby). This type of service tends to work well when consumers understand their preferences in various situations.

An alternative approach to identifying consumers' preferences is through inference based on given or available information, typically purchase-related behavior, such as online mouse clicks and previous purchases. Amazon.com is famous for its recommendations in a variety of product categories. Amazon and other organizations that use collaborative filtering to estimate consumer demand occasionally provide useful recommendations. In many instances, however, these types of recommendations are off the mark. At best, such recommendations are amusing and at worst they waste consumers' time. Poor personalized recommendations quickly wear out their welcome with consumers using technologically limited mobile devices for which they are paying for every minute of use.

Marketers rely on two general approaches to recognize consumers' need. They can wait for consumers to explicitly identify needs, as Benjamin did. Or, they can try to infer when and where a consumer may have a need, reaching out without an explicit request for them to do so. For example, some automobile salespeople holler out to anyone nearby, assuming that any person near their lot is in the market to buy a car.

Marketers must let wireless consumers state their preferences explicitly. At present, we are not fans of identifying customer preferences through inference, for example, relying on artificial intelligence or collaborative filtering to estimate what shoppers want. Too often, the quality of such preference estimates is poor, that is, personalized recommendations or information are off the mark. When consumers get such recommendations, they perceive the provider as wasting their time and energy and ignoring their needs; and they may believe that the provider focuses solely on satisfying its own needs. This is the antithesis of personalization. In a recent study summarized in the April 2001 issue of the *Harvard Business Review*, Nunes and Kambil of Accenture found that only 5 to 7 percent of customers want personalization that is based on inference.

Part of this lack of enthusiasm is certainly a reaction to the poor performance of recommendation systems based on artificial intelligence. We believe, however, that it is also a result of users' desire to maintain control of their Internet interactions and online information usage. We are not suggesting that marketers should avoid using personalization based on inference; rather we recommend using this approach only when it is likely to be the best alternative.

For example, when an OnStar-equipped automobile's airbags deploy, the car automatically transmits this information and its location to OnStar, which first attempts to contact the car's driver, and then automatically sends out emergency assistance if it gets no response. In automobiles not so equipped, when airbags deploy, the driver or someone else would have to call 9-1-1 or someone else for emergency assistance. Given the benefits of fast emergency response when it is needed, most people would likely be tolerant of OnStar sending assistance occasionally when it actually was not needed. In most cases at present, however, consumers are likely to value personalization only when it is based on their explicit preferences or requests.

Privacy, Security, and Trust

Privacy, security, and trust are important issues with respect to consumers in their use and adoption of online technology and resources. Consumers worry about the short-term and long-term implications of releasing, transmitting, and sharing personal information electronically. They are uncertain about what that information may reveal about themselves, how it will be used, who may obtain access to it, and whether they could ever retrieve it and bottle it up again once they released it. Many consumers today still refuse to provide credit-card or other sensitive information online because of security concerns, primarily the fear that this information will be stolen during transmission or from a database.

In response to these consumer concerns, many organizations have appointed a chief privacy officer or at least one person to take responsibility for privacy and security-related decisions, activities, and communications. This individual should educate external and internal audiences, about the organization's privacy policy. At AT&T Wireless, the privacy policy is built on four pillars: (1) customer education, educating consumers about the types of information the firms collects and the steps it takes to protect their privacy, (2) customer choice, telling customers how AT&T Wireless uses the information it collects and how consumers can choose what personal information they provide and how the firm will distribute it, (3) customer protection, explaining the security procedures the firm follows to protect consumers' personal information, and (4) customer communication, enabling consumers to inform the firm about their privacy concerns and preferences.

Privacy and security issues are crucial in any consideration of personalization in wireless environments. First, at the heart of successful personalization is the ability to obtain person-specific information. Second, inherent in the wireless infrastructure is the ability to identify individuals' current or past location, information that heretofore was typically known only by each individual. People may fear that Big Brother intends to track their movements, and to use that information as it sees fit.

The Internet's remarkable ability to record personal behavior was highlighted after the horrific terrorist attack of September 11, 2001 on the United States. The FBI and other law enforcement agencies pieced together a digital information trail, based largely on data stored on the Internet and on ubiquitous surveillance devices. For example, Kinko's, where some of the terrorists purchased their airline tickets online, had many video cameras installed on the ceiling. This digital trail allowed the law-enforcement agencies to gather information about the terrorists' pre-attack behavior, which they used in uncovering the organization responsible for the attack and in attempting to thwart it in potential further terrorist activities.

Consumers tend to release personal information when they believe it will be used for beneficial purposes; loosely, we can interpret this to mean that the consumer will benefit in some way. The rub is, however, that people do not know beforehand how the personal information they surrender will be used. They hesitate in releasing personal information when they believe its use will do nothing directly or indirectly for them, when its use could irritate them, or at an extreme, when it could be used against them. For example, some people maintain unlisted phone numbers to avoid receiving annoying telemarketing calls. Some avoid revealing their credit card information online because they fear that rogues will obtain this information.

Marketers will indeed find exciting the additional behavioral information they can obtain about individuals: their physical location at any time, and a record of their online activities. And, they will look for ways to profit from this information. Simultaneously, however, people will become aware of their vulnerability because of the availability of this information. On average, consumers will tend to distrust the intentions of organizations collecting and using this information. Marketers must show that their use of this information will improve people's lives.

We recommend strongly that providers of goods or services emphasize respecting people's privacy and garnering their trust. Only by doing this can they provide consumers with personalization experiences they will admire. By doing this, they will also be likely to maximize their returns from personalization efforts. Specifically, firms should not push uninvited or unsolicited information to consumers; and they should not share any personal information without the consumer's direction or consent.

The temptation to use available location information will be great, for example, to push an advertisement for a particular store to a person passing that store. If the individual did not explicitly ask for this type of information and did not find it useful, then the effect of this personalization experience will be negative.

Remember, effective personalization depends on people revealing their personal information and using personalized tools or resources. The likelihood that people will do either of these things is very low when a provider does not respect their privacy and when they do not trust the provider.

Partnership and Coordination

At an extreme, personalization would cater to every consumer's whim and situation. In general, that level of personalization is impractical and, in actuality, perhaps not best for consumers. Nevertheless, imagining such thorough personalization highlights the trajectory that it can take as consumers desire more, and as organizations extend, personalization capabilities. To deliver greater personalization, an organization needs to provide access to more services.

Given the varying needs of consumers and the situations in which needs can arise, an organization will likely have to partner with other organizations or service providers to enhance consumers' personalization experiences. Benjamin's and Selina's personalized buying experiences incorporated services provided by retailers, global positioning and mapping systems, customer relationship or preference systems, local detection and messaging systems, payment authorization systems, smart cash registers, personal service agents, handheld devices, and voice recognition. Without any one of these services, the consumer experience would have been different.

In many instances of personalization, the partnering will be opaque to consumers and perhaps should be. In any event, the consumer will assess the total experience and, ideally, will view the exchange as seamless. For example, sending customer identification information to the baby store so that the salesperson could recognize Benjamin when he arrived, greet him by name, and quickly hand over to him his purchase enhanced his personalized experience. End-to-end coordination of personalization processes is critical.

The success of personalization efforts will be a function of the performance of all the entities involved. For example, Benjamin evaluated the special treatment he received based on his perceptions of the performance of the personal service agent, the map and directions provider, and the retailer. Had one of these entities performed poorly, Benjamin would have been discouraged about the benefits of personalization. If the salesperson had been rude or had made Benjamin wait unnecessarily, Benjamin may have muttered to himself, "that was personalized service? Never again." Similarly, had Selina been pestered by bookstores near and far all week, she might have cancelled her personalization service and then shopped for books and other items without its blitz of ads. Success in personalization will depend on consumers' evaluation of the entire buying experience, which includes all stages in the consumer buying process.

Those who coordinate personalization should select their partners carefully. An organization's partners should increase (1) its knowledge and understanding of consumers in general and of its customers specifically, (2) its ability to provide information that helps consumers in their buying process, and (3) its breadth of product or service offerings.

Wireless Technology Realities

Wireless technologies used today differ in important ways from wired technologies commonly used today. Wireless handheld devices have smaller screens, smaller keyboards, shorter battery life, and smaller storage capacity. On average, their Internet connection speeds are slower. In addition, they drop connections more frequently; they cannot obtain service in all locations; and their owners pay for connections by the minute.

Design personalization solutions with these realities in mind. For example, the message the bookstore sent to Selina consisted of a brief headline and a list of reasonable action alternatives on a separate page that she could select or ignore. This concise information transferred quickly and fit on a small screen. In addition, the store spelled out action alternatives in order to minimize button pushing and to make responding easy.

The horizon looks bright for solutions to these constraints, for example, larger sized portable tablet computers, and faster transfer technology are on the way. In addition, the wireless Internet is gaining increased attention and momentum. Broadband fast 3G technology was launched in Japan during 2001 and available in the European Union during 2002; and reasonably fast 2.5G technology became available in the United States in 2002. Marketers can seek ways to implement personalization today with currently available technology and plan strategic and tactical enhancements for tomorrow's technology.

Connectivity and Access

The greatest benefits the Internet and related communication software and devices provide to consumers are connectivity and access to tremendous stores of information. In addition, this technology helps people keep in touch easily and affordably with other people and with organizations. To realize benefits from the Internet, one must be connected to it. Until recently, users had to operate cumbersome devices that were fixed in location and physically connected to hardware that facilitated Internet connections. Wireless Internet access relaxes these constraints and enhances consumers' connectivity and access.

Wireless Internet use is increasing as consumers adapt to it and as wireless technologies evolve. IDC predicts in its October 2001 research report (#1025160) U.S. Wireless Internet Subscriber Forecast and Analysis, 2000-2005, that the number of wireless Internet subscribers in the U.S. will grow to more than 84 million in 2005 from approximately 5 million in 2000 and notes that consumers want to access Internet information from their phones or PDAs. These consumers will be looking for tools to enhance their ability to obtain information and services in various situations.

Incrementalism and Integration

Wireless Internet resources are part of the customer solution, not necessarily the ultimate solution. Personalization solutions may consist of both online and offline components and may include various communication mediums that consumers use in their everyday lives. The wireless world is just one part of a consumer's universe. Nevertheless, situations will certainly exist where consumers find wireless Internet communications to be the most preferred alternative for a part or all of a personalized solution.

People are most likely to use the wireless Internet and seek personalized solutions when doing so will save time, provide convenience, allow for multitasking, reduce waiting or boredom, and enable them to take action.

In addition, integrated voice, video, text, and graphics can contribute to personalization experiences. For example, Benjamin talked with a personal service agent about his dilemma, while part of the personalized solution was delivered in text and graphical form on his mobile device — the name and phone number of the retailer and a map with directions to its location. Selina audibly stated her preferences for looking at the book later — and her preferences were stored digitally on her mobile device.

Personal Service Agent

In his quest to buy a gift, Benjamin sought help from his personal service agent, who happened to be a person. The personal service agent, however, could also be a machine or a computer. Whether a technological device can fill this role will depend on the consumer's problem, and the details of the situation.

The evolution of telephones from requiring human operators to place all calls to today's reliance on technology to perform almost all tasks effectively and efficiently with no assistance from actual persons indicates the progress we can expect in wireless technology.

With today's wireless technology, Benjamin could have accessed an online directory of stores and filtered them by location to choose a toy store to visit. Doing this would have taken more effort because wireless Internet and location services are fairly new. At present, assistance from a person was likely his best alternative. Very soon, wireless technology will perform such tasks more effectively and efficiently than people do today.

Wireless technology will perform various personalization tasks in the near future. Nevertheless, we are not convinced that technology necessarily makes life easy for consumers, even devices that manufacturers extol as easy to use; and, we are not convinced that consumers see technology as being personal. An important part of personalization is making life easy for a customer and providing personal support.

During the early stages of wireless Internet availability, providers will need people to play a prominent role in delivering personalized solutions to consumers. At present, in many situations, people are better than machines at listening, understanding needs and concerns, making decisions, creating new and flexible solutions as needed, providing a sense of warmth and personal attention, reading between the lines, cutting to the chase, empathizing, sympathizing, treating consumers well and forming deep, long-lasting relationships.

Providing a consumer with a personal service agent may seem counterproductive when considering the scalability inherent in wireless Internet technology. In this chapter, however, we are not considering the scalability of technology. Our primary focus is on making personalization more effective in a wireless world.

Summary

Effective personalization in the wireless world includes recognizing a consumer's situation-specific needs and preferences, and facilitating processes for satisfying them any time and anywhere. This type of personalization offers consumers additional access to solutions that will satisfy their needs; and it offers providers more opportunities to deliver highly valued goods and services, and greater long-term profits.

For firms to succeed in delivering valuable personalized solutions in a wireless world, they must pay attention to key success factors:
- They must take a consumer-centric approach to personalization.
- They must understand the principles of consumer behavior.
- They must understand the needs, preferences, and situations of individual consumers.
- They must make personalization easy to use.
- They must forego activities that would not benefit a consumer, particularly those which consumers would perceive as exclusively favoring the firm.
- They must recognize that consumers see their wireless handheld devices as personal.
- They must respect consumers and their privacy.
- They must treat customers well.
- They must earn consumers' trust.
- They must design solutions that recognize the realities of wireless technology.
- They must partner with organizations to offer services that enhance consumers' personalization experiences.
- They must integrate wireless and nonwireless resources.
- They must provide consumers with personal service agents who listen and respond to their needs.

References

Nunes, Paul F., and Ajit Kambil. 2001. Personalization? No Thanks. Harvard Business Review 79 (4): 32-34.

Vyas, Charul, Callie Nelsen, and Troy Bryant. 2001. U.S. Wireless Internet Subscriber Forecast and Analysis, 2000-2005. IDC, Report #W25160.

Weinberg, Bruce D. 2000. Internet Shopping 24/7 Project Initial Summary [online]. http:// www.internetshopping247.com/IS247Pv1.pdf.

4 Beyond Personalization

Experience Architecture

John Adcox, Vice President of Digital Media, Caribiner

International

Mike Wittenstein, Cheif Experience Architect, STORYMINERS

Personalization — Bringing Back the Good Old Days

Remember the good old days? No, you probably don't. But you may have seen them on TV. Think of *The Waltons*. Remember Ike Godsey, the man who kept the general store? Ike knew how to greet all the folks on Walton's Mountain by name — he could even keep all those Walton kids straight. More, he knew what the people in his community needed. That's how he stocked his store. He knew to keep favorite colors and new patterns of cloth for the ladies down the street, and he stocked grain for the

Baldwin sisters' "recipe," guitar strings for Jason, and tablets of white writing paper for John Boy.

For Ike on *The Waltons* — and for marketers in general — personalization began as something primarily social and evolved into a way to add value. Ike greeted his customers as friends and neighbors and modified his inventory as he got to know them.

In those days, personalization was pretty easy. Business owners knew their customers because they lived in small communities. They knew exactly what to order and for whom. They knew who liked flowered gingham and who needed turkey feed. They greeted everyone by name. Why? For two simple reasons. First, they could. Second, it kept them in business.

The times they have a changed, to paraphrase Bob Dylan. A few decades ago, personalization meant putting someone's name on a direct mailer. If you got a name wrong here and there, no big deal. Some one to five percent of them would respond, and that was a fair return on investment.

The first few people who got magazine sweepstakes offers and pre-approved credit card applications addressed to them by name may have been impressed. Now, however, that seems as quaint as Ike Godsey in his one-room store back on Walton's Mountain.

Somewhere between the good old days when shopkeepers knew your name and saved you a good pot roast for Sunday dinner and the Age of the Great Junk Mail Flood, something changed. The definition of personalization drifted, or personalization was misused so often that it lost its true meaning. Personalization became less about customizing products and services to fit customers' individual needs and more about gathering vast amounts of data to find customers that fit the products and services. Marketers mailed the same material to thousands or even millions of households, but they created the illusion of personalization by purchasing mailing lists in bulk and putting individual names on the address labels.

Marketers were trying to find customers that fit the needs of the enterprise, rather than shaping the enterprise to fit the needs of the customers.

Ironically, this was a step backwards for personalization. The attempt to appear social did nothing to add value for the customer. Direct marketing did something *to* the customer, not *for* the customer. People who realize that open their mail over the trashcan. Sound familiar?

Personalization continued to evolve. Rather than mass mailing blindly, marketers bought targeted lists and sent out fewer pieces with more specific offers to fewer potential buyers, eliminating demographic groups that weren't likely to buy. They followed the principle advertisers follow when they run ads aimed at men during the Rose Bowl rather than, say, the Oprah Winfrey Show. Targeted mailings improved response rates and return on investment. But, the marketers were still not practicing true personalization. Why? Their emphasis was on gathering information — finding customers to fit products — rather than on customizing products and services — and even business operations — to meet the needs of customers.

Let's say a company makes men's hats. Times change and trends evolve, and then John F. Kennedy doesn't wear a hat to his inauguration. Suddenly, men stop wearing hats. The company has several choices. It can start making some completely new products or it can establish itself as the premier supplier of fedoras for the few holdout customers. It can adapt to serve its customers, or it can find customers who fit the product. The latter may seem easier in the short run, but it's not likely to engender brand loyalty. The former would lead to long-term success. Balancing the transition from old to new products is the key to continued profitability.

How do you anticipate change? How do you *know* that your customers preferences are changing? More important, how do you find out *before* you have a backlog of unwanted products that you eventually have to dump at painfully low sale prices? Or, before your customers switch to someone else's product? More, how do you learn what kind of environment they want to shop in? Or what else they might like? In short, how do you learn what value you can you add to make customers prefer you to the guy down the street? And more importantly, how do you ensure that they will still prefer your brand when the market shifts? After all, you want your customers to prefer your enterprise, not just the products you sell!

The first step is to listen.

Gathering Personalization Data

Customers are eager to tell businesses what they want, how they want it, and what else they want to go with it. Moreover, they're eager to discuss the problems they face. Perhaps these are problems you can solve, either with your present products and services, or with some combination of them — perhaps something they can customize themselves.

The questions are:
- How do you capture this information?
- How do you obtain information early enough to make a difference?
- And how do you use it at the scale of a large enterprise?

You can track purchases, use click-tracing (a method of watching how customers move around on a Web site), or analyze hourly cash register reports. These methods will tell you what customers buy and when they buy, but it won't tell you *why* they buy. Seeing the motivation behind on-line or in-store activity is essential to understanding your customers and to anticipating their needs. Especially when you remember that people make decisions both emotionally *and* rationally.

Example Scenario:

At Kinko's, the 24x7 copy, printing, and now electronic imaging services center, entrepreneurs are often found at all hours putting the finishing touches on proposals, reports, presentations, and display materials. Imagine that you are one of them. You're up against a tight deadline and the pressure on you to land a new account tomorrow morning is intense. It's 11:30 p.m. and in the last hour you've completed the color copies, custom graphics, cover letters, contracts, and one-of-a-kind exhibits for your presentation. All the materials are collated and ready as you go to the hole punch machine. The last person to use it left the holes improperly spaced and you didn't notice. You happily punch all of your copies only to find out that they don't fit into your binders! Everything turns red in front of your eyes. Not only do you have to redo all the tedious hand copying and paste-up, but now you're also losing sleep — and you have to be at your best tomorrow morning.

Suzy, a veteran Kinko's associate who works the late shift and has seen this kind of situation before, sees your frustration. She comes over with a bright smile and offers to help. After you explain what happened, the work to be done, and its importance to you, Suzy suggests that Kinko's redo the work for you and deliver it before the morning meeting. Your eyebrows rise, then a smile starts to take shape. Let Kinko's do it, you think to yourself. The next day, you get a phone message from Kinko's saying that your order is checked and ready. The delivery location and time are also confirmed. When you get to your client's office, the materials are there and everything looks great. With the rest you've had, you're in peak condition. You do a great job and win the account!

What happened? Suzy anticipated her customer's needs and used the store's services (full-service, proofing, order assembly, and delivery) to meet a customer's needs. Not only did Suzy keep a customer happy, she contributed directly to brand loyalty, won a higher margin sale, and possibly helped convert a customer to full-service. Not only did Suzy do a good job, she felt good about it as well.

How did the customer feel? Frustrated at first, but then grateful and supported. These are excellent emotional outcomes for this Kinko's brand experience.

How can we learn from this scenario? More importantly, how can we learn how to learn so that, systematically, we anticipate customers' needs better? The cash register tape will only record the sale. The marketing analyst will never know this scenario happened, won't know the contribution to brand and loyalty that Suzy made, won't be able to identify similar trends at other stores, won't be able to draw insight that leads to new products, and other customers and employees won't be able to benefit from this customer's experience.

Achieving good customer service at scale is part of listening. Traditional market research alone won't work. So, how can we listen differently and better? Here are some new techniques you can employ to help you get at both the emotional as well as the rational aspects of why people buy. Remember, each company has to find its own answers.

- Ask — It worked for Ike Godsey, and it still works today.
- Draw — The Zaltman Metaphor Elicitation Technique (ZMET), from Harvard's Laboratory of the Mind, provides an in-depth understanding of how consumers feel about a product, a brand or an experience. Using an electronic composite or sketch, the way the customer sees the world becomes apparent. Zaltman and his team effectively provide insight on *why* people buy.
- Observe — Researchers watch people shop, and then systematically break down their behaviors, locations, and reactions to understand trends and needs.
- Track — On-line tracking is called click tracing. It's simply the counting and analysis of the "electronic exhaust" shoppers leave as they drive through a web site. The in-store equivalent is machine vision, which, using video, can see the outlines of shoppers as they stroll through a store. Customer waiting times, traffic jams, and employee locations are some of the real-time measurements machine vision offers.

These different methods share one thing in common. They seek the customer's point of view. Shifting from the seller's perspective to the customers' is essential to truly understand customers' wants. You must consider all viewpoints before taking action, as each offers compelling evidence to help you prepare for change.

Ike Godsey realized he had to look at the customer's needs and his own. He had limited space, but he always seemed to have exactly what folks were looking for. He didn't have elaborate tools like video analysis, but he knew what customers wanted and did his best to keep those things on hand. How did he know? Simple. He asked them. But shopkeepers who know all their customers (and their tastes and needs) have all but disappeared. Still, the principle remains: Ask. Listen. Respond.

Marketing begins with understanding what customers need and want. The best companies rely on a variety of sensors to find out what their customers are saying, doing, and thinking. In retail businesses, clerks hear complaints, listen to suggestions and watch traffic patterns. Sales people meet with customers every day. Cash registers today produce many reports. Customers congregate — especially business-to-business customers. Professional organizations, events, and publications provide information. Focus groups are powerful tools. The information is there, waiting to be noticed.

Fortunately, you can listen with more than your ears. You can use effective "hearing aid" technologies to gather information for analysis and improved decision making. Machine vision can count customers in your stores, tell you about their traffic patterns and record how long they wait. Electronic proximity sensors can tell you whether people are walking by a display or stopping to look. With a customer's permission, proximity sensors can identify individuals. Data-mining and business-intelligence systems can help you spot patterns and trends at the level of the individual customer and at aggregate levels: seeing the trees *and* the forest.

What you do with what you know is what matters. Once you hear, you must *respond*. Customers want you to make them feel good while reducing the effort, time, and resources they must expend to work with you. If you make buying a pleasure for your customers, focusing on the emotional outcomes they seek, they will reward you with their loyalty. That's exactly what corporate investors and directors want — customers' loyalty. That translates to sustainable competitive advantage.

Personalization and Operations

Let's jump ahead from Ike's store to the dawn of the 21st Century. Did Sam Walton know everyone (or heck, *anyone*) who shops at the local Wal-Mart? No way. But Wal-Mart knows how to identify its customers' needs. Sam Walton had strong opinions on how he wanted his stores run and how he wanted his customers treated. He managed the details of the entire encounter — from the parking lot through the entrance, up and down the aisles, through checkout, and back out again — with the customer in mind. He practiced doing things for the customer. He also coordinated his marketing with his operations and built an experience that continues to please his customers, often in unexpected ways — such as allowing customers to overnight their recreational vehicles in Wal-Mart's parking lots.

Wal-Mart has built a powerful brand by producing an experience that millions of customers have come to know. More, customers' attachment to Wal-Mart seems to be stronger than the feature set (lots of stuff at low prices) seems to merit. Something new and powerful is happening.

Personalization is evolving yet again. While the scale might be staggering, our pal Ike Godsey would recognize the thinking. It's evident in Wal-Mart's operations.

One unfortunate trend in current business is an ever more noticeable disconnect between marketing and operations. The operations side is busy making products (or providing services) while marketing is gathering data about who might buy these products. Marketing's job is to find the customers for the products, tell them about the features, and convince them to buy.

What if, in trying to form a strategy centered on the customers, the marketing team proactively gathered data about what the customers wanted, why they wanted it, and what problems they were facing? Then, when marketing communicated that data to the operations side, the company could respond by tailoring its products and its support services, such as check-out, shipping, customer relations, finance, and store design, to better please the customers. Ike Godsey didn't convince John Boy that he needed tablets of writing paper. When he found out that John Boy wanted to become a writer, he made sure he had the tablets on hand. He gathered the marketing data (John Boy writes), and he shaped his business to meet his needs (he ordered tablets).

Marketing is more complex today than it was in Ike's general store, and the scale is larger. But the point is that personalization is more than just being polite. It's about knowing intimately what matters to your customers and doing something *for* them with that knowledge. However, that's just the beginning. Remember, Ike Godsey ran the only store on Walton's Mountain. In today's crowded market, you've got to do more. Companies must see their brands as the experiences they are and manage them accordingly.

When customers choose between businesses that sell equivalent products, they opt for the one that offers the better experience —again, both intellectually and emotionally. Sometimes, people choose the experience even when the product is (arguably) inferior. The emotional elements are more important than the analytical ones. The non-food aspects of the McDonald's restaurant experience include playgrounds for kids, changing tables in the restrooms at interstate service centers, multi-lingual menus, plenty of parking, easy-to-recognize signage, food that is always consistent in taste and temperature, and *toys*. Is McDonald's the leading fast food restaurant because its burgers taste better? Maybe. Or is it because it has communicated its story — the McDonald's experience — better than its competition? More likely. In either case, the experience itself represents a valid value proposition. The customer decides when and if to revisit a restaurant by evaluating their total experience, not by intellectually considering and evaluating any single factor.

In America, we are "over retailed." Americans devote more square feet to retail space per capita than any other nation. Apparently, Americans aren't happy with all those square feet of shopping opportunity because so much of it is empty. The same is true of movie theatres and amusement parks. So what's to revitalize retailing and marketing in contemporary America?

Experience Architecture

Experience architecture is an emerging management discipline. By emerging, we don't mean "coming" or "untested." The world's best brands — Disney and Coca-Cola, for example — have been applying the principles of experience architecture successfully for years. As the author, futurist, and art critic Bruce Sterling is fond of saying, "The future is already here; it's just not well distributed yet."

Experience architects are people that work in marketing, operations, technology, research, human resources, and at the executive level to craft a meaningful and unique experience for customers to enjoy and appreciate. By looking at their business in a holistic fashion, they design the details of their businesses to appeal to customers. From the signage, to the entrance, to the merchandise layouts, to the check-out lanes, everything is designed to work with the customer in mind. That includes internal communications — like learning and performance or training tools — too.

Coca-Cola has converted its brand into an experience. Consumers think of it as a part of the very fabric of their lives and respond to it with affection and even genuine nostalgia. Again, the response is greater than the feature set (a sweet carbonated beverage with loads of caffeine) and the benefits (tasty and refreshing) seem to merit. This response is not an accident. The best brands create experiences for their core customers, and they design these experiences carefully. Experience architects at these companies take personalization to a whole new level.

Grounded in marketing, branding, personalization, and strategy, experience architecture is a way of crafting individual experiences for customers. It doesn't matter if a customer interacts with a business inside the store or on the Web site. *Every time a business comes into contact with a customer it creates an experience for that customer.* The way every interaction (a commercial, a Web site hit, an order, a call for technical support, a wait in a lobby) unfolds provides a clue that shapes a customer's perception of their total experience and affects their future purchase behavior.

In fact, people can't avoid having experiences. In every interaction with your business, a customer is going to have an experience. You must craft that experience to provide the specific and desirable outcome the customer wants — the one that represents value to that person.

Offline marketers may not be able to gather the wealth of data that such online marketers like Amazon.com can, or to customize each individual's experience to the degree that a retailer in cyberspace can (we'll talk more about them later). However, online and offline, every detail of each interaction shapes the way a customer perceives a brand. In a sense, how customers perceive you is as important as what you deliver when it comes to earning a customer's loyalty. The experience transcends rational analysis, and it goes beyond the feature values of the product or service. *Managing the customer's experience WELL earns preference and continued loyalty, leading to sustainable competitive advantage.*

Experience architects consider both the rational and emotional elements of decision making. Most accounting systems, for example, look only at the factors that contribute rational elements — features, advantages, benefits, and costs, if you will. Managers follow the numbers and run their businesses to improve the bottom line (because they can see only what they look at). On the other hand, qualitative market research focuses primarily on the emotional side. Something magical (and profitable) happens when a business designs the total experience to appeal to both the customers' emotions and rational needs.

Of course, Experience Architecture reaches beyond the customer alone.

Experience Architecture touches (and can be used to manage) all points in the employee-customer-shareholder value chain. Researchers have found (as have we) that *internal quality* drives *employee satisfaction*, which drives *employee loyalty*, which drives *productivity*, which drives *value*, which drives *customer satisfaction*, which drives *customer loyalty*, which drives *profitability and growth*. Whew! That's a lot of driving. In other words, build a good environment and design a good experience for your employees so that they can (and will want to) treat your customers well. The customers, in turn, will have a good experience and will return preference and loyalty to the brand or business. They will thereby increase shareholder value. It's simple, and it works.

A company's culture is at the heart of its brand. MindSpring, a top-rated Internet service provider, and Earthlink, its merger partner, taught this lesson when they thrived in a very difficult emerging market. Their cultures promoted employee satisfaction, which translated to industry-leading customer service. As a result, both employees and customers are extremely loyal to the Earthlink brand. Oh yeah, the company makes money too!

If you create a meaningful and pleasant experience for everyone involved in the enterprise — managers, employees, partners, and especially customers — they're going to remember it. More important, they'll respond positively when they encounter your brand again.

Experience and Technology

Five years ago, dot coms seemed to be the wave of the future. Every month, it seemed that the big research firms, such as IDC, Gartner, and Forester, were revising their estimates — upward, way upward — about how many people would be buying online in the coming months, and how much they'd be spending. Venture capitalists couldn't find enough dot com startups to fund.

Then came the so-called dot com crash.

What happened? Did people stop using computers and the Internet? Earthlink hasn't suffered. Did people lose interest in convenience? Unlikely. Did the Internet stop working? No way. Did business fail to use the Internet correctly? There you go. In many cases, they did.

In 2000, IDC Research reported that online e-commerce surpassed $100 billion. That sounds like a lot, but it's probably just the tip of the iceberg. E-commerce is still going strong, and it is getting stronger. So why aren't more companies succeeding? Our pal Ike Godsey might not be able to use a computer, but he would spot the problem right off. E-marketers aren't learning about their customers and adapting to serve them. In many cases, they're just using technology to lower the cost of reaching prospects and serving customers. They're certainly not creating delightful experiences.

The technology that's supposed to be making the shopping experience easier, better, faster, more convenient, and more enjoyable for customers is often getting in the way. Why, when we visit our favorite office-supply store (online or brick and mortar), does it let us leave with ink cartridges that are incompatible with our printers — only to have us to return (frustrated) later to get the right ones? The retailer knows what printers we bought from them and what cartridges we usually get. Or it should — it has the technology to track and store this data. Why doesn't it help us remember? Better yet, why doesn't it tell us when we're running low (based on previous purchase patterns) and suggest a new, improved photo-quality paper at the same time? Even better, why can't our ink cartridge trigger a PC to tell the retailer that we're running low? That would make marketing a creator of smart infrastructure. The retailer has missed an opportunity to create a positive experience for the customer and to build brand loyalty for the manufacturer while increasing repeat sales.

Instead of creating positive experiences, technology often gets in the way: Why do we have to enter our cell phone numbers, the last four digits of our social security numbers, **and** a PIN number just to wait on hold for so many minutes (now, they tell you how many minutes you have to wait) only to have a customer service person ask the identical questions and key them in again (while wasting more of our time)? We're ready to explode with frustration, and the company loses money because its call center operates inefficiently.

Once again, using the technology to do things *for*, not *to*, the customer is the key.

Amazon.com, for example, has problems creating a successful retail environment — an experience — because for many shoppers, buying online doesn't match the pleasure of browsing in a brick-and-mortar store. Book shoppers, who just want to buzz in, pick up one specific title, and buzz out seem ideal for Amazon. For them, home delivery probably makes Amazon more convenient than a trip to the closest mall.

But what about the book lovers who like to come in, browse through their favorite sections, and pick out some surprises? How does Amazon create a comparable experience for them? And how does Amazon adjust the experience to encourage impulse buys? Many stores depend on impulse purchases to move their statements from red to black. How does an online retailer provide opportunities for impulse purchases and, more to the point, recreate in cyberspace the experience that makes shopping a pleasure and increases sales?

Amazon is the pioneer in creating a personalized experience for each customer and making that experience useful and relevant (a service rather than an inconvenience). When you buy a book or a CD, for example, you'll see a list of recommendations based upon the additional choices of others who made the same purchase. When you return to the site, Amazon will immediately make recommendations based on your past buying habits. The more you visit and make purchases, the more attractive the recommendations become. Not sure if a recommendation is right for you? Amazon provides helpful reviews from other customers. The customer actually *participates* in co-creating that experience. Customers, for the most part, write the reviews. Now, these reviews are helpful, but they're also fun for the reviewers, many of whom become regulars. And Amazon's site receives the benefit of millions of dollars of "free content."

Can you find out what others think of a particular book, CD, or gadget in a brick-and-mortar store? Can you share your opinions? Can you share your favorite reading lists? Not very easily. Amazon has created a unique experience for each customer, an experience the customers can co-create.

The experience of publishing reviews and reading others' draws customers to the site. It inspires loyalty. Granted, that experience doesn't ensure that visitors will always (or ever) buy while they're on the site, but as Ike Godsey would be quick to point out, customers can't buy if they don't visit the store.

Every visit to the Amazon site is personalized. Amazon uses the information it gathers about its customers to do things for the customer. It provides additional, relevant service, and it purposefully creates an experience. Whether people want to buy once and forget the site (they set the rules for Amazon's handling of their accounts if they visit regularly), they feel that they are heard and that they are a part of the service delivery. Two-way communication is powerful stuff.

Why is the Amazon experience powerful? For rational reasons? Partially. The reviews and recommendations are helpful. But it's more than that. Customers *like* participating in the process. They like seeing their names on reviews, and the regulars like being part of an online virtual community of people with similar tastes and interests. Amazon's customers aren't simply pleased with the products they buy or the convenience of online shopping and delivery. They like the experience of shopping on Amazon. Shopping on Amazon is appealing to both reason and emotion. The experience is complete and rewarding, and it's personalized for each individual.

Amazon uses the information it gathers to craft a better experience. Customers are happier, and Amazon's sales have increased. Amazon also uses the information it gather to steer customers to other product areas— book buyers look at DVDs and electronics, gardeners can buy power tools, and everyone has access to auctions in the areas that interest them.

Too often, personalization systems haven't been used to their full potential. For all the learning that personalization systems do, so far their insights seem dedicated to selling another pair of pajamas or one more book. They're missing the true opportunity. *The best use of this wealth of customer understanding is to better meet customer's needs so that they have positive experiences and are inspired to return.* Enterprises can mine the information the businesses gather to help them to continually adjust to the customers' needs and priorities. Companies should *improve the way they work*, not force customers to be better numbers for the shareholders. When companies use the information they gather to create services that more efficiently and more completely meet customer's needs, they offer greater value and inspire brand loyalty. They achieve long-term preference, loyalty, and profits.

Amazon provides a carefully crafted brand experience for its customers. For example, Amazon lets you track orders on its site (like the killer application by FedEx that lets you track air bills). And it keeps your MY ACCOUNT page up to date and easy to access (just click on a link in the confirmation e-mail message you receive when you place an order). It sweats the details, and customers return the favor with their loyalty. Other book, CD, video, and gadget sites may be cheaper, but customers prefer Amazon's model. Amazon may be the only online retailer that has achieved household-name status like Coke or Kleenex. To Amazon, it doesn't matter whether the customer experience is online or in a store. The feelings and the theme (story) are the same and that's what customers come back for.

Experience and Measurement

Measuring the effect of customers' experiences on the bottom line is difficult. Experience Architects designs simultaneously affect multiple parts of the business, coordinating marketing, operations, training, information systems, promotions, and design to produce emotional outcomes that line up with customers' preferences. But the measurement systems currently in use can't track the multi-component adjustments or their outcomes. Traditional measurement systems focus on the individual pieces of a solution and they follow the notion that if you can't measure it, you can't do it. Unless you pass out mood rings and track the color changes, it's difficult to record and measures emotions.

Managers are trained to optimize each piece individually. However, optimizing piecemeal can't yield results as good as a more holistic experience architecture approach.

Like a living organism, an enterprise is more than the sum of its parts. Individual parts, optimized independently, may not, when combined, create a complete, unified experience that pleases customers. Working separately on the parts of an enterprise is like treating symptoms one by one instead of curing a disease, or, better, promoting total health. Optimizing a single, independent unit might satisfy an immediate need, but it is unlikely to inspire brand loyalty.

Traditional measures, such as those found in many accounting and customer satisfaction systems, usually apply only to the rational side of the purchase decision, capturing preference for features, such as price, size, color, and options. These are the attributes that matter the most to the seller. Remember, in many situations, sellers are in the business of finding customers for their products.

It is preferable to focus some measurement activity on those attributes that matter the most to the customer. Understanding how customers perceive their own experience and knowing how customers feel about the emotional side of the purchase decision provides valuable information for experience architects. Experience architects use this information to create better experiences for customers, deriving profits, loyalty, and sustainable competitive advantage over time.

New technologies provide us insight into customers' thinking processes. Coupled with our understanding of emotional outcomes, new insights can be obtained that help in the management of experiences.

Easy to say, but how do you make it work in the real world? Let's consider an example. Suppose we could use machine vision and direct observation (researchers) to map the paths shoppers take through stores and plot the time they spend on a timeline. Suppose we could correlate that information with their store receipts.

This kind of measurement accompanied by a customer-centric method of interpretation can help business managers make decisions that improve the customers' experiences at the scale of big business. In this example, the researcher could analyze what customers respond to, and what they ignore. Increasing the elements that contribute to a positive experience should boost those sales receipts. More, they should help us spot the trends that help us, as marketers, to anticipate customers' needs and preferences, even as they change and evolve over time.

It's all but impossible to measure whether a particular customer leaves intending to make another purchase in the future. Emotional response is, almost by definition, intangible. But emotion ***does*** factor in to the decision making process. In fact, emotion, more than rational thought, is at the heart (pun intended) of brand loyalty. While we may not be able to measure emotional response in a cost-effective, timely, or accurate way, that doesn't mean we should leave out the emotional part of decision-making. In fact, we should design explicitly for it. The intangibles are just as important — if not more so — in building a leading brand.

To continue using retail as an example, you can't measure Experience Architecture by the number of neckties or hammers a customer buys when they visit your store. But you can measure by how often they return, how many other shoppers they recommend to you, and how long they stay when they come back.

So how do you measure the effects of Experience Architecture? How will you know the approach worked? When customers refer to your brand in the same way they refer to Coke or Kleenex (at least in the "world" of your specific niche or market), you can be pretty sure the effort was successful. That may seem like a lofty goal, but Experience Architecture is a powerful tool.

Experience and Value

In Ike Godsey's good old days, proprietors knew that what they earned came from what they gave to their customers. Their future value was in their customers' wallets, not in some exotic combination of balance sheets.

Products and services can create extrinsic value, but experiences can create ultimate, or intrinsic, value: fun, aesthetic pleasure, self-esteem, trust, and security. People want the total experience that comes with buying the product. Moreover, they decide on their future purchases, in large part, because of their previous experience. The product and the purchase are only parts of the total experience.

People often buy the experience rather than the product. How many people do you think go to Hooters primarily for the food? Why do families save to vacation at Disney World when they could visit excellent amusement parks closer to home?

When Personalization is a NEGATIVE Experience

Personalization should be used to do things *for* customers, not *to* them. Using personalization to do things to customers also creates experiences for customers, but those experiences are seldom positive ones.

If we try to optimize what's right for the enterprise and its shareholders, all too often we abuse customers by using information about them improperly. We forget that in the long run, what's good for the customer is also good for the enterprise.

The enterprise must decide what to do with the information it gathers from customers — whether it's personal information (like names and addresses), buying habits, or even their motions as they wander through a store. Do you use the information to push more information at customers, hoping they'll buy one more pair of pajamas? Or do you use it to reshape your business to better meet their needs?

This isn't rocket science. Have you ever known anyone to enthuse over junk mail or spam? Ninety percent or more of the material sent out in many direct-marketing campaigns ends up in the trashcan. And if 10 percent doesn't, the junk mail campaign is considered enormously successful. The targeted customers aren't happy and may feel invaded, and the return on investment isn't attractive. Who is winning here?

Focusing on using customer data to market current products leads to shortcuts that destroy customers' interest. It doesn't inspire brand preference and loyalty. Worse, it ultimately fails to fill the purses of shareholders.

Enterprises can use the information to improve their businesses. Marketing and operations must connect to make the business better for customers. Remember, it's the customers we're trying to please.

Making a Company Customer-centric

We're all too familiar with brands that make some promise that operations can't or doesn't deliver. The company has lied to its customers. It hasn't met its customers' expectations, and it hasn't solved its customers' problems. The enterprise didn't make its customers' lives better, and it may have made them worse. Ouch. Such negative experiences color customers' expectations of the company and may never overcome the irritation arising from one bad experience.

How could the firm avoid such disconnects? It must build a solid connection between marketing and operations. Marketing should listen to the customers, and gather meaningful information about what they want and need. Operations should use that data to ensure that everything the company does is designed to meet those needs and provide positive experiences for customers. Marketing should make sure customers are aware of the company's message. The customer responds. Profits increase. Everybody is happy.

The recipe may sound simple, but in many cases, the disconnect persists. Marketing goes on seeking customers that fit the company's products instead of gathering information the enterprise can use to develop products the customers need within experiences they crave. Communication travels in only one direction — from the business to the customer. Communication *should* be two-way. Marketing talks about communicating the company's message. That's great, but the other half of the marketing team's responsibility is to listen.

Marketing is the company's advocate, telling the company's story. But marketing should also be the customer's advocate. It can be the customer's voice in the enterprise. If the business listens and responds when customers speak, customers will be likely to listen and respond when the company speaks (markets) to them. Personalization and experience architecture are about two-way communication.

Businesses everywhere, especially those in retail and business-to-business sales, are looking for better value propositions. They are looking for better ways to add value and to inspire brand loyalty. The key is listening first, then using that information to design an ideal experience for the customer. If that means changing the way the company works so that it works for the customer, so be it. *This is the work of the experience architect.*

The experience architecture methodology helps business designers to focus on both the rational needs of customers and on the emotional aspects of the buying experience and to coordinate the two by building an ideal yet tangible vision that can be built in logical steps.

While the customers always come first, theirs isn't the only experience that experience architects need to craft with specific emotional and rational outcomes in mind. They must also consider employees, managers, partners, and even shareholders. The employee-customer-shareholder value chain is a good map for understanding the relationships that make brand experiences succeed or fail.

Creating a successful brand experience depends on understanding what customers need and what they're likely to respond to and then adjusting the business to please the customers in such a way that all the constituents have positive experiences. The business must change and it must change the way people (inside and out) think about it. The business designer must pay attention to even small and seeming insignificant details. For example, perfectly maintained gardens you see and smell while you're in line for the rides at Walt Disney World appeal to multiple senses and create a pleasant overall experience. The business must tailor its products to suit individual customers. It should shape every aspect of its customers' experience, from advertising and first contact to deal making and follow-up service and support. It must develop a culture that fits the people who do the work. MindSpring (now merged with Earthlink) has done all of these things.

Charles Brewer, the founder of MindSpring, says he crafted the company's core values and beliefs — an emphasis on service and support, a work environment that employees love and thrive in, and dedication to absolute integrity — before he had decided what the company was going to do. The essence of the MindSpring experience was in place before the company developed its product. MindSpring made its internal culture into an experience that its employees, and later its customers, embraced. It became the company's most valuable asset.

Brewer foresees a day when Earthlink may no longer provide its core product, Internet access, but he believes the brand experience will endure. The company's brand experience is excellent service and support, so Brewer believes that the company may someday evolve into an outsource for— customer service and support.

Products, features, and advantages come and go, but strong brand experiences endure. They become a part of the fabric of people's lives.

How do you get there? How do you convince others in your organization to work with you on improving the customer and employee experiences?

Don't talk about building a better experience. Build one.

Show them. Create a tangible vision of what the future experience will be and show it in a way that all stakeholders understand the new experience from their own points of view. You can use a literal prototype built in the brick-and-mortar world or perhaps an experimental model built in cyberspace. This kind of collaborative creation makes the business context clear and motivates your colleagues to fight to get new ideas supported and adopted. Visions held in common are powerful.

Communicating the Experience — Clues and Brand Stories

Once you craft an experience, you must communicate it to customers. Every detail that shapes people's experience — an advertisement, a store layout, a Web page, a conversation with an employee, a corporate lobby — all provide clues that trigger responses in customers. Each detail shapes the experiences the customers have of the brand and determines their propensity to patronize the enterprise.

Again, think of Walt Disney World. The brand experience begins long before customers arrive — in advertising, in videos and Web sites that help them plan their vacations, in the way cast members (Disney's term for all its employees) respond when customers call to make reservations and travel plans. The experience continues in the parking lot, where spaces are marked with colorful signs. It continues in the parks, where everything — from the color of the sidewalks (a special red developed by Kodak to make it easier to spot steps and obstacles) to the scents in the breeze — is carefully architected to enhance the experience. It even lingers when the visit ends.

Experience architects work with every aspect of a business — from marketing and advertising to training to information systems to operations — to prevent experience disconnects. They make sure that individual clues work together seamlessly to shape an appealing brand experience.

What makes the world's best brands — Disney, Coca-Cola, and McDonald's, for example — different from others? The difference can be summed up in a single word: *experience*. The very best brands carefully craft every single clue that helps shape an experience for core constituencies, an experience that more often than not transcends the feature set of the products these brands represent.

How Disney creates its customers' experiences is well known. The company pays unmatched attention to detail and story. Audiences expect a certain kind of experience when they see a Disney film or visit a Disney theme park. They expect a story every time. Kids love visiting, say, Six Flags, but whole families dream of visiting Disneyland. They want the experience the Disney brand represents.

The park experience at any Disney property centers on a single concept: story. Some animators are better than Disney's, many filmmakers are better than Disney's, and some theme park developers are better than Disney's. But no one understood story better than Walt Disney himself. Walt Disney was famous for cutting complete animated sequences from his movies because they didn't advance the flow of the story. He scrapped rides and attractions even after expensive construction had begun because they didn't fit with the theming — or story — of the park. For the Disney experience to work, every clue must always be spot on.

Disney tells this story internally, too. The Disney enterprise bills its employees at the parks and retail stores as cast members. Why? To remind them that they are always on stage, and they are always an integral part of the show. They are always telling the story. Employees buy into it, too. After all, the brand experience begins with them.

Disney uses its skill at telling stories to turn the elements of its brand into a compelling brand experience.

The Disney organization is an obvious example, but it is not the only company to use experience architecture to create a brand experience that audiences love. McDonald's and Coca-Cola have done the same thing. Other fast food restaurants may have products superior to McDonald's. But McDonald's set the benchmark for success in its industry. Kids plead to go to McDonald's. Why? McDonald's has used the media at its disposal, from television commercials to its menus with their family-friendly design and its stores, most of which now boast playgrounds, to tell a story that creates a "McDonaldland" experience for its target customers.

Coca-Cola arguably creates brand experience better than anyone. The product — sweet syrup in carbonated water — doesn't seem all that special. But consumers react to the brand in an emotional way that goes beyond what the product itself seems to warrant. Coca-Cola has managed to convince its public that Coke is a part of its past and of its life in a very compelling way. It has told a story, and consumers in every corner of the world respond. Coke isn't just a soft drink; it's an expectation of an *experience*, and it always delivers.

The best brand experiences are timeless, and do not depend upon the products, their features, or their advantages. When the first Disneyland debuted in California, customers lined up hours before it was scheduled to open its gates, even though the park had no track record, and Disney had no experience in the amusement park industry. Why? Because the audiences for Disney's films had faith in the Disney experience. The story at the heart of Disney's brand was already part of their lives.

Experience Architects

The best brand experiences don't happen by accident. Experience architects understand the elements of a company's brand — its products and services (along with their features, advantages, and specific benefits for the company's customers), its culture, its champions, and more.

Experience architects work inside companies to design people's experiences and they serve as customer advocates ensuring that customers have great experiences. They listen to what customers say, and they use their information-gathering sensors to learn more. As a result, they know their customers, and they know how the brand can make their lives better. They know how the audience responds emotionally. They know how customers perceive the brand and how they could perceive the brand. Brand architects understand the customers' problems, and how the brand can solve them. They understand how customers gather and use information, where they congregate to share information, and how and why they are likely to respond to a brand experience. They make themselves the customers' advocates within enterprises.

Experience architects also know how to work their own organizations to obtain the internal changes that lead to better employee and customer experiences. Management must empower them and facilitate their efforts.

Experience architects gather marketing data. Then, they use this information to shape the enterprise — on both the marketing and operations sides — to ensure that it is designed to satisfy its customers. Then, they ensure that every clue — every experience customers have with the brand — contributes to shaping a wonderful emotional and rational experience.

The Experience Architecture Method

Experience Architecture is the ultimate extension of personalization. It's a powerful tool for connecting marketing and operations to respond to customer needs and to build brand experiences customers will respond to.

In using experience architecture:
* First, remember that change doesn't happen overnight.
* Perform an audit to understand the experiences your customers and employees are having today — with your enterprise and with your competition.
* Listen to your customers, and understand their needs and wants, how they gather and use information, and what their rational/ emotional triggers are. Learn how your customers see you in their world (not the way you see them).
* Identify the emotional highs and lows (the threads) that are linked and pay particular attention to them. For example, customers might expect a restaurant-quality meal at home when they heat up the restaurant's branded canned soup, but they find it doesn't taste the same and that they don't feel as pampered as they did in the restaurant.
* Find the core theme that links the experiences. Look for the emotions common to each experience that carry meaning for the customer.
* Develop clues (human, physical, informational, process) that reflect the theme.
* Enforce the business design by aligning all the clues to the theme.
* Establish feedback loops so that everyone learns how each part of the new system works.
* Measure your success.
* Repeat the process.

Experience architecture helps people to work together, leveraging mutual efforts, ideas, and designs to create on-target, high-value experiences. Experience architecture begins with a motif: a set of target emotional outcomes compatible with the values of customers, employees, and other key constituents. The motif provides creative governance as experiences are built, one detail at a time.

Some of the tools experience architecture uses are blueprints to show the big picture supported by the details, and narratives for the roles people play. You can use experience architecture to envision the future state of the business; to listen to customers and create a vision that meets their needs; to manage the enterprise to make the future vision real; to communicate that vision to the customers. You can use experience architecture for more than big picture and strategy work. You can use it get at the details that make ideas real, such as; building computer applications and processes that touch customers and employees, coordinating multiple projects and initiatives; continuously learning, and completing the listen and respond cycle.

Experience architects are the customer's advocates as surely as they are the advocates of the enterprise, its employees, its managers, and its stakeholders. Led by the chief experience architect (CEA), the individual responsible for creating customer strategy, they're the ones who listen and respond — who shape the experience that creates a leading brand that thrives and endures even as market conditions change.

Experience Architecture and Personalization

Experience architects are the modern Ike Godseys. They may not be able to greet every customer by name, but their efforts are effective at large scale because they know how to listen, how to shape the enterprise, and how to provide the clues that make up the powerful brand experience that customers will respond to. Experience architects craft compelling experiences that add value for the customers and inspire brand loyalty.

Experience architecture is personalization taken to the ultimate level. It's no longer about putting someone's name on a piece of junk mail or finding more customers that fit the needs of the company. In the long run, that thinking dooms the company to failure. Untapped markets are finite resources.

Experience architecture isn't about a quick fix; it's not about selling one more pair of pajamas. It's about creating true value for the customer, a more inspiring environment for employees, and, in the end, greater returns for shareholders. Most of all, it's about creating positive experiences that inspire enduring brand loyalty.

The best brands are doing it right now. You can too.

5 Personalization of Global Sales and Marketing Activities in the Digital Economy

A Strategic Perspective

Venkatesh Shankar, Ralph J. Tyser Fellow and Professor of
Marketing, Robert H. Smith School of Business, University of
Maryland

Mary P. Donato, Vice President of Global Teleweb Channel, Dun
and Bradstreet

Personalization of global sales and marketing initiatives is increasing in the digital economy. Personalization of global sales and marketing online can be defined as the set of sales and marketing actions that tailors a company's web site to different needs of users or groups of users around the world. What are the key managerial issues in personalizing online global sales and marketing? What strategic framework is useful in analyzing personalization issues in global sales and marketing? How can a firm formulate a good personalization strategy for global sales and marketing? What is the likely future of personalization in global sales and marketing? We address these important questions in this chapter.

Introduction

Consider the following projections.

- By 2005, more than 70 percent of the one billion Web users around the world will be non-English speakers (www.idc.com).
- By 2007, Chinese will be the number one language on the Web (www.accenture.com).
- In 2002, U.S. e-marketplaces expected 44 percent of their volume to come from abroad (www.forrester.com).

Given these projections, international business growth is a critical factor for the success of firms in the digital economy. International markets hold the promise of new customers and efficiencies in manufacturing, distribution, management, research and development, and marketing. Companies that can leverage valuable resources globally will be the most competitive and have the greatest potential to grow. Companies that remain mired in local markets, with static cost structures and limited resources, will face increasing competitive pressure and risk becoming marginalized or extinct.

The Internet is becoming an intrinsic part of an effective global marketing and sales strategy. For example, Lands' End, Inc. started an online operation in 1995 and now generates 16 percent of its total sales online. In late 1999, Lands' End launched online stores in the United Kingdom, Germany and Japan, and then Ireland, France, and Italy in 2000. Today, 14 percent of the company's business is outside of the United States and the first three international subsidiaries account for 11 percent of total sales. The company ships to 185 countries, all from its Dodge, WI, headquarters.

With the emergence and growth of e-business and the Internet, enterprises increasingly recognize that successful globalization and localization of their products, services, and Web sites is a strategic imperative and competitive requirement. Globalization refers to standardization of offerings and web sites across different cultures and countries. Localization refers to adaptation of offerings and web sites to different cultures and countries according to their needs. Firms are providing a spectrum of personalized globalization and localization services online to improve worldwide communication, marketing, selling, and fulfillment to their customers, suppliers, partners, and employees. The International Data Corporation (IDC) predicts that personalization of global sales and marketing activities online will grow quickly during 2002 and 2003. Personalization online refers to actions that tailor a company's Web site to the different needs of users or groups of users (Shankar 2001). Personalization of global sales and marketing online can be defined as the set of sales and marketing actions that tailor a company's Web site to the different needs of users or groups of users around the world. Because sales and marketing activities are the primary customer-facing activities of any firm, personalization initiatives in sales and marketing are focused predominantly on customers. The goal of personalization is to enhance the firm's attention to its customers and improve its relationships with customers. Online personalization is closely tied to managing customer relationships electronically (e-customer relationship management [e-CRM]). Companies typically tailor their Web sites to the needs of their customers in the following ways:

- Creating and maintaining customized content (for example, MyX.com),
- Providing customers with access to their accounts and maintaining the accounts,
- Collecting information on customer preferences,
- Offering express transactions,
- Offering personal-productivity tools,
- Providing wish lists,
- Providing saved links,
- Recognizing returning customers,
- Targeting marketing or advertising to customers,
- Individualizing the appearance of the Web site,
- Offering customized prices,
- Tailoring email alerts,
- Recommending products,
- Configuring products online,
- Organizing the Web site around customer needs,
- Managing a customer service knowledge base,
- Maintaining multiple profiles for billing and shipping, and
- Integrating all customer data.

Key Issues in Personalization of Online Global Sales and Marketing Activities

According to the Personalization Consortium (a group of firms involved in personalization efforts) (www.personalization.org), the goals of personalization are to

- Better serve customers by their anticipating needs,
- Make interactions between the firm's Web site and its users efficient and satisfying for both parties, and
- Build relationships that encourage customers to return for subsequent purchases.

Customers increasingly expect enterprises to offer and price goods and services based on such variables as customer, channel, and product groupings. They look for customized interactions with the Web sites. They are more loyal to those firms from whose Web sites, products, and services they perceive that they derive greater personalized value. Firms face some key issues in this regard:

When should a firm configure its sales and marketing activities for personalization?

An enterprise must decide whether it will personalize its Web pages and content, or set simple cross-selling and up-selling rules. It could do any of the following:

- Assemble or engineer products to order,
- Ship products to order when customers specify multiple attributes for a product family,
- Establish a complex structure of pricing based on customer, channel, and product groupings, and
- Employ mobile field salespersons.

To decide when to use personalization, firms may find the following framework useful (Figure 1). This framework has two key dimensions, customer needs worldwide and life time value (LTV) (Shankar 2001). When customer needs worldwide do not vary much and the values of customers to the firm over their lifetime are similar, firms can practice standardized mass marketing. When customer needs vary around the world and the lifetime values of the customers vary significantly, firms should consider personalized global marketing solutions.

	Customer Needs Worldwide	
Distribution of LTV	Undifferentiated	Differentiated
Similar	Standardized mass marketing	Adaptive marketing
Different	Global frequency marketing	Personalized global marketing

Figure 1. Personalized Global Marketing
Source: Adapted from Shankar (2001), Personalization in the Digital Environment in Pushing the Digital Frontier, by American Management Association.

What should the firm's personalization strategy be?

Once a firm has determined that it should personalize its global sales and marketing activities, it must decide on its personalization strategy for its customers worldwide. A strategic framework and the key questions for formulating a personalization strategy are as follows.

A Strategic Framework for Personalization Decisions

Firms should think about personalization strategically. A strategic framework for making decisions about personalization starts with the firm's business goal. The business goal determines the potential personalized solutions. The similarities and differences among customers around the world drive the degree of personalization the firm can employ at its Web site. Personalized content, in turn, affects the sales and marketing activities that the firm can undertake on its Web site. The firm chooses what initiatives to undertake based on the costs of personalization technology and for online sales and marketing activities and the returns it expects from its investment.

Evolution of Personalization
In theory, personalization entails personalized interactions with every member of the target audience. In practice, however, personalization has evolved through four generations (Figure 2), going from static sites to more individualized sites. In the first generation, static sites comprising brochureware or product and company information were common. Web sites that greet known visitors by name or portals that allow users to select the content appearing on the site are examples of low-level forms of personalization associated with this generation. The second generation personalization offered targeted features, such as search engines and Web pages for user categories. The third generation of personalized Web sites offered such features as rules-based matching, context-based matching, alerts and targeted e-mail, and dynamic profiling. The fourth generation offers a global personalized interface, cross-sell and up-sell features, in addition to the features from the third generation.

Evolution of Customer Relationships
Firms should address three phases of customer relationship in their global personalization efforts (Figure 3). In the first phase, the firm defines the rules for customer interaction and organizes its relationships with its customers. In the second phase, it uses its Web site to establish trust and to develop its relationship with its customers. In the final phase, it develops a fully personalized site based on an integrated view of the customer. Over time, the Web site features directed toward the community

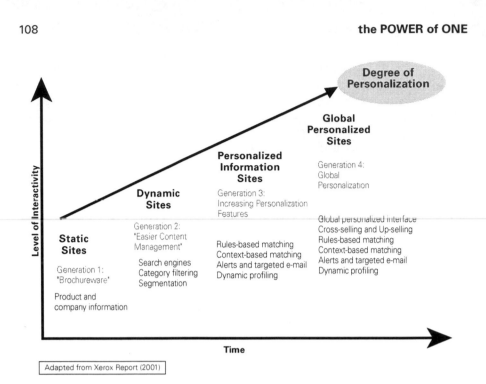

Figure 2. Evolution of Personalization

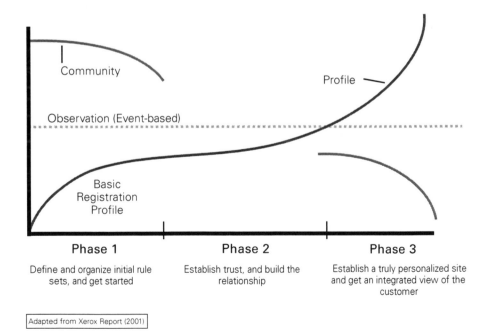

Figure 3. Evolution of Customer Relationships

of users become less important and the firm updates the individual user profiles, which becomes valuable sources for personalization.

Several examples illustrate the different types of personalized services currently available. These examples are described below. Providing information (including news) and purchasing appear to be two key areas for personalization. The Xerox example offers some personalization features and the use of personalization tools to develop a model to assist sales and marketing. Services that allow great selectivity of the content coverage are typified by MyYahoo (Bonnet 2000). A specific application area, namely, customized television listing, is also described. For those who want to make a longer-term investment in using a personalized service, repeated purchases are supported by sites such as Staples.com. Amazon.com provides an example of how personalized recommendations are employed as a marketing tool for users worldwide.

Sabre's Virtually There offers an example of personalized reservation tools in multiple languages.

MyXerox.com

Personalized Marketing through Predictive Modeling of Order Cancellations
Xerox's business objective was to improve customer-retention rate for high volume, high profit, light-lens products around the world. It wanted to predict order cancellations and to develop mechanisms for salvaging relationships with canceling customers.

Personalized Solution
A number of factors drive Xerox's relationship with its customers, including sales coverage, product performance, price, service, response time, billing, contract types, overall business relationships, and competitive presence. When a customer decides to cancel its order for a specific product, it probably does so for a combination of reasons, not just one. In addition, every customer values each aspect of her or his relationship with Xerox differently, so each relationship has to be assessed individually.

Xerox wanted to develop a model that would predict order cancellations by customer and that would also identify the factors that would trigger cancellation by that customer. By knowing some triggers in advance, Xerox would be better able to salvage its relationship with that customer and retain that customer. The model building approach consisted of three steps:

- Data Integration: The first step was to integrate customer data relevant to each potentially important driver of customer cancellations. The resulting integration brought together over 1,000 variables from multiple systems, integrated at the level of individual product serial numbers.

- Historical Study: In the second step, Xerox identified customers who had canceled the targeted products during the previous three years. Using statistical techniques such as regression analysis to identify the significant triggers for cancellations, Xerox built a model that quantified the variables and narrowed the list of 1,000 potential variables to the 20 most significant variables.
- Application to Current Customers: In the third step, Xerox applied the model to all its current customers worldwide for the targeted products. The final output of the model was a probability of cancellation for each targeted product by serial number.

Implementation

Because Xerox was able to identify the red flags, it could craft individualized messages for all of its customers (segment size of one). In the first implementation of this high-risk customer program, Xerox combined direct mail and the Xerox TeleWeb Channel using virtual sales executives (VSE) to make personalized follow-up calls. By proactively seeking to understand the current cancellation triggers (or the lack of such triggers) in the customer's relationship with Xerox, the VSE can address problems before they become worse, and it can anticipate the needs of the customer. Because the cancellation triggers include product issues, service issues, sales concerns, and the type of contract signed, the VSE's message is likely to hit home with the customer and put Xerox in a proactive role, instead of in a reactive position. The model was extremely accurate in predicting which serial numbers each customer was likely to cancel, when validated against 2001 actual order cancellations.

Future Personalization Efforts

Xerox plans the following for the future:

- It plans to profile all existing customers using different touch points such as the telephone, the Web, email, and face-to-face interactions, and to offer one-to-one, customized messages based on the findings for each customer.
- It plans to customize direct mail messages based on cancellation triggers for each customer. For example, if Xerox determines that a customer has had service problems, but is using its machine at a rate greater than recommended, it may send a specific mailing that addresses the service issues and shows the customer that

Xerox can reduce the customer's total cost of ownership by moving the customer to a product better suited the customer's needs.

• Xerox plans to target its customers who appear to loyal, or unlikely to cancel, for additional offerings, thereby leveraging Xerox's current good relationships and increasing its share of the customer's purchases.

Source: Xerox Report (2001)

Xerox

By signing up for MyXerox, visitors to Xerox's Web site can get the following benefits.

• They can log-in once and have access to all Xerox service offerings.
• They can view exclusive offers and promotions.
• They can track the status of their orders online.
• They can reorder based on their online order history and their stored or update shipping and billing addresses.

My Yahoo

Yahoo is one of the largest information portals in the world. It has Web sites and customers in 23 countries. After registering at the U.S. personalization site, MyYahoo, users can customize the Web site layout and select content from a choice of modules. Modules include news items, stock prices, weather reports, TV listings, and traffic reports. Users can control the modules according to their needs and manipulate the arrangement of content on the screen. Users can also determine how frequently content is updated (Figure 4). Yahoo offers different personalization features in its Web sites in different countries such as Canada, India, and France.

Staples

Staples is an 800-pound-gorilla superstore in office supplies in the U.S. with operations in Canada, UK, and Germany. At www.staples.com, the Web site for its U.S. customers, customers can compile the products they buy often into a list of favorite items (Figure 5). They can also ask for email reminders for reordering. They can customize their browsing by using the Favorite Aisles feature to create lists of the product categories they visit frequently. Groups of people, such as companies or organizations can define group profiles so that members of the groups (for example, employees) can use commonly set up features. At www.staples.ca, its Canadian Web site, these features are available under a space titled "Time Savers" which comprises features such as favorite items, email reminders, past purchase history, product

Bienvenue - Yahoo! - Aide - Ouvrir session

YAHOO!

POUR PARTIR EN VACANCES   votre adresse   votre ville

YAHOO! Cartes

Nouvelle Page   mardi - avr. 29

[Choisir couleurs & options] [Choisir le contenu de la page] [Modifier la mise en page] [Ajouter pages]   [Cacher les boutons]

Yahoo! Actualités • Cliquez ici pour suivre en continu les développements de la crise irakienne

Ouvrez une session Yahoo!

Vous n'êtes pas inscrit

Inscrivez-vous

Déjà inscrit sur Yahoo!

Compte Yahoo!

Yahoo! Mot de passe:

Mémoriser compte et mot de passe

[Ouvrir session]

Un peu perdu? À l'aide

Cours de la bourse [Modifier] [X]

▽ Cours

CAC-40	2940,80	-8,77
DJIA	8462,30	-9,31
NASDAQ	1465,47	+3,23
EURUSD-X	1,106700	0,0000

[Trouver cours]

Symbol Lookup

Quote data provided by Reuters. délai : 30 min -

* infos pendant les dernières 24h

Météo [Modifier] [X]

Marseille	13...22 C
Montreal	1...14 C
Paris	12...18 C
Toulouse	13...24 C
Tunis	16...29 C

cliquez sur une ville pour des prévisions détaillées

Photo du jour 29 avr. 20 h 40 [X]

La France veut accroître la protection de sa façade maritime
LES PRINCIPALES MAREES NOIRES EN EUROPE

Nouvelle Page Actualités 29 avr. 20 h 40 [Modifier] [X]

Personnalisez vos dépêches d'actualité pour ne lire que ce qui vous intéresse

France: Monde   29 avr. 20 h 24

- Tripoli accepte sa responsabilité civile dans l'attentat de Lockerbie
- Treize Irakiens tués par les troupes américaines, Moscou contre la levée des sanctions
- Abbas et son gouvernement obtiennent la confiance du Parlement palestinien

France: Politique   29 avr. 20 h 31

- Sarkozy annonce une hausse des expulsions de clandestins
- La France veut accroître la protection de sa façade maritime
- Les députés adoptent le projet Plagnol sur les simplifications administratives

France: Sport   29 avr. 20 h 26

- Dakar 2004: arrivée de nouveau à Dakar, modifications du règlement
- Sporting Portugal: l'entraîneur Laszlo Boloni ne sera pas reconduit
- Egypte-France Espoirs: les Bleuets rodent le groupe en Egypte

Programmes télé [Modifier] [X]

20:00	20:30	21:00	21:30

Et sur Yahoo! [X]

Actualités
- Actualités
- Finances
- Météo
- Sport

Commerce
- Enchères
- Petites Annonces
- Shopping
- Voyages

Communautés
- Clubs
- Tchatche

Communication
- Agenda
- Carnet d'adresses
- Cartes de voeux
- Courrier
- Messenger
- Mobile
- Photos
- Porte-Documents

Loisirs
- Astrologie
- Encyclopédie
- Jeux
- Musique
- Télé

Personnalisation
- Compagnon
- Mon Yahoo!
- Signets
- Musique
- Télé

Recherche Yahoo! [X]

[Rechercher]

Agenda [Modifier] [X]

◁ avril 2003 ▷

Di	Lu	Ma	Me	Je	Ve	Sa

Aujourd'hui: 29 avril 2003

Today   Ajouter un évènement

Sign up for Yahoo! Calendar and be reminded of today's and upcoming events.

Calculatrice [X]

7	8	9	√
4	5	6	%
1	2	3	MR
0	.	%	M-
CE	BCK		M+

[Choisir couleurs & options] [Choisir le contenu de la page] [Modifier la mise en page] [Ajouter pages]

--Ajouter modules en colonne gauche-- ⬧	--Ajouter du contenu au centre-- ⬧	--Ajouter modules en colonne droite-- ⬧
Ajouter	Ajouter	Ajouter

POUR PARTIR EN VACANCES   votre adresse   votre ville

YAHOO! Cartes

Figure 4. MyYahoo's French Web site

Figure 5. Screenshot from Staples' U.S. Web Site, Explaining the Use of the Favorite Items Feature

matchmaker, ready made lists, and rebates. At its German Web site (www.staples.de), personalization is lowest. Thus, Staples personalizes its sites differently in these different countries.

Amazon

Amazon.com, the popular online book retailer has Web sites in many countries including the US, UK, France, Germany, Japan, Spain, and Austria. It was an early mover in personalization. Among other activities, Amazon suggests products of interest to visitors browsing its Web site. Amazon infers a visitor's interests from previous purchases and from ratings it gives to titles. It compares the individual's inferred interests with those of other customers to determine the titles to recommend using collaborative filtering. It can remove from the recommended list books the customer has already bought. A visitor who removes titles from a recommendation list by the books on the list helps Amazon to create new recommendation lists (Figure 6).

Sabre's Virtually There

Getting personal in a global economy with a Web-based business is a challenge for every company. Not only does the Web take away most face-to-face interaction, it has forced companies to do business 24 hours a day, 7 days a week in languages in which most of us couldn't say much more than "hello." New personalization tools are helping many online businesses connect more directly with their customers, but most of these tools tend to ignore the multi-cultural and multi-lingual client base companies are now serving via the web. Sabre® Virtually There™ is a success story that demonstrates one such tool that is helping the travel industry personalize business on a global scale using the web.

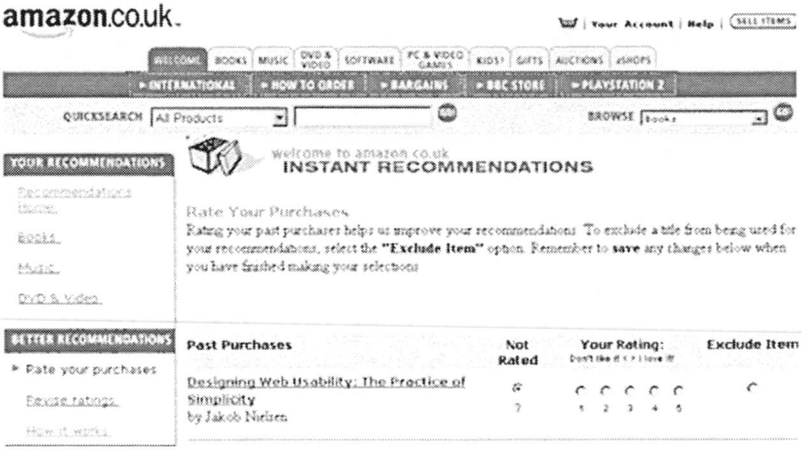

Figure 6. Screenshot of Amazon's Ratings Facility from its UK Web site

Virtually There provides personalized, real time itinerary, destination information and travel tools (Figure 7). When a trip is booked through a Sabre Connected travel arranger or the online booking site, a personalized itinerary with real-time information is set up for the traveler. The personal itinerary, accessed through the www.virtuallythere.com Web site, coordinates information on flights, gate assignments, hotels, rental cars, and the weather, all of which are instantly updated if travel plans change.

Because travel is often global, it was important that Virtually There be able to develop this personal relationship with customers in many different countries. Virtually There's personalization effort begins by making all of its features and functionality available in seven languages: English, Italian, German, French, Spanish, Dutch, and Portuguese. Destination information, such as attractions, museums, restaurants, theaters, sporting events, insider tips on local hot spots and maps, is produced by people living in that particular city, in the local language.

Virtually There also enhances the services offered by in-house or third party travel arrangers and is a cost saving tool for travel agencies. The Sabre reservation system is used by more than 66,000 travel agencies in 112 countries on 6 continents. Virtually There enables these travel arrangers to give superior customer service to their clients 24 hours a day, 7 days a week; something they would never be able to do without significant expense. In fact, research shows that more than 7 out of 10 travelers say that Virtually There increases their satisfaction with their arranger.

Virtually There also reduces agency costs associated with printing and faxing of itineraries. As Amy LaFave of Travel and Transport told

essential **travel** information

Members   Privacy Policy   Help

HOME   MOBILE SERVICES   DESTINATION SERVICES

Language:
[English ▼]

View an Itinerary

Reservation code
[   ]

Passenger last name
[   ]

Time displayed in:
12 Hour (6:00pm)
24 Hour (18:00)

[View Itinerary]

Virtually There®
Now all of your important travel information is in one place so you can travel smarter.

Looking for your itinerary? Just enter your **reservation code** and last **name** into the form to the left and we'll pull it up.

Don't have a current trip planned?
▸ View a sample itinerary

Newsletter 🗔
SIGN UP NOW
for travel e-newsletters and special offers from *Virtually There* partners

Weather
Get the five day forecast for your destination
Enter city, state, country, province or zip:
[   ] [Go]
Weather maps
[Select a region ▼]

City Guides
Discover what to do and see in over 2300 cities worldwide.

Select a region:
[Select a region ▼]

Top 19 cities:
[Select a city ▼]

Flight tracker
Check flight status
Airline:
[Select airline ▼]
Flight Number:
[   ] [Go]
▸ More search options:

Travel Alerts and Information
▸ Worldwide travel warning updates
▸ Need to know telephone numbers
▸ Answers to the most frequently asked questions we have heard

Your travel arranger is the best source for pertinent information regarding your specific trip plans.

Valuable *Virtually There* Services

▸ **Passport/visa information**— No more standing in line. This service does the work for you. (US citizens only.)

▸ ***Virtually There* "Travel News"**— An exclusive free newsletter for *Virtually There* subscribers brimming with comprehensive destination insights, travel tips and travel news that helps you travel smarter. Sign Up Now

▸ **Currency converter**— Calculates the conversion rate for currencies in 164 countries. Plus, print out the Currency Cheat Sheet and World Currency Chart to have powerful tools at your fingertips.

▸ **Flight Notification**— Register now to be notified of changes to your departure gate and terminal information, delayed flight departure, and departing flight cancellation via a text message to e-mail, pager, or mobile phone.

▸ **Add to Calendar**— If you are a user of Microsoft Outlook, Lotus Notes, Act 2000! Or Palm Desktop, you can download your trip plans directly to your desktop organizer.

About Us | Advertise | For Travel Agents
Privacy Policy | Copyright and Trademark Notices

Sabre
virtually
there

Figure 7. Sabre's Virtually There Home Page

us, "Our clients can print their own itineraries and e-ticket receipts from the Virtually There Web site, a feature which has dramatically reduced the costs and time associated with these documents. Making business personal worldwide means giving our customers the information they need and want, when they want it, in their choice of languages and media formats. This service and delivery enables us to establish a personal relationship with our customers on a global scale that paves the way for customer satisfaction and retention."

What type of personalization software should the firm use?

A firm can select from three primary types of software, namely, rule-based, collaborative, and learning agent technology based or dynamic personalization (Shankar 2001). Rule-based software uses business rules to deliver certain types of information to different user groups based on user profiles (e.g., Kodak Picture Center, www.kodak.com). Collaborative filtering tools identify common patterns between the purchase behavior of one customer with that of another (e.g., www.amazon.com). Learning agent technology uses behavioral click-stream pattern to dynamically learn customer preferences and deliver suitable content and interactive experience.

What vendor(s) should the firm select?

The final issue is the choice of the vendor. Companies have a range of vendors to choose from. At the high end are vendors such as ATG, Broadvision, Edify, Grouplens, Learn Sesame, and Vignette. At the low end are companies/products such as ColdFusion, LikeMinds, Neuromedia and Web objects. Other vendors include Silver Stream, Blaze, Brokat, Broadbase, and Manna.

Privacy Issues

Because much of personalization entails intensive collection and use of personal information, companies must consider the implications for users' privacy and its protection of the information users supply. For active personalization at least, users must knowingly provide personal information to benefit from personalization features. Once users see benefits, they may be willing to provide further information, if they know what the company intends to do with their information. In passive collection of information, users may often be unaware of what data the company is collecting about them. To guard all personal information, companies must encrypt passwords and sensitive data and also evaluate the procedures or have an external organization do it. Many sites have privacy statements (or disclosure statements) that describe exactly what kind of information they gather and their policies about how they use and share that information. Platform for Privacy Preferences (P3P) is a World Wide Web Consortium (W3C) proposal for controlling the use of personal information on Web sites. P3P provides a way for Web sites to disclose how they handle user information and for users to describe their privacy preferences. P3P-enabled Web sites make this information available in a standard, machine-readable format. P3P-enabled browsers can read this snapshot automatically and compare it to the consumer's own privacy preferences. The aim of P3P is to "communicate to users, simply and automatically, a Web site's stated privacy policies, and how they compare with the user's own policy preferences. P3P does not set minimum standards for privacy, nor can it monitor whether sites adhere to their own stated procedures" (http://www.w3.org/P3P).

Personalized news is likely to become a regular feature of our daily lives. Kevin Kelly, former executive editor of *Wired* magazine, thinks that news will soon follow us wherever we go. "In addition to static Web sites, there will be an entirely new species of things following you around at your general invitation. Devices that chime on your wrist when there's a traffic jam ahead and pagers that broadcast the scores of your favorite teams as their games are being played. If the president is assassinated, the news will pop up in the middle of the spreadsheet on your home computer."

For consumers, such a world may be an information nirvana — or a vision of privacy hell. Companies will amass personal profiles listing consumers' shopping habits, their surfing behavior, and perhaps their personal traits and beliefs. Someone somewhere will have a record that includes the style and size of the underwear a consumer ordered online. In some cases, companies will know consumers by name and address; in other cases, they will know the consumers only by the identifying number on their computers. This, of course, is the flip side of personalization. The price of the Daily Me is the surrender of some measure of privacy. Every online transaction is an exchange of services or products for money and an exchange of information.

Are the personalized offerings worth the price? That's a question every user must answer for himself or herself. But two things are clear: Companies must become much more forthright in disclosing exactly how they are using or sharing data about consumers. And users must be adamant in refusing to surrender personal information until they are satisfied that the company collecting information is properly safeguarding their privacy, using their information only to offer greater value.

Establishing policies regarding online privacy is complicated for personalization in the global context. Different countries have different laws on online privacy. In most European countries, privacy rules are very stringent compared to the U.S. rules. These differences in privacy regulations have important implications for personalization in global marketing activities. Companies may have to use very different types and degrees of personalization to conform to the regulations of various countries.

Formulation of Strategy for Global Sales and Marketing Personalization

When formulating a strategy for personalizing global sales and marketing, companies should ask the following questions:

- *How much value can I offer to my customers through personalization? What is my value proposition to my customers? How much will it differ across customers worldwide?* The answers to these questions depend on the global distribution of customers by lifetime value and the differences in their needs.
- *Who are additional target users of the site (for example, employees, partners, suppliers)?* If the firm has many additional potential users, then it should decide what degree of personalization to use for them and whether it is compatible with the degree of personalization used for customers.
- *What are the firms' objectives for personalization?* A firm's objectives for personalization typically follow from its business goal and could include sharing information, providing online support, and enabling e-commerce.
- *How much do customers' needs differ around the world?* If different countries have very different needs, the firm may have to design separate Web sites for the different countries perhaps with different types of personalization.
- *What are the costs of personalization?* The costs of personalization vary with the type and degree of personalization. In deciding the extent of personalization, companies should consider the costs and benefits of proposed personalization strategies and compare the costs of personalization with the costs of not undertaking it (such as loss of market share and loyalty).
- *How long will the firm take to adopt different levels of personalization?* Companies that intend to adopt personalization in stages should plan their future personalization strategies, carefully estimating the time required for each stage.
- *Can the firm use personalization as the main differentiator of its brand?* Some firms can stay ahead of their competitors by using personalization to maintain close relationships with their customers. Others, however, may offer average levels of personalization or even try to catch up to their leaders.
- *What is (will be) the firm's position compared to its competitors in personalization?* Since personalization of global sales and marketing activities is constantly changing, firms should compare themselves to their competitors from time to time.

- *Will the firm's personalization be consistent and integrated with its overall global business strategy?* A firm's global business strategy is a key driver of its personalization efforts for its customers worldwide. Firms that try to standardize across countries may use personalization that are common to similar customer segments around the world. Firms that adapt their strategies to suit individual countries should pursue country-specific personalization strategies.
- *Will the firm integrate its personalization for global sales and marketing with its technology strategy?* And will it integrate its online and offline marketing channels and its customer information databases and systems?
- *How do various countries' privacy rules affect the firm's personalization strategy?* If the countries in which the firm markets its products differ very little in their privacy rules, the firm may be able to pursue similar personalization strategies for all of them. If, however, they differ a great deal, the firm will have to fine-tune its personalization strategies by country.
- *What metrics should the firm use to monitor and evaluate its personalization strategy?* It could use repeat visits, time spent on

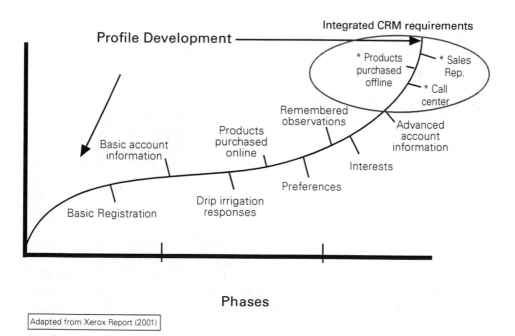

Adapted from Xerox Report (2001)

Figure 8. Building Customer Relationships

the Web site, customer satisfaction, customer loyalty, number of transactions, amount of billings, or share of wallet.

Based on its answers to these questions, the firm can decide how to use personalization to build customer relationships (Figure 8). This firm starts by profiling its customers when they register at its Web site. It gradually moves toward integration of activities with the efforts of multiple channels in the firm.

Future Issues in Personalizing Web sites for Global Sales and Marketing

As personalization of global sales and marketing activities evolves, two trends are emerging. First, firms are moving from personalization based on popular offerings to personalization based on preferences for particular product or service attributes. Most current personalization schemes are based on popularity. For instance, Amazon.com might recommend Johnny Cash CDs to people who buy Willie Nelson's latest album, because Cash tends to be popular among Nelson fans. That kind of personalization just pushes the best sellers. The consumers often don't benefit, because they already know about the popular option that's being foisted upon them. And the retailer has missed an opportunity to push an attractive product that the consumer might have been happy to learn about.

A personalization technology that can recommend appropriate offbeat products could offer greater value to individuals. Instead of relying on popularity as the determining factor, attribute-based personalization makes recommendations to customers based on who they are and what they like. The retailer creates a profile of each customer and then uses that profile to match customer attributes with those of various products.

The downside to this method is that it requires merchants to compile a list of attributes for each product they offer. Such lists aren't lying around waiting to be plunked into a database, so compiling them takes work. In addition, customers have to be willing to complete surveys and fill out their own profiles.

Allaire plans to release a personalization product based on this idea. If consumers can see real value in filling out the profiling forms, Allaire's product should be widely adopted. Retailers won't mind the extra work if they find that it makes inventory move faster.

The second trend is that firms are personalizing Web sites for global customers, such as multinational corporations. A global company could have a single one-stop personalized account with its supplier, and its employees in different countries could log in and get similar interfaces and standard experiences. In addition to the supplier's common personalized Web site across the world, users from each country may also make their country-specific personalizations. Thus, personalization will be available in multiple layers enhancing customer value.

Conclusions

Personalization of online sales and marketing activities worldwide is increasingly important in the growing digital economy. Firms must decide whether they need to personalize and if they need to personalize, what should be their personalization strategy and what types and from which vendors of software to buy. Firms should adopt a strategic framework starting with the firm's business goal and ending with concrete sales and marketing activities. When formulating a personalization strategy, a firm should ask questions ranging from the value derived by the customer through personalization to the metrics that could be used to monitor and evaluate personalization efforts. In the future, we should see more flexible personalization technologies and a focus on providing one-stop personalization for global companies.

References

Bonnet, Monica. 2000. Personalization of Web Services: Opportunities and Challenges, Working Paper.

The Personalization Consortium, http://www.personalization.org/personalization.html

Shankar, Venkatesh. 2001. "Personalization in the New Digital Environment," in Pushing the Digital Frontier, American Management Association, New York.

Xerox Report. 2001. Enabling a Customer Focused Web Site, Presentation.

6 Learning About Customers Without Asking

Alan L. Montgomery, Associate Professor of Marketing, Carnegie
Mellon University

Kannan Srinivasan, H. J. Heinz II Professor of Management,
Marketing, and Information Systems, Carnegie Mellon
University

Introduction

Personalized marketing refers to customizing offers and content to the individual consumer. This individualized approach to marketing is also called interactive marketing (Blattberg and Deighton 1991, Haeckel 1998) or one-to-one marketing (Peppers, Rogers, and Dorf 1999). At the heart of an interactive marketing strategy is the ability to learn about individual consumers and adapt the marketing messages correspondingly. The purpose is to create more value for consumers to increase the consumers' loyalty to the supplier, and thereby increase the supplier's profitability.

A fundamental question is how do we learn about a consumer so that we know what level and type of personalization is valuable to the consumer? The obvious answer is to ask the consumer directly, which we call active learning. Examples of actively seeking information from users online include log-ons, surveys, forms, and shipping information. These are frequently the fastest and easiest techniques for collecting information that suppliers use to personalize the products and services they offer. Unfortunately, active learning techniques have many shortcomings:

1. The direct approach requires too much effort on the part of the consumer. Imagine a visitor to Ford's Web site who would like to build a car and must select every one of the 4,000 component systems that make up the automobile. Clearly this would be too intensive an exercise.
2. The consumer may not know the correct answer, either lacking the proper knowledge or experience to evaluate the alternatives. For example, our visitor to Ford's Web site may lack the expertise to answer questions about engine options.
3. Consumers may be unwilling to reveal correct answers. Suppose Ford was to ask what price the user would be willing to pay for a customized car. Clearly consumers might bias their answers anticipating that Ford might use the information to set the price.
4. The direct approach is inefficient since it ignores information consumers reveal about their preferences in their past interactions and purchases. A good deal of internal and external information to the company can be used to supplement actively collected information. A repeat visitor to the Ford Web site, for example, who reviews the product information several times, shows a higher interest level than a one-time visitor; this is useful internal information in targeting and relationship building. Additionally, Ford may have access to previous car purchases through external sources that could also be used to customize the user's online experience.

Another type of learning is passive learning, and it is the subject here. Passive learning focuses on learning about consumers through the information they reveal online in browsing the Web. Active learning is still useful, and sometimes is the only method for learning about a consumer. Consider a company that needs a customer's mailing address. One could guess that the previous mailing address was still correct, which is a form of passive learning. But the direct approach of asking for a new mailing address is preferred. However, combining active and passive learning may yield a superior approach. For example, one could give the consumer a choice of shipping to the address used in the past or to a new address, which combines active learning (asking for a new address) and passive learning (presenting a previous address).

Many managers are unfamiliar with passive learning and they may be losing out on its benefits. Passive learning requires some sophistication on the part of the manager, which may explain why passive learning is less commonly used than active learning. A primary benefit of the Web is that it is a wonderful tool for collecting and processing information passively.

An Example of Passive Learning

To understand passive learning, consider a Web visitor to altavista.com who searches for an online stock broker using the keywords "online brokerage." AltaVista responds with a Web page that contains text, graphics, and links. One of the graphics is a banner advertisement. However, this graphic is not generated by AltaVista but is provided by another company, DoubleClick. DoubleClick provides advertising services for many Web sites.

Most Web browsers are configured to retrieve any graphics embedded within a page. Additionally, browsers automatically provide the referring Uniform Resource Locator (URL) when requesting graphic or other files. The user's search at AltaVista will result in a request for a graphic file (or the banner advertisement) from DoubleClick. Hence, the user has unknowingly started an opportunity for DoubleClick to use passive learning. In this case, AltaVista's referring URL signals to DoubleClick that the user is looking for financial information, which indicates that AltaVista directed the user to the site during a search for "online brokerage." DoubleClick can remember previous requests from this user by assigning the user a unique identification number and depositing this ID in a cookie on the user's browser. (A cookie is a small file of information that the Web server can store on a user's local PC). Using this cookie DoubleClick can identify this same user at any site that offers DoubleClick banner ads, such as U.S. News or the Dilbert Zone. DoubleClick's server uses the information it compiles on the user's history and profile to determine an appropriate advertisement and relays this ad to the user's browser, which displays it automatically. In this wonderful example of passive learning, DoubleClick learns about users without ever actively asking them questions.

While this system may seem complicated, it is transparent and automatic to the consumer. Its primary advantage is that it allows DoubleClick to display a banner ad on a finance topic targeted to an individual who has just visited a finance site or to rotate banner ads to maintain their effectiveness. DoubleClick can also display banner ads chosen on the basis of search terms and keywords. For example, if a user performs a search for "online brokerage" at altavista.com, a banner ad for Datek, an online brokerage, may be returned along with the results of the search. DoubleClick reports that the "click-thru" of targeted banner ads for Datek constructed in this way was over 15 percent, far beyond the usual 0 to 3 percent range. The cost for such a targeted banner ad may be $.085 per viewer, which is more than four times the cost of a nontargeted banner ad. In comparison the average cost of a 30-second commercial on television during prime time is about $.012 per viewer. Targeted advertisements are more costly, but their greater effectiveness may outweigh their costs. The use of passive learning goes far beyond targeted banner ads; it can be used in many contexts to customize the offers and content provided to users.

The Inputs of Online Learning

Learning occurs when we take the raw data and turn it into knowledge. We can measure the value of knowledge by the impact it has on a decision. Unfortunately, many managers do not know how to extract knowledge from the data they collect. Hence, the data have no value because it has no impact on their decisions. Fortunately many tools are available for turning data into action.

Online environments provide many sources of data. A natural byproduct of users accessing Web pages is a dataset that contains the sequence of URLs they visited, how long they viewed them, and at what time. This dataset is called the clickstream, and it is a rich resource for online learning. To maximize its potential, managers can merge the clickstream with demographic and purchase information or other external databases. The different types of data available online include purchase and transaction data, clickstream data, information collected from cookies, and e-mail data.

Purchase and Transaction Data

Generally, as marketers we wish to predict purchases so it is only natural to start with transaction data. In many retail contexts, transaction data are already collected automatically. For example, when you check out at your local supermarket, a computerized bar-code scanner records all your purchases, the prices you paid, any specials or coupons, and may associate these purchases with you using a frequent-buyer or affinity card. Besides the obvious uses of this information for accounting and inventory purposes it can also be used for marketing purposes. For example, we can compile these data through time and use them to predict a consumer's next purchase. In marketing research, we find that the best predictor of a future purchase is what the consumer has purchased in the past. For example, if we are trying to predict whether a shopper will purchase Tide or Wisk laundry detergent on a particular visit, the most valuable information is not age, gender, or other demographics. The most valuable piece of information is whether that person bought Tide in the past.

In addition, if we want to determine whether the shopper should get a coupon, the most relevant question is not what they have bought, but how will they respond to price promotions in the future. Rossi, McCulloch, and Allenby (1996) consider how purchase histories can be used to determine couponing policies. They estimate a statistical model known as a multinomial probit model to determine the price sensitivity of a supermarket shopper using information from previous purchases in a single product category, canned tuna. They used the model to determine what value (if any) of coupon to offer a shopper at the checkout stand and the expected profits for different coupons based on various information sets (Table 1). The blanket coupon drop assumed that all consumers received a coupon for 10¢ off on their next purchase. This blanket coupon drop is used as a benchmark to compare other strategies. Using demographic information to choose who received a coupon, they increased expected profits by 10 percent over a blanket coupon drop. In comparison, by using only data on the last purchase, they increased profits by 60 percent. Clearly purchase information is more valuable than demographic information in this context. In the full information case, they used information on both previous purchases and demographics and obtained a 160 percent increase in expected profitability over the blanket coupon drop. Purchase information used properly is an incredible resource.

Information set	Profit gain
Blanket coupon drop	1.0
Coupon drop using information from consumer demographics	1.1
Coupon drop using information from last purchase	1.6
Coupon drop using entire purchase history	1.9
Coupon drop using entire purchase history and demographics	2.6

Table 1. The relative value of information sets for the distribution of a coupon as estimated by Rossi, McCulloch, and Allenby (1996). Expected profits increase as more information is used. The most dramatic profit increases come from using purchase histories and not just demographic information.

Clickstream Data

Just as we can collect purchase data in physical stores, we can collect purchase data in virtual stores. However, the data set is much richer. In the brick and mortar retail store, we know what the customer purchased and what items and prices were available within the store. But imagine that we also record shopper movements through the store, what items they looked at and considered and those they ignored, how long shoppers considered their decisions, and whether they bought cake mix and then put cake frosting into their carts. This is exactly the kind of information we can collect in online shopping environments.

Consider a web user who visits the portal AltaVista, searches for "automobile," and selects the first site from the list of results, which is labeled "Automobile Magazine Just $11.95 a Year!" This Web session is illustrated in Figure 1, and the corresponding clickstream data set is provided in Table 2.

Date and Time of Access	Seconds Viewed	URL
18 Jul 2001:18:55:57	20	http://www.altavista.com
18 Jul 2001:18:56:17	38	http://www.altavista.com/sites/ search/Web?q=automobile
18 Jul 2001:18:56:55	18	http://store.yahoo.com/ magazinecity/9675-12.html

Table 2. This table provides in tabular form the clickstream dataset that would be collected from the session in Figure 1.

The browser does many tasks for the user automatically. When the user requested the second URL the document called for had many graphic images to be imbedded. The browser automatically requested these images from their servers and displayed them appropriately in the browser window. Three of the graphics were logos (Avsmall.gif) or navigational symbols (blended_icon.gif and truste_mark.gif) that were located at akamai.net. The other was a banner ad located at ad.doubleclick.net/click. Each of these requests created a trace on the servers at akamai.net or doubleclick.net and hence further opportunities to learn about the user for these companies.

There are four potential sources of clickstream data:
1. The host server (the computer of the site being visited) keeps a record of visits, usually called a server log. When a user

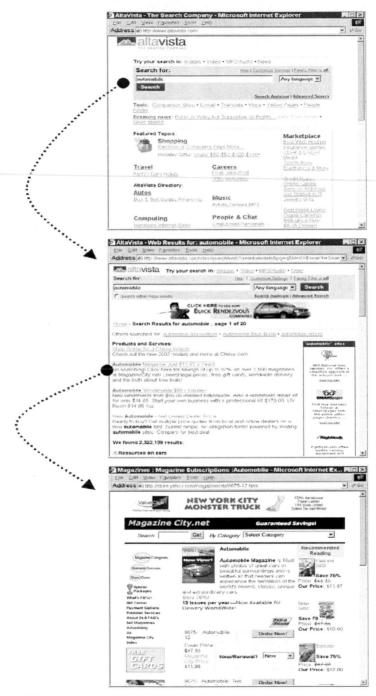

Figure 1. This sample clickstream session illustrates a search at the portal AltaVista for "automobile." The arrows illustrate the controls selected by the user and the flow of the session.

requests a page, the server records identifying information (the user's IP (Internet protocol) address, previous URL visited, and browser type) in the server log. In the example given in Figure 1, altavista.com would know that this user requested two different URLs from their server.

An advantage of collecting clickstream data from server logs is that they contain a record of everything done at a Web site. Unfortunately, they can also be difficult to process because they contain so much data. A practical problem with many server logs is that they become large very quickly. The Internet portal Yahoo! received 1.2 billion page requests per day as of July 2001. This generates terabytes of information to be stored every day.

Learning how to access and store this information can be incredibly challenging. Many companies provide products to summarize and analyze these logs, for example, Accrue, IBM SurfAid, IRG, MINEit, Macromedia, NetGenesis, NetIntellect, and WebTrends. Other companies, such as Accrue, CommerceTrends, Digital Archaeology, E.piphany, Hyperion, Informatica, MicroStrategy, Personify, and Sagent, provide consulting services that process clickstream data and aggregate them with online sales data and e-mail data to create a comprehensive picture of their client firm's business (Mena 2001).

To make its logs useful for later analysis the server should record what it presented to the user. This is a problem because servers generally offer large amounts of content and change it frequently. Many URLs and the content these URLs contain are dynamically created, which means that requests for the same page by two different users may result in two different pages. To manage the resulting data set and extract useful information, some companies scan each Web page presented to a user for titles or metatags. This process is called packet sniffing.

2. A major limitation of clickstream data collected from server logs is that the data come from only one site and do not enable tracking across sites. For example, in the previous example, AltaVista would not know what the user did before or after he or she left its Web site. One way around this is to provide links to content, such as graphic images, that are stored at other sites. For example, when DoubleClick provides graphic images at AltaVista, it can collect clickstream data from AltaVista's users without their intentionally visiting DoubleClick's Web site. Of course, AltaVista must be willing to place these images on its Web site. Many firms besides DoubleClick provide advertising placement services: 24/7Media, Ableclick, Advertising.com, AOL, BURST!Media, Cybereps, Engage, Go4Media, L90, Phase2Media, Premium

Network, RealMedia, Sonar, and ValueClick (Mena 2001). Large providers, such as DoubleClick and Engage, can leverage the large number of sites they do business with and track users across Web sites. For example, DoubleClick can remember that a visitor to iVillage.com is the same one that visited altavista.com last month, even though iVillage and AltaVista have no direct relationship.

Other third parties that can collect clickstream data by working in conjunction with Web servers are Application Services Providers (ASPs), such as Angara, Cogit, CoreMetrics, DigiMine, Interelate, Informative, Keylime, and WebMiner (Mena 2001). Frequently, these companies do not provide graphics the user will see as DoubleClick does, but 1x1 pixel images called Web bugs. These graphics are so small that they are invisible to Web visitors. CoreMetrics holds a patent for one type of Web bug. For example, walmart.com places Web bugs on its site that allow CoreMetrics to record a visitor's movements at walmart.com. CoreMetrics can then analyze these movements and make recommendations to walmart.com about its Web design and marketing policies. Another example of a Web bug is one used by zanybrainy.com in 2000. Whenever a customer made a purchase at zanybrainy.com, it placed a Web bug that relayed the purchase information to DoubleClick. Web bugs allow one company to communicate information about its Web visitors to another company.

3. Clickstream data can also be collected by a third party because of the network topology of the Internet. Users' requests for Web pages on their computers are relayed by a series of computers attached to the network before they finally reach their destination. Most users are connected to the Internet through an Internet service provider (ISP) or a commercial on-line service (COS), such as AOL. For example, when an AOL user makes a request, AOL's servers receive the request before it is relayed through the Internet. When an ISP or COS routes a request, it can record the routing information and create its own clickstream data set. (What AOL does with this information depends upon its privacy policy.) Because many ISPs and COSs cache their users' page requests, they do not always pass all requests on to the server. Instead, ISPs and COSs may serve many pages from their own archives to speed up responses to user requests. Unfortunately, this means that the server logs we discussed in (1) and (2) may contain only a subset of the users' viewings. Dreze and Zufryden (1997) discuss some of the challenges of using server log data to measure advertising effectiveness.

4. A final — and perhaps the most reliable — source of clickstream data is a meter program that can record what users do on their computers. This meter program can "watch" the user and record the URLs of all pages viewed in the browser window and any other application programs the user is running. Because this program works on the user's computer, it avoids problems with cached pages mentioned in (3). Such a program can also record how long users keep windows active, instead of simply when they request URLs.

A drawback to this technique is that the individual must be willing to run such a program. Most companies that use this method to collect clickstream data are marketing research companies, such as Jupiter Media Metrix and A. C. Nielsen. These companies create large, representative samples of households that own personal computers (PCs) and have consented to participate in such a panel. The companies use statistical techniques to project usage from these small samples to the overall population.

Cookies

Cookies are small text files that are stored by a user's browser. Cookies are important because they overcome a major shortcoming of the original design of the World Wide Web (WWW), the lack of memory about a user. Originally, those who developed the Web envisioned that users would view static text or content that would not change. Hence they saw no need for the system to remember that the user viewing one page was the same one who viewed another page. The content of a page was always the same, regardless of what content the user viewed previously. However, as the Web has evolved, a page may depend strongly on the previous page. For example, users may want to create shopping carts, avoid logging in every time they visit sites, or simply save their preferences from one click to the next.

Cookies allow Web servers to maintain memories about users. When a browser makes a request to a Web server, it also checks to see whether it has any cookies that the server has asked it to save from previous visits. The first time a user visits a Web server, he or she will not have any cookies for that site. The Web server can ask the browser to create cookies or change cookies when it responds to a user request.

The Web server determines how to use the cookie. For example, DoubleClick uses a cookie to assign every visitor who requests one of its files a unique identification number. Other servers use a cookie to identify the shopping basket, to save preferences about a Web site, or to identify which requests from a given computer are coming from the same browser window. Users can decide whether they want to accept a cookie, but most users do not change the default setting of "accept all cookies." Given that the primary use of the cookie is to track users, many privacy advocates are very concerned about the use of cookies, although no consensus has developed concerning privacy (Smith 2001).

E-mail

E-mail is one of the most frequently used applications on the Internet, and marketers can use it to reach customers. People use e-mail to communicate with colleagues, friends, and family. One property of e-mail that makes it different from Web browsing is that it is asynchronous. Generally, when a user requests a page from a Web server, it is displayed immediately and then removed after a short time. E-mail messages, however, may not be viewed for many hours or days. Also, they can persist for a long time, since users can save them for future reference. It is possible to embed Web bugs or references to graphic images in e-mail messages that will cause them to make requests to a Web server. When the user reads the e-mail message, the browser will request the server to display the graphic or Web bug, leaving a trace in a clickstream dataset. Hence, clickstream data and data on e-mail browsing can be combined.

Many companies have begun using e-mail for direct marketing. Companies such as Brigade, Brightware, Digital Impact, eGain, FaceTime, Kana, LivePerson, Message Media, and NetCentives (Mena 2001) provide e-mail systems that can be intelligent and can interface with other functions that their clients provide. For example, LivePerson provides facilities to monitor chat sites and to use advanced text-processing techniques to respond to user comments.

Passive Learning

Online data sources are valuable only if they change our actions as marketers. Most of the data sets we have mentioned are easy to collect but can be large and difficult to process. Data mining (Berry and Linoff 1997) is useful for processing these datasets. Data mining combines algorithms developed in computer science with statistical techniques to automatically search for patterns in large data sets. Currently, data mining is made up of diverse methods, such as regression analysis, decision trees, neural networks, Bayesian learning, genetic algorithms, and clustering. Many software providers provide data-mining tools: Angoss, BusinessMiner, Data Distilleries, IBM, Megaputer, Quadstone, Urban Science, Visual Insights, SAS, and SPSS. Unfortunately, these tools can be expensive and require trained analysts to process the data sets into actionable knowledge. These techniques extract knowledge from data collected passively, and several are very promising in turning data collected online into valuable intelligence for managers. Hence, data mining is another example of passive learning.

User Profiling

Frequently we want to identify users in terms of demographic characteristics or attitudes. For example, if we have separate clothing lines for men and women, determining users' genders could be useful for personalizing their experience. Answering questions can be burdensome for users—if they are willing to answer questions at all. We can use passive learning with clickstream data to make inferences about users' demographic characteristics and attitudes based upon the choices they made while visiting Web sites or pages. For example, visitors to sports sites are likely to be men. The question is how much can we learn and can we trust what we learn?

Montgomery (2001) developed a user-profiling technique using clickstream data. Consider the example of one user who visited 22 Web sites during a month (Table 3). Jupiter Media Metrix estimated the percentage of people visiting each domain at least once during the month who were women. For example, it estimated that 66 percent of visitors to ivillage.com are female. (This percentage is not weighted by the number of pages requested, and men may account for a lower percentage of page requests since they may request fewer pages per visit than women.) Without knowing anything about a user except that he or she visits ivillage.com, the odds are two to one that the user is female. These odds are quite reasonable because ivillage.com offers content geared towards women. For similar reasons, a gaming site may appeal primarily to

Domain Visited	Percentage of Visitors who are Female	Domain Visited	Percentage of Visitors who are Female
aol.com	48%	libertynet.org	63%
astronet.com	64%	lycos.com	39%
avon.com	75%	netradio.net	27%
blue-planet.com	52%	nick.com	57%
cartoonnetwork.com	56%	onhealth.com	59%
cbs.com	54%	onlinepsych.com	83%
country-lane.com	76%	simplenet.com	44%
eplay.com	47%	thriveonline.com	76%
halcyon.com	41%	valupage.com	59%
homearts.com	70%	virtualgarden.com	71%
ivillage.com	66%	womenswire.com	66%

Table 3. In this list of domains visited by a female user over the course of one month, Jupiter Media Metrix estimated the percentage of people who visited the domain at least once during the month that were female.

teenage boys, and sports sites may predominately attract men. On the other hand, portals such as Yahoo! and Excite draw audiences that are fairly representative of the Web as a whole and their use provides little information about gender.

If we did not know the gender of a Web user, we might form the hypothesis that the user was female since the user visits Web sites oriented towards a female audience (Table 3). Initially we could use the information that 45 percent of Web users in this month were female. If we knew that the user visited ivillage.com, 66 percent of whose visitors were female, we could update our inference that our hypothesis (the user is female) was true using this new piece of information. Statistically this is known as a Bayesian hypothesis-updating problem, and we could apply the following rule to recompute the probability that the user is female:

$$\ddot{p} = \frac{\dot{p} \cdot p}{\dot{p} \cdot p + (1 - \dot{p}) \cdot (1 - p)} = \frac{.45 \cdot .66}{.45 \cdot .66 + .55 \cdot .34} = .62$$

The original probability that the user is female is denoted by $\dot{p}$ = .45. The new information indicates the probability is .66, p=.66. The updated probability or posterior probability of our hypothesis is denoted by $\ddot{p}$ = .62. In other words, the probability that this is a female user has increased from 45 to 62 percent. Based on information from all 22 sites, the probability that the user is female is 99.97 percent (derived by updating the probability that the user is female by using information on all the sites listed in Table 3).

To assess the accuracy of this technique, we applied it to actual usage information from a sample of 19,000 representative Web users with one month of usage and known gender. Users in this sample vary a great deal; some visit only one site, while others may visit hundreds. If the model predicted that a user was male with more than an 80 percent probability, then we predicted the user to be male. We made similar predictions for female users. We had enough information to classify 60 percent of users as either male or female. Of the users we classified as male, 81 percent were male, and of the users we classified as female, 96 percent were female. The agreement between the predictions and actual gender validates the accuracy of the technique. More advanced techniques that account for statistical dependence between Web-site visits could increase the accuracy of these predictions.

In this example, we knew all the Web sites a user visited, but such thorough tracking is not necessary to employ a user-profiling technique. For example, we could determine the probability that a user who visited cnn.com were male by examining what categories he or she visited. Or we could guess whether a random visitor to ppg.com was an industrial buyer or technician by examining the types of pages visited. The technique does not require huge amounts of information. If we knew only that this user visited cbs.com, ivillage.com, libertynet.org, nick.com, and onlinepsych.com, we could still predict with a 95 percent degree of certainty that this was a female visitor. This is precisely the information that the DoubleClick network would have about this visitor.

Predicting the genders of Web users seems innocuous, but we can use the same techniques to predict incomes (for example, does a user make more than $75,000?). Just as some sites provide information about gender, some provide information about income (for example, millionaire.com, wsj.com, and businessweek.com). In fact, we could apply this technique to any characteristic as long as we had a sample of users with known characteristics to compare with our unknown user. With user-profiling techniques, managers can accurately predict the characteristics of their Web-site visitors without asking them to fill out surveys.

User profiling has potential problems. First, it makes errors. Even with a 99.97 percent chance that site visitors are female, we will incorrectly label some males as females and vice versa. For example, in a sample of 10,000 users that we predicted were females, on average three would be male. Therefore, we must consider the costs associated with making a wrong prediction. We might display the wrong advertisement or insult a female user with a male message. In addition, a company should assess its users' privacy concerns and determine whether the value of personalization outweighs its costs.

Collaborative Filtering

Another approach to providing customized content is to recommend new products based on an individual's previous purchases or on expressed preferences for particular products. A popular technique for doing this is collaborative filtering. Collaborative filtering works by comparing a consumer's past purchases or stated preferences to the purchases or stated preferences of similar consumers from an existing database. The firm can make recommendations by identifying products that similar consumers have purchased that this consumer has not yet purchased.

Amazon and CDNow, for example, use collaborative filtering to recommend books and CDs to customers. For example, if someone bought albums by the Rolling Stones, the Beatles, the Who, and Jefferson Starship, a collaborative filtering system might recommend Hot Tuna, Kaukonen*Jorma, Quicksilver Messenger Service, and Love. iReactor, an Internet data mining firm, says this system has doubled CDNow's sales of recommended albums over a system of having its employees make recommendations based on their own experience. For additional references about collaborative filtering and its applications, see Shardanand and Maes (1995).

Many collaborative filtering techniques are based on cluster analysis. In an example by Ungar and Foster (1998), six individuals have seen various films (Table 4).

People	Favorite Movies
Lyle	Andre, Star Wars
Ellen	Andre, Star Wars, Hiver
Fred	Star Wars, Batman
Dean	Star Wars, Batman, Rambo
Jason	Hiver, Whispers

Table 4. The favorite movies of six individuals are given in this Table. This data is the raw input of a collaborative filtering system.

In using K-means clustering (MacQueen 1967), the analyst assigns each item to the cluster having the nearest mean, following three basic steps:

1. Assign the N items to K initial clusters.
2. Reassign each of the N items, to the cluster having the nearest mean. When you reassign an item, recompute the means of the clusters losing and gaining the item.
3. Repeat step 2 until you need to make no more reassignments.

To create a collaborative filtering system, we can apply this technique by first clustering the users and then clustering the movies. On the next pass, we can reapply this technique to cluster the people based on the movie clusters from the first pass, and then recluster the movies based on the user clusters. We can repeat this process until we reach a good solution. For example, from the data shown in Table 4, we might find the solution shown in Table 5.

User	Batman	Rambo	Andre	Hiver	Whispers	Star Wars
Lyle			X			X
Ellen			X	X		X
Jason				X	X	
Fred	X					X
Dean	X	X				X

Table 5. An example of the clustering solution found by a collaborative filtering system. There are apparently three clusters of movies (action, foreign, and classic) and two clusters of users (intellectual and fun). We might recommend Hiver to a new user who likes Andre but dislikes Batman since this user most likely belongs to the "intellectual" group.

In a real application, thousands of users might have seen thousands of movies. The idea behind collaborative filtering is to group similar users and similar products. To make reliable predictions, collaborative filtering requires a large amount of information. Many firms, such as Gustos, LikeMinds, NetPerceptions, and Webridge (Mena 2001), create software to implement collaborative filtering systems. The strength of collaborative filtering is that is can turn passively collected information into valuable intelligence. Unfortunately, it may be costly to implement, require large amounts of data, and may not scale well to massive data sets.

Path Analysis

The path a user takes through a Web site can reveal a great deal about the purpose of a visit. A user navigating the Barnes and Noble Web site (Figure 2) starts at the home page and searches for "information rules," then selects the first item in the search list, a book by Shapiro and Varian (1998), and adds this item to the shopping cart and moves to the checkout.

The user could have ended up at the Information Rules page on the Barnes and Noble Web site in a myriad of ways. He or she could have found this book by browsing the business, computer, or nonfiction book sections, or even found this book after searching for the authors. The user could have come to the Barnes and Noble Web site, entered the business-book section, viewed a number of bestsellers, then searched for pricing, and eventually found the Information Rules page after two dozen clicks.

Path analysis is an attempt to infer information about users' goals from the navigation decisions they make. Some users make directed searches with distinct goals in mind (Figure 2). People in this directed mode would likely see additional information as irrelevant since their goal is to find a specific book. In fact, any additional information on the page, such as specials and advertisements, could be distracting and could lower the probability that they would stay at that site. On the other hand, users surfing the site are conducting nondirected searches and can be strongly influenced by the content of the session. An appealing Web-page design may capture the attention of such users and cause them to look at a book they would not have considered previously. With path analysis, managers can personalize users' sessions by responding with relevant information, can intervene by making special offers to users who are likely to leave the site, or can identify users who are simply browsing and locating products they might never otherwise have considered (and perhaps display recommendations from a collaborative filtering system).

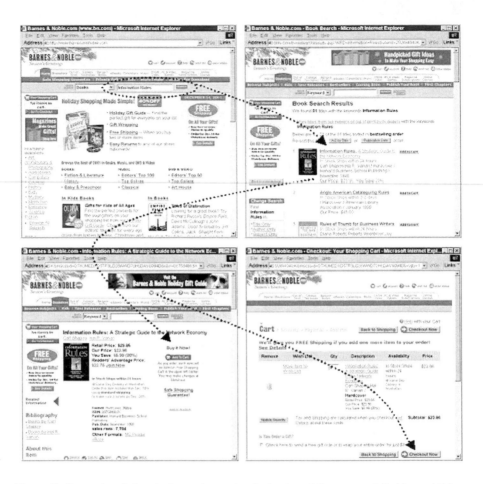

Figure 2. Example of directed user browsing behavior at Barnes and Noble and this user searches for Information Rules.

Browsing behavior at online stores differs from that at offline stores. In an offline store, shoppers must take time to move through the store, which gives the retailer time to present products in an order that maximizes profits. For example, supermarkets put their dairy, produce, and bakery departments at opposite ends of the store even though they offer items that are commonly purchased. The supermarkets thus force consumers to navigate through the entire store. However, an online store does not have that luxury. Users can enter or leave the store from any point. This implies that online retailers need to be more cognizant of the paths users take through the store. Unfortunately, research on path analysis both in academia and in business is just beginning. However, path-analysis technology could have a huge impact on Web-site design and on the use of passively collected data to infer shoppers' goals and desires.

Proactive Learning

In active learning, one focuses on asking questions and allowing users to dictate the course of personalization. In passive learning one focuses on using information collected passively or as a byproduct of browsing to learn about users and personalize their experiences. Another form of learning, which we call proactive learning, combines these two elements. With proactive learning, one leverages the strengths of the two methods to improve the interface with users. Specifically, we will describe a marketing technique, conjoint analysis, to illustrate proactive learning.

The principle behind conjoint analysis is that consumers attach values to all the attributes of a product. The total value or utility of the product is the sum of the values of its components. However, attribute values are latent, and consumers cannot state them directly. For example, we could ask consumers directly for the probability that they would purchase a wool coat at $98 and a rayon one at $89. Unfortunately, consumers would not know the answer to these questions or if they did answer such questions, the answers would be of doubtful reliability. However, consumers would be able to answer directly whether they would purchase a wool or a rayon coat. If the analyst varies the attributes of products and asks consumers to compare a series of coats with varying attributes and prices, the analyst can then infer the value of each component using a statistical model of choice, such as a multinomial logit or probit model. The use of a statistical model helps the analyst to infer how consumers make decisions.

In Lands' End's personal shopper feature (Figure 3), consumers are asked to choose between outfits presented in pairs. Based upon these choices, Lands' End determines the value of each of the attributes of the outfits to each consumer. Lands' End can use this information to predict whether a consumer would like a new outfit that they have not seen. Lands' End can also use this information to personalize a consumer's shopping environment. Instead of displaying a lot of products that are not relevant to the individual shopper and that detract from the shopping experience, Lands' End can create a store that is designed to enhance that person's shopping experience. Imagine a customer visiting an online store in which every product has been selected to be of personal interest to that shopper.

Conjoint analysis can also be used in the context of a shopbot (a shopping robot). A shopbot might be used to help consumers find low-priced items. The shopbot asks the user to request a product and then launches a search at all the online stores it can access. For example, a search for the book <u>John Adams</u> by David McCullough at dealtime.com yields a range of prices between $20.99 and $50.95 after searching scores of online stores. The offers made by the various stores are for the same book but differ in price, shipping options, availability, and reputation of the store.

Figure 3. An example of a conjoint task at Lands' End's Personal Shopper. The consumer is asked to choose between two outfits. Lands' End can use choices like this
one to infer the value a consumer attaches to various designs and materials.

In the context of conjoint analysis, we can think of each of these features
as an attribute. As the shopbot visitor makes choices, we can find out
what features this person values. Without asking the consumer to make
dozens of comparisons, the shopbot can determine which offers are likely
to interest each consumer. It can then improve the shopping experience for
the consumer, which should make that consumer more profitable and loyal
for the shopbot (Montgomery, Hosanager, Krishnan, and Clay 2001).

Discussion and Conclusions

The Internet offers many firms ways to reduce their costs and ways to
passively learn about opportunities to sell products and services. They

can often reduce costs for customer service. By providing information online, firms can save on their call centers for customer service. The celebrated example in this area is Federal Express's migration to the Internet, where it gives customers the ability to track their own shipped packages. The firm provides detailed information on the progress of the shipment, including where the package is in the transit process. Customers switched to the Internet to obtain information, and FedEx's call center volume decreased dramatically. FedEx has reduced its call-center personnel from several hundred to dozens. The firm also has an opportunity for passive learning. Individuals who often track overnight packages are apparently far more time sensitive than other customers. They may become ripe targets for future services that further reduce shipping time or allow them to track shipments using remote network appliances, such as cell phones or PDAs (personal digital assistants).

Firms in several sectors are following Federal Express's lead. Mutual funds, inundated with calls from customers who want their current account balances, have flocked to the Web to minimize costly call volume. Appliance firms provide electronic manuals to customers who have misplaced them reducing the need for call centers to support customer requests. The cost reduction is immediate, and the scope for passive learning is immense.

Through passive learning, firms can tailor different strategies for customers with different levels of expertise. Financial service firms can provide vast amounts of information on instruments ranging from the simple to the complex. By mining collected data on the extent and depth of information customers seek, firms can develop prospect lists for their product offerings. In addition, based on customers' information-search patterns, firms can distinguish expert customers from novice customers. For the former, providing information on complex offerings might suffice, while for the latter, far more personal counseling may be required.

Passive learning has enormous potential for business-to-business interactions as well. Firms providing maintenance have a major opportunity to keep their customers' machinery up and running. For the next generation of networked copiers, suppliers will continuously monitor usage patterns, recognizing when the system might break down and providing timely preventive maintenance. Suppliers will be able to offer customized maintenance plans instead of standard plans that may not serve all customers optimally. The suppliers can also identify opportunities to sell consumables, additional services, and even new products. For example, customers who use color copiers heavily, need far more related consumables than do other customers. The supplier can deliver such consumables frequently and may even figure out that a different copier would better serve the customer. Some customers may use copiers intensely during certain periods. For example, an accounting firm's usage would peak just before April 15. By tracking firms' peak loads, suppliers can schedule preventive maintenance and supplies appropriately. Finally, such passive monitoring systems also provide a plethora of information about which features of the product the customer uses heavily.

Many firms do not have the in-house expertise to leverage the data they collect. Fortunately, many companies produce e-commerce suites and e-Customer Relationship Management (eCRM) systems that help them to reap the benefits of these techniques. Some of these companies are ATG, BEA, Blue Martini, Broadbase, Broadvision, eHNC, Harte-Hanks, Manna, MarketSwitch, Microsoft, Oracle, SAP, Siebel, and Xchange (Mena 2001).

Today's technology appliances are loaded with features, and disentangling their value is critical for developing the next generation of the products. Along with such well-known market-research methods as conjoint analysis, inferences drawn from usage patterns might provide valuable information about customer needs. The opportunity for passive monitoring and maintenance is enormous. United Technology has proposed real-time wireless information gathering and engine monitoring to various airlines. Using intelligent inference engines, the firm aims to schedule maintenance dynamically. It also plans to leverage the information it collects to forecast requirements for parts and labor.

Passive learning is not limited to making inferences about customers. The Web provides a wealth of information about competing firms. By leveraging information found through the customized intelligent searches offered by such companies as WhizBang Labs! (www.whizbang.com), firms can develop the ability to monitor the changing prices of competitors' products. In fact, computer programs that systematically search the Web (crawlers) can alert managers and sales people to competitors' price changes in real time and to content changes such as announcements of new products or services or of promotions.

Individualized marketing makes new demands on managers and on accounting. In the past, marketers thought in aggregate terms over a few quarters. However, this is no longer efficient, because marketers can now track customers' responses by the individual over long periods. Marketers should focus on analyzing the lifetime value of consumers, as done by some direct marketing firms (Mulhern 1999). Managers need to track and compute the cost of acquiring each consumer and then relate this cost to the profits the customer produces over his or her lifetime. Given that it is much more expensive for a firm to acquire a new customer than to keep an existing one, long-term analysis can help it to increase profits.

References

Berry, Michael J. A., and Gordon S. Linoff. 1997. Data Mining Techniques: For Marketing, Sales, and Customer Support. New York: John Wiley and Sons.

Blattberg, R., and J. Deighton. 1991. Interactive marketing: Exploiting the age of addressability. Sloan Management Review 33 (1): 5-14.

Dreze, Xavier, and Fred Zufryden. 1997. Testing Web site design and promotional content. Journal of Advertising Research 37 (2): 77-91.

Haeckel, Stephan H. 1998. About the nature and future of interactive marketing. Journal of Interactive Marketing 12 (1): 63-71.

MacQueen, J. B. 1967. Some methods for classification and analysis of multivariate observations. Proceedings of the Fifth Berkeley Symposium on Mathematical Statistics and Probability. Berkeley, California: University of California Press. Vol. 1, 281-297.

Mena, Jesus. 2001. Web Mining for Profit: Beyond Personalization. Woburn, Massachusetts: Butterworth-Heinemann.

Montgomery, Alan L. 2001. Applying quantitative marketing techniques to the Internet. Interfaces 32 (2): 90-108.

Montgomery, Alan L., Kartik Hosanagar, Ramayya Krishnan, and Karen B. Clay. 2001. Designing a better shopbot. Working paper, Graduate School of Industrial Administration, Carnegie Mellon University.

Mulhern, Francis J. 1999. Customer profitability analysis: Measurement, concentration, and research directions. Journal of Interactive Marketing 13 (1): 25-40.

Peppers, Don, Martha Rogers, and Bob Dorf. 1999. Is your company ready for one-to-one marketing. Harvard Business Review 77 (1): 151-162.

Rossi, Peter E., Rober E. McCulloch, and Greg M. Allenby. 1996. The value of purchase history data in target marketing. Marketing Science 15 (4): 321-340.

Shardanand, Upendra, and Pattie Maes. 1995. Social information filtering: Algorithms for automating Word of Mouth. Proceedings of the CHI-95 Conference. Denver, Colorado: ACM Press.

Shapiro, Carl, and Hal R. Varian. 1998. Information Rules: A Strategic Guide to the Network Economy. Cambridge, Massachusetts: Harvard Business School Press.

Smith, Jeff H. 2001. Information privacy and marketing: What the U.S. should (and shouldn't) learn from Europe. Harvard Business Review 43 (2): 8-31.

Ungar, Lyle H., and Dean P. Foster. 1998. Clustering methods for collaborative filtering. Working paper, University of Pennsylvania.

7 Personalized Product Presentation

The Influence of Electronic Recommendation Agents on Consumer Choice

Gerald Häubl, Banister Professor of Electronic Commerce and
Associate Professor of Marketing, University of Alberta

Kyle B. Murray, Ph.D. Student in Marketing, University of Alberta

Valerie Trifts, Ph.D. Student in Marketing, University of Alberta

Introduction

Personalized Product Presentation

Imagine that a retailer is able to organize its store in such a way that, when a customer looking for a tent enters the store, the first products she sees are tents. In addition, imagine that the customer wants a backpacking tent for about $250 and that, therefore, the retailer has displayed the tents of this type and in this price range right by the door. Moreover, the retailer has organized the tents from lightest to heaviest because this customer is more concerned about the weight of the tent than about its durability. If the customer moves beyond the first tent, which — according to the vendor's understanding of her personal preference — most closely matches what she is looking for, she will come to the tent that is the next closest match to the retailer's estimate of her preference. In essence, the entire store has been arranged to suit this one customer's preference. The next customer who enters the store wants to buy a stereo, so the retailer quickly moves the tents to the back of the store and stocks the shelves closest to the door with stereos, arranging them to match that shopper's personal preference for stereos.

Such a scenario is unthinkable in a traditional retail setting, where customers with very different goals and preferences continuously pass through the store. However, this degree of personalization is attainable in an electronic store, where the traditional bricks-and-mortar constraints on space and organization do not apply. In fact, with the advent of online decision aids, personalization of product presentation is available to any consumer with access to the Internet who is willing to answer a few questions. For example, if you are in the market for a running shoe, you may use nike.com's online shoe advisor. It asks you how competitive you are, where you like to run, what sort of features you prefer, and how much you are prepared to spend. After a brief discussion with this advisor, it gives you an initial recommendation that it has personalized for you based on your expressed preference (Figure 1). In fact, it has rated Nike's entire line of running shoes for you based on the information you provided. The artificial intelligence of the electronic advisor has relabeled all of the shoes on nike.com's virtual shelves, leaving you to browse a product line personalized specifically for you.

This type of personalized shopping assistant is often referred to as a shopbot, which is shorthand for a shopping robot. A shopbot does the work of shopping: it searches through the marketplace to find the products that best suit the subjective preference of the consumer for whom it is working. Often, such robots simply search for the lowest price for the item the consumer wants. Examples of this type of shopbot include allbookstores.com (finds the lowest price on a book) and destinationrx.com (finds the lowest price on prescription drugs and other health products). Another such example, dealtime.com, will even page shoppers when it finds a good deal on the merchandise that they are interested in. However, price-comparison robots are helpful only after a consumer knows what he or she wants to buy, and, therefore, they do only part of the work for the shopper. The consumer must consider the product's nonprice attributes before the robot can go to work. Another class of shopbots is designed to help consumers to find the product that, given their subjective preference in terms of product attributes, is right for them. In some cases, such digital decision aids may search across a number of stores (e.g., activebuyersguide.com), or they may search the database of products

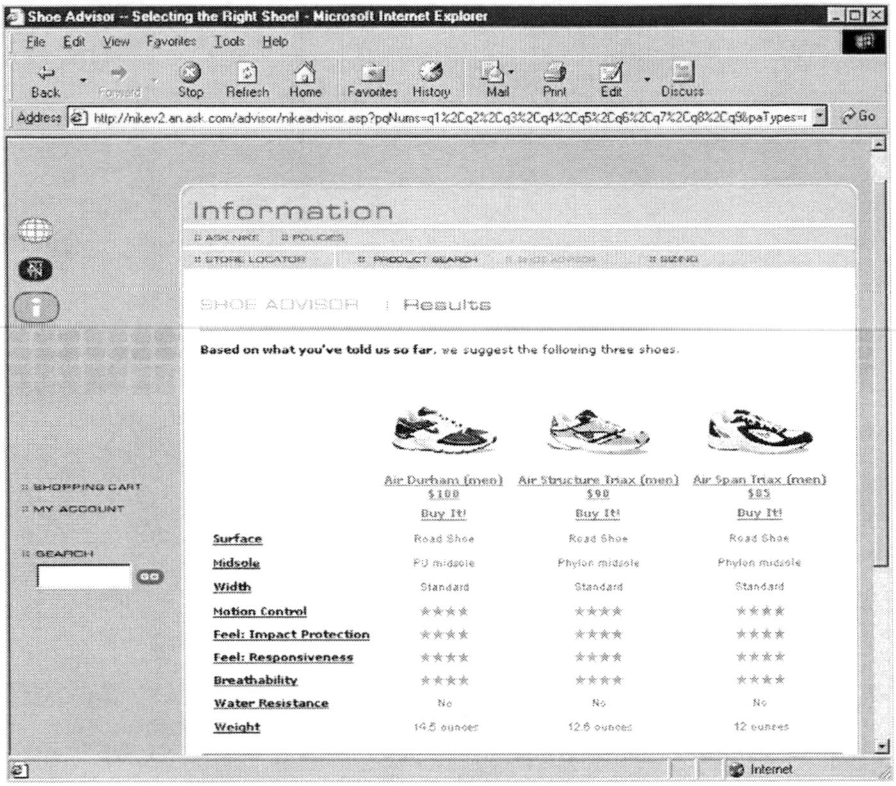

Figure 1. Nike.com's Online Shoe Advisor

offered by a particular retailer or manufacturer (e.g., Nike's shoe advisor). We refer to shopbots that gather information on a consumer's personal preference or taste in a particular product category and then base product recommendations on this information as recommendation agents. This type of shopbot, which actively seeks to understand a consumer's preference and makes personalized product recommendations based on this understanding, is the focus of this chapter.

The Trade-Off Between Effort and Accuracy

The amount of thought that a human decision maker devotes to making a particular choice depends largely on the degree of difficulty, or thinking cost, associated with the decision (Shugan 1980). This cost of thinking is positively related to both the complexity of the decision (in terms of the number of relevant dimensions) and the desired level of confidence in having made the best possible choice, and inversely related to the difference in the decision maker's preference between the available options. As a result, complex and important decisions are more costly in terms of cognitive effort than simple and routine decisions. Individuals often settle for less accurate decisions in return for a reduction in effort (Bettman, Johnson, and Payne 1990). Because of this trade-off between effort and accuracy, decision makers often choose options that are satisfactory but would be suboptimal if decision costs were zero (Simon 1955). This is particularly true when alternatives are numerous and/or difficult to compare (Payne, Bettman, and Johnson 1993).

Unlike bricks-and-mortar shopping environments, digital marketplaces are not constrained by limitations in physical space in their organization of product information. Online vendors have virtually unlimited shelf space and can, therefore, offer a very large number of products to their customers. As a result, a potentially vast amount of information about market offerings is available to consumers. Searching through a marketplace composed of many such retailers would require consumers who wish to make well-informed decisions to expend a great deal of effort.

For shoppers, easy access to large amounts of product information is both a blessing and a curse. It is a blessing in that, given more information, they may make better purchase decisions (e.g., select products that better match their personal preferences) than they would otherwise. However, it is a curse in that, given vast amounts of information but limited cognitive capacity, consumers may be unable to adequately process the information. The idea that human decision makers have limited resources for processing information — whether those limits are in memory, attention, motivation, or elsewhere — has deep roots in the fields of psychology and marketing (e.g., Payne, Bettman, and Johnson 1993; Shugan 1980; Simon 1955).

Because of the limitations of human information processing, recommendation agents may be of great value to online shoppers. While people tend to do quite well at selecting the criteria they wish to use in making a decision, computers are good at methodically searching through a problem (or product) space in order to compile and retain large amounts of information. For example, a recommendation agent may ask a consumer a set of questions in an attempt to understand his or her preference, and then do the work of searching through the products in the marketplace to find the most appropriate alternative(s) to recommend. Clearly, such a recommendation agent has the potential to assist consumers in their decision making by reducing their effort and increasing the quality of their purchase decisions.

While different types of recommendation agents exist (see, e.g., Ansari, Essegaier, and Kohli 2000), we focus on attribute-based agents — i.e., on those that ask a consumer about his or her preference in terms of product attributes and then, based on this preference information, estimate a model that can be used to rate all available products for that individual. (In both of the studies reported in this chapter, a weighted additive utility model was used for this purpose.) Having estimated such a model, the agent is able to provide personalized product recommendations to the shopper. The Nike shoe advisor follows this type of process to make shoe recommendations. However, more general recommendation agents also exist. For example, activebuyersguide.com can assist shoppers in selecting products in categories as diverse as automobiles, family pets, online stockbrokers, beer, and belt sanders. Moreover, such an agent can recommend products across multiple manufacturers, brands, or retailers. In each case, the agent asks the consumer a series of questions, estimates a model of his or her preference, rates the products in its database (which may be compiled from a variety of vendors) based on this preference model, and makes personalized product recommendations (see Figure 2 for an example). The question is, do consumers benefit from this type of electronic assistance in deciding what to buy? In the following sections, we discuss the findings of two recent studies that, taken together, address precisely this question.

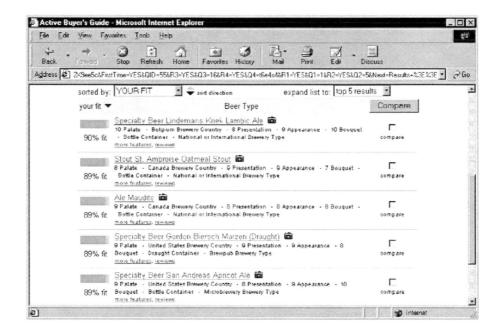

Figure 2. Example of Personalized List of Recommended Products (Active Buyer's Guide)

Overview of Empirical Evidence

We will review some of the findings of recent research on how electronic recommendation agents may influence shoppers' purchase decisions. In particular, we will discuss the relevant results of two major empirical studies that examine different aspects of consumers' agent-assisted product choice behavior in personalized digital shopping environments.

The first study focuses on the impact that use of a recommendation agent has on both the quality and the efficiency of consumer decision making in an online shopping environment, i.e., how good a choice the consumer makes given the set of available products and how much effort he or she must expend to make a decision. This study provides evidence that a recommendation agent can benefit consumers, because it does much of the work of searching the product space and personalizing the information environment by presenting those alternatives likely to be most attractive to a shopper first (i.e., at the "front" of the store). However, for a recommendation agent to benefit consumers, it must do its work in an accurate and unbiased fashion. The electronic agent must be effective at determining what the consumer wants and at searching for a product that meets the consumer's needs.

The second study concerns recommendation agents that perform their search of the marketplace based on an incomplete conversation with the consumer. In this context, "conversation" refers to the dialogue between a computer-based recommendation agent and a consumer, in which the electronic agent asks the human questions designed to elicit information regarding his or her personal preference in terms of the features or attributes of a product. The second study examines the impact on consumer behavior of a recommendation agent that elicits limited preference information before making a personalized product recommendation. The findings suggest that, when an electronic recommendation agent is selective in its conversation with a shopper, it goes beyond merely eliciting preference information and, in fact, may influence the consumer's preference.

Recommendation Agents and Consumer Decision Making (Häubl and Trifts 2000)

The primary objective of the study by Häubl and Trifts (2000) was to obtain an understanding of the possible effects of using an electronic recommendation agent on both the quality and the efficiency of consumer decision making in online shopping environments. To that end, they examined the impact of the availability of such an electronic decision aid on three aspects of consumer decision making: (1) the amount of search that the consumer undertakes before making a purchase, (2) the set of products the consumer seriously considers purchasing (i.e., the consideration set), and (3) the quality of the consumer's ultimate purchase decision.

Method

Häubl and Trifts conducted a controlled experiment to examine the effects of an electronic recommendation agent on the above aspects of consumer decision making in an online shopping environment. A participant's task consisted of shopping for, and making a hypothetical purchase of, a product in each of two categories, backpacking tents and compact stereo systems, in an online store. These purchase decisions were tied to a lottery incentive that was designed to increase the validity of the findings by making the shopping task more consequential (see Häubl and Trifts 2000 for details). The availability of the recommendation agent was manipulated systematically. Half of the participants in this study completed the task with the help of the electronic agent, while the other half received no such assistance. In addition, the order in which subjects shopped for the two products was varied independently. Study participants were randomly assigned to one of the experimental conditions.

The data for this study were collected in a university computer lab in small group sessions of 15 to 20 subjects. The study was completed by a total of 249 participants. Upon arrival at the laboratory, subjects were assigned to personal computers and informed that they would be pilot-testing a new online store by shopping for two products, a backpacking tent and a compact stereo system. The experimenter then held a 10-minute practice session during which she demonstrated the features of the electronic shopping environment. Before starting their first shopping trip, participants rated their levels of knowledge about, and interest in, each of the product categories (using 9-point rating scales). They then read a detailed description of the task and of the lottery incentive.

In each product category, 54 products were available (9 models for each of 6 brands). Actual brand names and fictitious model names were used. The following tent attributes were varied across the 54 alternatives (number of levels in parentheses): pole material (3), warranty (3), weight (12), durability rating (12), and price (12). In addition, fly fabric and vestibule were used as filler attributes with levels that were the same for all backpacking tents. For stereos, the varied attributes were CD player type (3), tuner presets (3), output power (12), sound quality rating (12), and price (12). Cassette decks and remote control were used as additional attributes, and their levels were identical for all stereo models.

An innovative method for measuring the quality of shoppers purchase decisions, as well as of their consideration sets, was used in this study. Since consumer preferences are not subject to direct observation, it is impossible to accurately measure decision quality in uncontrolled real-world settings. In the Häubl and Trifts (2000) study, the sets of available products were constructed in such a way that, irrespective of an individual's subjective preference, the purchase of particular alternatives represented a poor decision. This approach is based on the idea of an objective standard for quality and requires a combination of objectively dominated and nondominated alternatives. An alternative is dominated if there is at least one other alternative that is superior on at least one attribute while not being inferior on any attribute. By contrast, an alternative is nondominated if no other alternative is superior on an attribute without, at the same time, being inferior on at least one other attribute. For each product category, 6 nondominated alternatives—one for each brand—were constructed. While these 6 products were mutually nondominated, they did dominate all other products. Whether or not a participant purchased an objectively attractive (i.e., nondominated) alternative was used as one measure of decision quality, and the share of nondominated products in a subject's consideration set was used as the measure of consideration set quality.

Subjects in the no-recommendation-agent conditions were taken to a hierarchically structured Web site with all six brands listed at the top level and all models for a brand listed at the lower level. They could access detailed information about a product by first clicking on a brand name and then on a model name. In the conditions in which the attribute-based recommendation agent was available, participants started by providing attribute importance weights using a 100-point constant-sum scale, specifying minimum-acceptable attribute levels, and selecting the maximum number of alternatives to be included in the recommendation. Based on this information, the electronic agent produced a personalized list of recommended products. In this list, products were identified by their brand and model name, and sorted by their likely attractiveness to the shopper (in descending order). From the recommendation list, subjects were able to request detailed information about particular products. In all conditions, participants could complete their purchase from any of the screens containing detailed information about a product via a checkout procedure that included the confirmation of the selected product.

After finalizing their purchase, participants completed a short online questionnaire. Next, they were presented with a list of the alternatives they had looked at and asked to report their consideration set ("Please indicate which of these products you considered seriously before making your purchase decision."). Subsequently, participants completed a switching task in which they were given an opportunity to switch from the purchased alternative to each of several nondominated alternatives, all of which had been available during the shopping task. The number of switching opportunities depended upon whether a subject had initially chosen a dominated alternative (6 switching opportunities) or a nondominated alternative (5 switching opportunities). The switching task consisted of a series of pairwise comparisons. Participants were encouraged to switch whenever they saw an alternative that they preferred over their initial choice, and informed that the lottery incentive would reflect any changes to their product selection that they made during this task. Response behavior in this task was used as the second measure of decision quality, with switching to another, previously available alternative indicating poor initial decision quality.

Key Results

As to the extent of information search, shoppers who had access to a recommendation agent looked at far fewer products in detail than did those who were shopping without agent assistance. Across their two shopping trips, subjects requested detailed information for an average of 6.57 alternatives when the electronic agent was available, compared to 11.78 alternatives when it was not available (Figure 3). Furthermore,

Number of Alternatives for Which Detailed Information Was Viewed (Means)

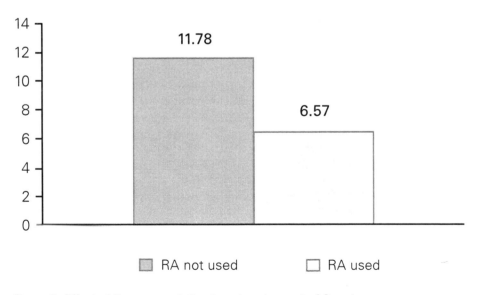

Figure 3. Effect of Recommendation Agent on Amount of Search

although the availability of a recommendation agent had no substantial effect on the number of products that participants considered seriously for purchase, agent-assisted shoppers had a much higher percentage of objectively desirable products in their consideration set. In particular, the share of nondominated alternatives in subjects' consideration sets doubled as a result of using an electronic recommendation agent when making purchase decisions (Figure 4). The level of statistical significance for both of these effects is very high (p < 0.001).

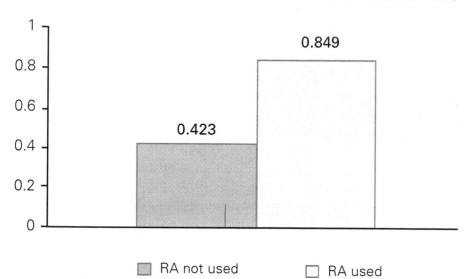

Share of Considered Alternatives That Were Nondominated (Mean Ratio)

Figure 4. Effect of Recommendation Agent on Consideration Set Quality

The recommendation agent also had a strong positive effect on the quality of shopper's purchase decisions. First, participants who had the assistance of the electronic agent were much more likely to select a product that was objectively of high quality than unassisted shoppers. Specifically, while only 65 percent of subjects purchased a nondominated product when no recommendation agent was available, this share increased to 93 percent when shoppers had the assistance of the electronic agent (Figure 5). In addition, consumers who were able to use a recommendation agent on their digital shopping trip were significantly less likely to abandon their initial choice during the subsequent switching task than were those who had no such assistance. The share of participants who switched to another, previously available product was 59.5 percent of those who shopped without agent assistance and only 21.5 percent of those who did use the electronic recommendation agent during their shopping experience (Figure 6). The effects on both measures of decision quality are highly significant (p < 0.001).

Share of Subjects Who Purchased a Nondominated Alternative (Percent)

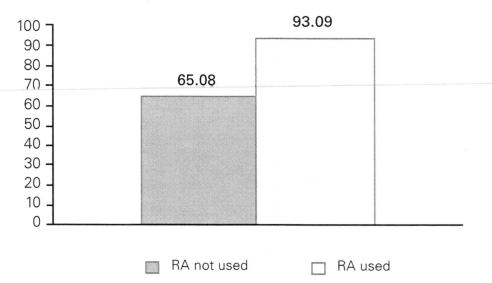

Figure 5. Effect of Recommendation Agent on Decision Quality (1)

Share of Subjects Who Switched to Another Product During the Switching Task (Percent)

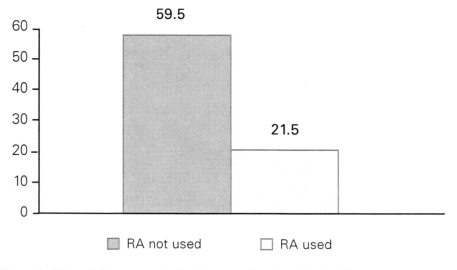

Figure 6. Effect of Recommendation Agent on Decision Quality (2)

In sum, these results indicate that the personalization of product presentation through an attribute-based recommendation agent allowed consumers to engage in less search, while improving the average quality of the products they considered and, most important, the quality of their ultimate purchase decisions. In sum, use of the electronic recommendation agent enabled consumers to make *better decisions* with *less effort*.

The findings of Häubl and Trifts (2000) show how a recommendation agent implemented in an online shopping environment can transform the way in which consumers search for product information and make purchase decisions. Given that the trade-off between effort and accuracy has been demonstrated consistently in the offline world (Payne, Bettman, and Johnson 1993), it is remarkable that an increase in decision quality would not require an increase in effort. This study provides strong evidence that consumers can greatly benefit from the personalization of product recommendations. However, it is important to note that the recommendation agent available to shoppers in this study was fully cooperative and was carefully designed to effectively screen the marketplace on behalf of the consumer based on preference information provided by the consumer. Real-world recommendation agents may not be as altruistic or as complete in their design. For example, they may not cover all available products but instead represent only the products of a particular vendor. They may fail to ask questions or elicit information about some important product attribute, or they may be biased in the way they process the information that they do elicit, either of which may result in recommendations that do not reflect the true preference structure of the consumer. While Nike's shoe advisor is overtly a tool for recommending only Nike shoes, a recommendation agent could be much more covert about its algorithm and its objectives.

Recommendation Agents and Consumer Preference Construction (Häubl and Murray, 2003)

Almost inevitably, real-world attribute-based recommendation agents are selective in that they consider only a subset of all the relevant attributes in a product category. This is apparent in the implementation of many commercial recommendation systems for online shopping (e.g., Active Buyer's Guide or Nike's shoe advisor). The reasons for such selectivity in electronic recommendation agents include (1) the large number of attributes that exist in many product categories, (2) the substantial amount of data about, or interaction with, a consumer that would be required to develop an accurate understanding of the consumer's subjective preferences for products with many attributes, (3) an inclination to use only those attributes that are common to most or all available products, and (4) a tendency to include only attributes that are quantitative in nature (i.e., whose levels can be represented numerically). Apart from these reasons, the attributes to include in a recommendation agent may be chosen for strategic reasons (e.g., to de-emphasize specific attributes) by the designer of the agent.

An electronic recommendation agent may be made available either by a particular online vendor (e.g., Nike's online store) to help shoppers choose one of the products in its own assortment or by a third-party provider (e.g., Active Buyer's Guide) to help consumers choose a product from those of various vendors. The two types of providers may have different motivations for including certain attributes in these decision aids. Häubl and Murray's work pertains equally to the two provider scenarios (vendor and third-party provider), if the recommendation agent is selective in the attributes it includes.

Häubl and Trifts (2000) found that an attribute-based recommendation agent in an electronic shopping environment can result in a substantial reduction in the amount of consumers' pre-purchase information search. This finding suggests that, due to the limited information-processing capacity of the human mind, consumers rely heavily upon an electronic agent's recommendations to reduce the effort required to make a purchase decision. Given this tendency to rely on the recommendations of these agents and given the rapidly increasing prevalence of such decision aids in digital marketplaces, it is important to examine whether and how electronic recommendation agents may *influence consumers' preferences.*

The information-processing approach to decision making recognizes that human information-processing capacity is limited (e.g., Bettman 1979) and that most decisions are consistent with the notion of bounded rationality in that decision makers seek to attain some satisfactory, although not necessarily maximal, level of achievement (Simon 1955). As a result of these constraints, individuals typically do not have well-defined preferences that are stable over time and invariant to the context in which decisions are made (Bettman, Luce, and Payne 1998). That is, in a domain (e.g., a product category) in which the alternatives have multiple attributes, individuals typically do not have specific pre-formed strategies pertaining to exactly how important each of several attributes is to them personally, what kind of integration rule they should use to combine different pieces of attribute information into overall assessments of alternatives, or precisely how they wish to make trade-offs between attributes. Instead, decision makers tend to construct their preferences on the spot when they are prompted to evaluate alternatives or to make a decision (Payne, Bettman, and Johnson 1993).

The constructive preferences perspective adheres to two major tenets: (1) that expressions of preference are generally constructed when individuals are required to evaluate an object, and (2) that the process of preference construction is shaped by the interaction between the properties of the human information-processing system and the properties of the decision task (Payne, Bettman, and Schkade 1999). In a similar vein, Slovic (1995) notes that preferences appear to be remarkably labile, i.e., sensitive to the way in which a choice problem is described or framed and to the mode of response used to express the preference (see also Bettman, Luce, and Payne 1998).

Given the large amount of empirical evidence suggesting that the characteristics of the decision environment play a central role in individuals' construction of preference (e.g., Slovic 1995), digital shopping environments, which are interactive (rather than static) and personalizable (rather than standardized), have great potential to influence consumer preferences and, ultimately, purchase decisions (Johnson, Lohse, and Mandel 1999). In a recent study, Häubl and Murray (2003) examined this possibility by looking at the choice behavior of consumers shopping online with the assistance of an electronic recommendation agent that is selective in its conversation with consumers, i.e., that elicits preference information in terms of only a subset of the relevant product attributes.

Method

The main task for participants in this study was to shop for a backpacking tent in an experimental online store. All participants used an electronic recommendation agent, which asked shoppers to specify their preferences for particular tent attributes. However, unlike the tool used in the Häubl and Trifts (2000) study, this recommendation agent was *selective* in the information it asked for from different shoppers. All available backpacking tents were described on four quality attributes, and price was the same for all tents. Participants were randomly assigned to one of two agent conditions. In one, the electronic agent asked shoppers to indicate (on a 100-point scale) how important weight and warranty were to them when choosing a tent. In the second condition, the agent asked subjects how important durability and fly fabric were to them when choosing a tent (see Figure 7). The recommendation agent used in this study was selective, eliciting preference information from a shopper in terms of only two of the four relevant attributes.

The electronic recommendation agent then searched the product space based on this fragmentary preference information and provided the shopper with a list of backpacking tents, sorted based on the attribute preferences the shopper had expressed. As a result, although all available products were displayed, their presentation was personalized

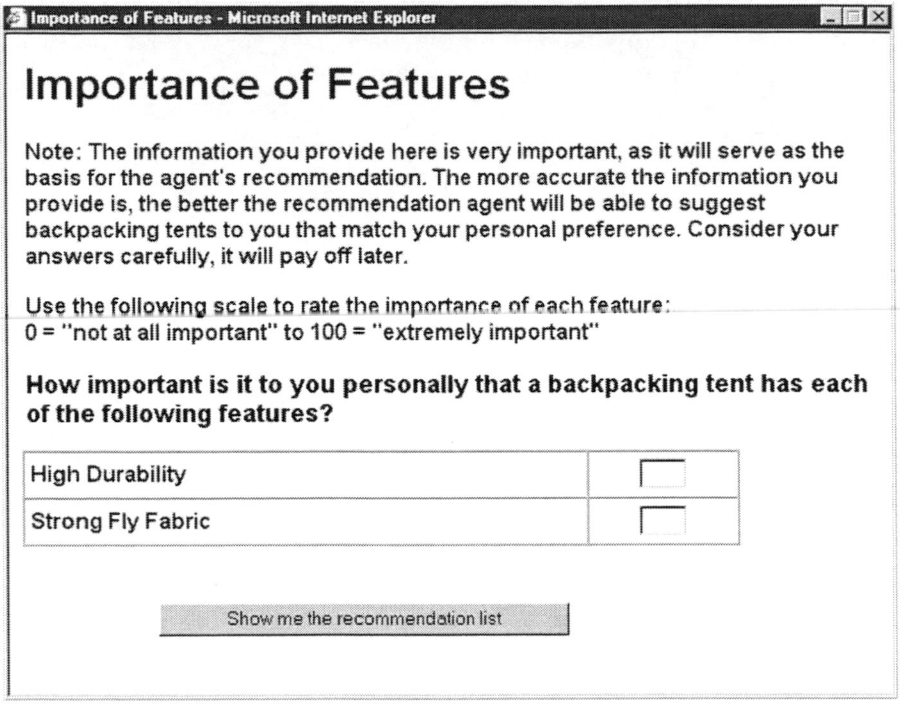

Figure 7. Preference Elicitation by the Recommendation Agent

based on consumers' subjective preferences in terms of a subset of the relevant attributes. From the recommendation list, subjects were able to request detailed descriptions (i.e., on all four attributes) of individual tents. Participants could complete their hypothetical tent purchase from any of the screens containing detailed information about a product via a checkout procedure that included the confirmation of the selected product.

Given that preferences are often constructed on the fly rather than pre-formed, Häubl and Murray were interested in examining whether and how consumers' preferences would be affected by the selective inclusion of product attributes in a recommendation agent. They expected to find an *inclusion effect*: all else being equal, included attributes would be more important in a consumer's decision process simply because they had been included by the recommendation agent. If this is the case, then it is also important to examine whether such a preference-construction effect may *persist* over time, especially into situations where no recommendation agent is available. To investigate the possibility of the effect's persistence, Häubl and Murray asked subjects to perform a follow-up choice task after the initial shopping experience.

The experiment was conducted in a research laboratory equipped with state-of-the-art networked personal computers. All stimuli were embedded in a dynamic Web environment, which subjects accessed via a standard Web browser. Participants entered all of their responses via this Web interface. In addition, subjects' interaction behavior with the experimental environment was recorded electronically. Data were collected in group sessions with 10 to 15 participants per session. A total of 347 subjects completed the study. Participants were informed that the overall purpose of the study was to test a new electronic shopping environment. The main task was taking an online shopping trip for a backpacking tent in an electronic store equipped with a recommendation agent.

To allow for a clear and simple test of the predicted inclusion effect, the set of available tents was constructed such that a subject's product choice was informative as to which attribute was the most important one in making his or her decision. Shoppers had to choose a product that had the most desirable level of one attribute, but not of the other attributes. As a result, which of the attributes the selected alternative was superior on served as an indicator of the relative importance of the attributes in a subject's purchase decision. We refer interested readers to the detailed description of this method in Häubl and Murray (2003).

Two different market scenarios were used for this shopping task: the inter-attribute correlations across the set of available products were either positive or negative. In a market with positive inter-attribute correlations, an alternative that is favorable on one attribute tends to also be favorable on other attributes. By contrast, in a market characterized by negative inter-attribute correlations, a more attractive level of one attribute tends to be associated with a less attractive level of another attribute and, therefore, purchase decisions require trade-offs among attributes. Subjects were randomly assigned to one of these two market conditions.

After finishing their shopping trip by selecting their subjectively most-preferred tent, participants completed an extensive online questionnaire. The final part of the study involved a series of preferential-choice questions, whereby subjects were asked to consider 6 two-alternative choice sets containing new backpacking tents, i.e., ones they had not encountered in the shopping task. All alternatives were described in terms of the same four attributes using in the shopping task. The pairs of tents were personalized using a dynamic choice design (for details see Häubl and Murray, (2003). In addition to choosing their preferred tent from each choice set, subjects also indicated the strength of their preference on a five-point rating scale with end points 1 = "just barely prefer" and 5 = "very strongly prefer." The choice response and the strength-of-preference rating were combined into a 10-point graded-paired-comparison response variable representing an individual's relative preference for the 2 alternatives in a choice set. This task allowed for a test of whether the inclusion effect persisted into a choice environment in which no recommendation agent was available and all products were new to consumers.

Key Results

First and foremost, Häubl and Murray were interested in whether or not a less than perfect recommendation agent (which in this case was selective in its elicitation of preference information) would affect consumers' construction of preference. The results of this experiment provide strong evidence for the proposed inclusion effect. However, the authors found this effect only in connection with a market that required consumers to make trade-offs between product attributes, i.e., one with negative inter-attribute correlations. Such a marketplace is more efficient and more analogous to real-world markets than one characterized by positive inter-attribute correlations. For example, when consumers can buy a tent that is both the lightest and the most durable (where it doesn't matter which attribute they base their choices on), Häubl and Murray found no evidence of an inclusion effect. They observed such a preference-construction effect only in marketplaces in which consumers must to make trade-offs among product attributes — for example, when a more durable tent is heavier and a less durable tent is lighter.

Figure 8 shows the choice shares for a market with negative inter-attribute correlations of (1) the products with the most desirable level of an attribute that was included in the electronic recommendation agent (i.e., an attribute that the agent asked the shopper for preference information about) and (2) the products that were superior on an attribute that was excluded from the recommendation agent (i.e., an attribute that the agent did not ask about). Note that, because each attribute was included in the recommendation agent for half of the shoppers, equal choice shares (50 percent each) in Figure 8 would have indicated the absence of any effect of attribute inclusion in the electronic agent on consumer preference. However, subjects tended to prefer products that were superior on an attribute for which the agent had elicited preference information (71 percent choice share). This inclusion effect, measured as the departure from equal choice shares, is highly significant ($p < 0.001$).

Having demonstrated that a selective recommendation agent can influence shoppers' construction of preference, Häubl and Murray also examined whether this effect would persist in future decision making. Subjects' responses to the 6 preferential-choice questions, which followed the agent-assisted shopping task and an online questionnaire, were used to test for such persistence. The graded-paired-comparison responses (see

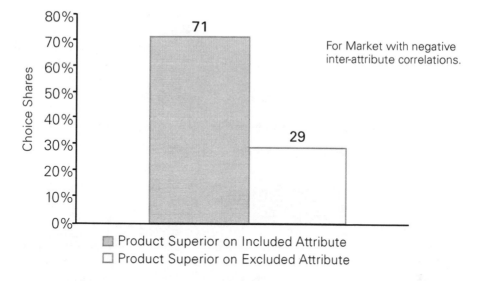

Figure 8. Agent-Assisted Shopping Task: Choice Shares

above) indicate that participants attached significantly greater overall importance to the attributes that had been included in the electronic agent during the earlier shopping task than to those that had not been included (p < 0.01). This shows that the preference-construction effect based on attribute inclusion in the recommendation agent persisted over time and into a setting in which no recommendation agent was available. Once again, we refer interested readers to Häubl and Murray (2003) for a more detailed discussion of this study's findings.

Summary of Findings

The two studies described here provide some initial insights into the potential of electronic recommendation agents to affect consumer decision making. A well-designed recommendation agent can help consumers to increase the quality of their purchase decisions and, at the same time, reduce the amount of effort required to make these decisions. However, these results also suggest that the potential for systematically manipulating consumer behavior in digital marketplaces through the design of electronic decision aids is very significant. This was demonstrated in the Häubl and Murray (2003) study despite the fact that their recommendation agent was, apart from being selective in its inclusion of attributes, perfectly cooperative. For example, it considered all available products and provided product recommendations that were fully accurate (given an individual's input about his or her preference).

Less cooperative recommendation systems may silently omit certain products or entire classes of products (e.g., all models of certain brand) or use a biased algorithm to generate a "personalized list of recommended products" (e.g., by attenuating the importance of price in a consumer's subjective preference model or by boosting the rank-positions of certain alternatives). The findings discussed in this chapter are conservative in the sense that they tend to understate the potential for influencing consumer preferences and purchase decisions through non-cooperative recommendation agents.

Conclusion

The type of personalization we have considered in this chapter is important because consumers like to make good decisions with low effort, and personalized product recommendations can be very helpful in this regard. However, when consumers rely on an electronic recommendation agent to screen the marketplace, they open the door to influence in much the same way they would by relying on a salesperson in a bricks-and-mortar store. While we know a lot about how people can influence other people (e.g., Cialdini 2001), we know very little about how electronic entities, such as recommendation agents, can influence people.

Unlike flesh-and-blood salespeople, electronic agents can control the choice environment. Although a retail salesperson at Niketown may come to understand a particular customer's product preference over time, she or he cannot rearrange the store and personalize the presentation of products in the same way that Nike's online shoe advisor can. A human sales assistant may change his or her behavior and advice for different customers, but the electronic agent can alter the entire online shopping environment in response to each individual consumer.

While we are just beginning to develop an understanding of how this level of personalization may affect consumer behavior and consumer preferences, the research findings reported in this chapter show that the personalization of electronic shopping interfaces through recommendation agents can not only improve consumer decision making, but also systematically influence consumer preferences.

References

Ansari, A., S. Essegaier, and R. Kohli. 2000. Internet Recommendation Systems. Journal of Marketing Research 37 (August): 363-375.

Bettman, J. R. 1979. An Information Processing Theory of Consumer Choice. Reading, MA: Addison-Wesley.

Bettman, J. R., E. J. Johnson, and J. W. Payne. 1990. A Componential Analysis of Cognitive Effort in Choice. Organizational Behavior and Human Decision Processes. 45: 111-139.

Bettman, J. R., M. F. Luce, and J. W. Payne. 1998. Constructive Consumer Choice Processes. Journal of Consumer Research 25 (December): 187-217.

Cialdini, R. B. 2001. Influence: Science and Practice (4th edition). Needham Heights, MA: Allyn & Bacon.

Häubl, G., and K. B. Murray. 2003. Preference Construction and Persistence in Digital Marketplaces: The Role of Electronic Recommendation Agents. Journal of Consumer Psychology. 13, 1 and 2, in press.

Häubl, G., and V. Trifts. 2000. Consumer Decision Making in Online Shopping Environments: The Effects of Interactive Decision Aids. Marketing Science. 19, 1: 4-21.

Johnson, E. J., G. L. Lohse, and N. Mandel. 1999. Designing Marketplaces of the Artificial: Four Approaches to Understanding Consumer Behavior in Electronic Environments. Working Paper. Columbia University, New York, NY.

Payne, J. W., J. R. Bettman, and E. J. Johnson. 1993. The Adaptive Decision Maker. New York, NY: Cambridge University Press.

Payne, J. W., J. R. Bettman, and D. Schkade. 1999. Measuring Constructed Preferences: Towards a Building Code. Journal of Risk and Uncertainty. 19: 243-271.

Shugan, S. M. 1980. The Cost of Thinking. Journal of Consumer Research 7: 99-111.

Simon, H. A. 1955. A Behavioral Model of Rational Choice. Quarterly Journal of Economics 69 (February): 99-118.

Slovic, P. 1995. The Construction of Preference. American Psychologist 50 (May): 364-371.

8 Personalizing Your Web Site

A How-to Guide

Anindya Datta, Chief Executive Officer, Chutney Technologies

Helen Thomas, Assistant Professor of Management Information
Systems, Carnegie Mellon University

Debra VanderMeer, Director of Technical Services, Chutney
Technologies

Personalizing visitors' experiences has become a high priority for many Web sites, e-businesses, and bricks-and-mortars. Executives at many Web sites have discovered that the "one-size-fits-all" metaphor does not necessarily apply to the Web.

In the context of the Web, personalization refers to a paradigm of site design through which users receive content and services specific to their individual needs, and e-businesses tailor their site's interaction with visitors.

In sites that incorporate personalization technology, users can quickly and easily access information they want without spending time and effort searching for it. This ease of use improves the visitor's overall experience, leaving users with positive impressions of the site. This, in turn, encourages visitors to take further advantage of the site's offerings, becoming repeat customers and giving the Web site "increased stickiness." Case studies (Colkin 2001, Kemp 2001) and published research (Reichheld and Sasser 1990) show that the increases in stickiness and customer loyalty that result from personalizing visitors' experiences increase the probabilities that they will buy.

Given the potential benefits of personalization, you may want to integrate personalization into your own site's design and architecture.

How Web Personalization Works: An Overview

We can think of the process of generating a personalized Web page in terms of a simple input-process-output model (Figure 1). This model consists of five basic components:

1. A set of customer data (an input component),
2. A set of Web site content (an input component),
3. Business logic (a process component),
4. A set of dynamic scripts (a process component), and
5. A personalized Web page (the output component).

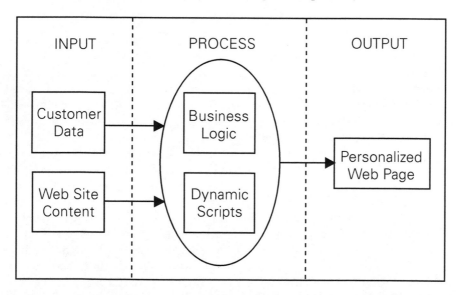

Figure 1. A Process Model for Generating a Personalized Web Page. Generating a personalized Web page can be viewed as an input-process-output model. The inputs are customer data and Web site content. The business logic and dynamic scripts take these inputs and produce a personalized Web page as output.

Essentially, you want to use the information you have about your customers to choose content appealing to each customer. Your knowledge of your customers allows you to make educated guesses as to what products or services will be of interest to a particular customer. Based on these guesses, you can present the information you think is most relevant to each customer prominently on the output Web page, while displaying content you think is less relevant less prominently.

Your personalization business logic codifies the educated guesses your Web site will make in choosing specific content for a particular user, depending on what you know about him, and what he has requested on your site. For example, if you know that a visitor purchased romance movies in the past, you might present him or her with recommendations for newly released romance movies.

The actual personalized Web page your site sends to a user is the result of running a *dynamic script.* A dynamic script is a piece of executable code that builds the output HTML page in response to a user's request. The script considers the information about the user that is available on the site and in the contents of the site, then applies the business logic associated with the URL the user requested to determine the specific content to include in the output HTML response. Once it has chosen a content item to include in the Web page, the script formats the content so that it will appear in the appropriate place on the page.

Building a Personalized Web Page

To personalize your Web site, you need a thorough understanding of Web architectures. Web designers typically build Web sites using a layered design approach called the n-tier architecture. At the heart of such n-tier architectures is a set of *dynamic scripting technologies*, which generate HTML in response to user requests.

Web sites employ dynamic scripting technologies to generate content in response to user requests. For example, when a visitor to an online book site chooses the Fiction category link, the request Uniform Resource Locator (URL) may appear as follows: http://www.books.com/catalog.jsp?category=Fiction. This request will invoke a program or dynamic script called "category.jsp" and pass the parameter name-value pair "category-Fiction." This program will execute the logic defined by the Web site designer to generate the page corresponding to the Fiction category. For instance, this logic may include submitting a query to a content database to retrieve the content to be displayed for the Fiction category, e.g., names, descriptions, and images for the subcategories of the Fiction category. The category.jsp program may execute additional logic as well, such as formatting or personalization logic. Once the program has executed all the page generation logic, the resulting HTML page is delivered to the visitor (Figure 2).

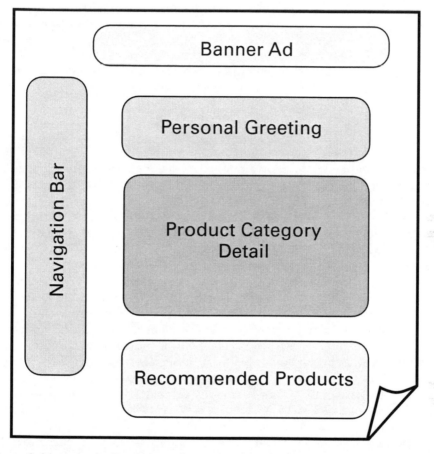

Figure 2. Mockup of a Dynamically Generated Web Page. A page that is generated dynamically typically consists of a number of fragments, such as a *Banner Ad, Navigation Bar,* and *Personal Greeting.*

The resulting page contains the content associated with the Fiction category (shown as the **Product Category Detail** block in Figure 2), along with several other components or fragments, some of which are personalized. For instance, the **Personal Greeting** and **Recommended Products** fragments would typically be generated by running personalization logic that is invoked by the script.

Dynamic scripts usually run on a special server called an *application server.* Whereas Web servers primarily manage connections to the site, application servers primarily manage the complexities of executing application logic including managing memory, scheduling tasks, executing page generation logic, and managing connections to back-end services (e.g., database systems). Various application servers are available on the market, offering varying levels of features and functionality. For instance, most application servers provide the functionality mentioned above. High-end application servers, such as BEA's WebLogic (BEA Systems, Inc.) and IBM's WebSphere (IBM Corp.), also provide advanced features, such as load balancing and real-time priority management. Some application servers provide personalization functionality as well. For instance, ATG's Dynamo (Art Technology Group), WebSphere, and WebLogic Personalization Server all offer built-in personalization functionality.

Application servers can also be classified according to programming model. If your site is based on the Java 2 Enterprise Edition (J2EE) programming model, you have many J2EE-compliant application server products to choose from (e.g., WebLogic, WebSphere, iPlanet [Sun Microsystems, Inc.], Macromedia's Jrun [Macromedia Inc. b], Hewlett-Packard's Total E-Server [Hewlett-Packard Company]). On the other hand, if your site is based on the Microsoft COM/MTS/COM+ model (to be replaced by the .NET programming model), you must use the Microsoft Internet Information Server (IIS) product (Microsoft Corp. a).

Choosing an appropriate application server will depend upon the characteristics of your Web site. Furthermore, keep in mind that some Web servers (e.g., the Apache Web Server [Apache Software Foundation]) offer some of the management functionality of an application server.

Dynamic scripts can be written in a number of programming languages. Java-based languages — Java Servlets and Java Server Pages (JSP) — are widely used for dynamic page generation. Another common choice for dynamic scripting is the Microsoft Active Server Pages (ASP) family of languages, which includes VBScript, Jscript, and C#. Other languages available include Perl and PHP.

Designers of modern Web sites typically use an n-tier architecture. An n-tier architecture is based on a layered design, which partitions application functionality into independent layers. The layers in a typical n-tier architecture (Figure 3) include the following:

- **Presentation**. The presentation layer is responsible for displaying information to users and includes formatting and transformation tasks. Presentation layer logic is usually handled by dynamic scripts.
- **Business Logic**. The business logic layer handles the execution of business logic for the enterprise. Business logic is typically implemented using component technologies, such as Enterprise Java Beans (EJB) or COM. In many Java-based Web applications, servlets are used to invoke these components.

- **Data Access.** The data access layer facilitates connections to the underlying data sources, such as database systems or legacy systems. It uses standard interfaces, such as JDBC or ODBC, to access these data sources.
- **Back-end Systems.** The back-end systems layer includes resources that provide such services as database systems, legacy systems, and directory servers.

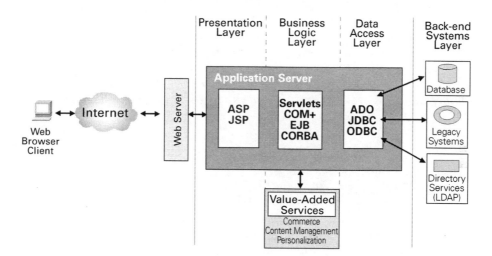

Figure 3. Example of an n-tier Web Architecture. An n-tier architecture partitions application functionality into independent layers. The presentation layer is responsible for the display of information to users. Presentation logic is usually written in a dynamic scripting language, such as JSP or ASP. The business logic layer handles the execution of business logic. Business logic is often implemented using component technologies, such as EJB or COM. The data access layer facilitates connections to underlying data sources using standard interfaces, such as JDBC or ODBC. The back-end systems layer includes the resources that provide services, such as database systems, legacy systems, and directory servers.

To better understand this architecture, recall the earlier example request for the Fiction category page on the books.com Web site. Serving this request may proceed as follows:

1. The application server executes the **category.jsp** script.
2. The **JSP**, running in the presentation layer, invokes a **servlet** in the business logic layer.
3. The **servlet**, in turn, invokes an **EJB** (also in the business logic layer) to create a User Profile object.
4. The **EJB** requests the User Profile data (e.g., name, preferences) from the **directory server** (in the back end systems layer).

5. The data request is handled by **connectivity software** (e.g., JDBC) in the data access layer, which connects to the **directory server**, once a connection becomes available.
6. Once the **directory server** serves this request, control passes back (through the same path) to the **JSP**, which produces a personal greeting fragment containing the user's name.

The system would follow similar steps to generate the remaining fragments. For instance, it would query the content database to create the fragment containing information from the *Fiction* category information. The resulting page would appear similar to the one shown in Figure 2.

Additional services, such as commerce, content management, or personalization systems, may be invoked to serve requests (Figure 3).

Managing Web-based Content

An important aspect to consider when deploying a personalization solution is *content management*. Web pages are constructed using a variety of types of content, such as text, images, or video. Different groups within an organization are typically responsible for managing different types of content. For instance, in an online store, the content includes product information, product reviews, and customer service information. Product information may be maintained by the product management group, whereas customer service information may be maintained by the customer service group.

Content management is the combination of rules, processes, and workflows used to create, edit, manage, and publish Web content according to the organization's requirements. Many organizations use *content management systems* to manage Web content. Content management systems are software tools that enable efficient authoring, editing, and publishing of Web content. Examples of content management systems that are available on the market currently include Content Suite from Vignette (Vignette Corp. 2001a) and TeamSite from Interwoven (Interwoven Corp.).

In general, content management systems allow content to be authored and submitted using a variety of tools, such as word processors. This ensures that authors need not be programmers to submit content. For example, a financial analyst may write and submit an article for an online financial portal. The content management system handles the associated workflow, e.g., review, approval, and publication of the content. The content itself may be stored in a variety of systems, e.g., relational databases, XML repositories, or file systems (Figure 4).

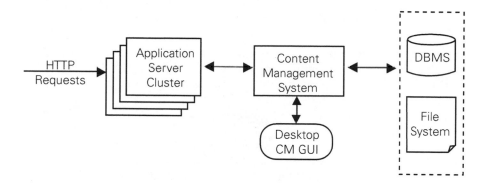

Figure 4. Typical Content Management System Architecture. When a user request is received, the application server invokes the content management system, which, in turn, retrieves the appropriate content from the back-end resources. Internal users submit content to the system through the Desktop Content Management (CM) GUI.

When the system receives a request from a user, the application server invokes the content management system to retrieve the appropriate content. The *Desktop Content Management* (CM) GUI box in the figure represents the user interface used to submit content to the system.

Content management systems offer a number of benefits. For example, these systems help to separate presentation from content, allowing content to be served to a variety of devices. By providing expiration policies, these systems also help ensure that Web content is served fresh. In addition, content management systems enable distributed contribution of content and information.

While content management systems can help to ease content management tasks, the cost of these systems must be considered since most of these systems are quite costly. For instance, Vignette's Content Suite V6 starts at $200,000 (Vignette Corp. 2001b), while Interwoven's TeamSuite typically costs $35,000 or more (CAMWorld). A few less expensive solutions are available, such as Macromedia's Spectra (Macromedia Inc. a), which is about $8,000 per server (CAMWorld).

Web Personalization Paradigms

Web personalization comes in many forms. We will focus on the most prevalent personalization paradigms, providing not only a detailed discussion of each category, but also examples of software available to support it. Web personalization methods can be classified into two general categories: filtering methods and rule-based methods.

Filtering-based Personalization

Two types of filtering-based personalization methods are widely used: (1) simple filtering and (2) collaborative filtering (IBM High Volume Web Site Team 2000).

Simple Filtering

Simple filtering allows you to deliver content to users based on *classes* of users. This allows you to customize the experience of a particular type of user based on the class(es) to which he or she belongs. This type of filtering works by recognizing the user as belonging to a particular class of users, and providing the content and services associated with that class. For example, a Web site for an industry research company (such as Gartner or Forrester) might offer both free content as well as subscription-based services. Here, a non-subscribing user might be able to access abstracts of industry research reports, while a subscribing user would have access to the full text of the company's research reports.

Implementing simple filtering requires that the system identify a visitor's user class at run time, and build the page with the content appropriate for the user class. A visitor's user class might be encoded in his or her profile, or determined by a referrer (a data item that reveals the site from which the visitor came). Once the class has been determined, the dynamic scripting logic can choose the appropriate content for the visitor's user class and build the page. This requires no specific software beyond basic dynamic scripting technology; you can, in most cases, easily explicitly code all the logic required for simple filtering: recognizing the user class, retrieving the appropriate content for the user class, and building the output page.

Simple filtering works well for sites where users can be easily categorized into classes, and the site's content and services can be associated with those classes. For example, an airline might offer special services, such as automatic upgrades to first class, to members of its frequent flier program who fly more than 100,000 miles a year, but not to other site visitors. In contrast, using simple filtering will prove difficult in the context of a more complicated personalization scheme. For examples, consider the case, where a site makes recommendations based on the customer's purchasing history, or his personal interests. In such cases, other types of filtering, or other categories of personalization technologies, such as rules-based or learning-based personalization methods, may be appropriate.

Collaborative Filtering

Collaborative filtering works on the principle that visitors with similar interests can be clustered into groups. The behavior and opinions of users within an interest group can then be used to generate recommendations for other members of the same group. This type of personalization is *inferential* — using collaborative filtering, your site can recommend content or products in which the user has not previously indicated interest. This, in turn, encourages the visitor to spend more time on the site, and potentially purchase more from the site.

A site enabled with collaborative filtering analyzes user rankings to form *user interest groups*. Based on this analysis, the site generates recommendations for each user, and delivers these recommendations at run time. For example, consider a particular visitor to an online bookseller's site who shows an interest in *Wildflower Gardening and Landscape Architecture,* perhaps by purchasing books in these categories. Suppose that analysis of this user's interests, in combination with those of the other visitors on the site, reveals that his interests are most similar to a group of people interested in a variety of gardening topics. Here, the site might recommend a book on rosebushes, based on the interests of other users in the same interest cluster — *even though the user has never expressed an interest in rosebushes previously.*

This type of personalization requires a particular type of software, specifically a *collaborative filtering recommendation engine*. Products in this category available on the market include Net Perceptions personalization solutions (Net Perceptions [NETP]) and Macromedia's LikeMinds product (Macromedia Inc. c).

These engines take as input user rankings or opinions associated with particular content items. These inputs must come from your users, either *explicitly*, by requesting that your users identify their interests and preferences in a user profile, or *implicitly*, based on individual users' purchase behavior. There is much debate over whether implicit or explicit rankings are better. Information gathered implicitly (where the user does not need to provide additional information) may not represent the full range of a user's interests, while only a fraction of your users will provide the explicitly gathered information, which requires that the user actively input information.

Collaborative filtering works well for sites having high traffic, a large user base whose members return often looking for new content or products. A large user base provides enough information to generate distinct interest clusters. If a site has few repeat visitors, the interest clusters derived may have only a few users each, limiting the usefulness of the recommendations. The frequency of user return is also important.

The ability to generate recommendations using collaborative filtering is dependent on having some knowledge of a user when he visits, i.e., the recommendation engine will not be able to generate meaningful recommendations for first-time visitors. Thus, if a site's traffic consists mostly of first-time visitors, this type of technology may not be effective.

One of the biggest drawbacks of collaborative filtering technology is the cost. Prices for collaborative filtering recommendation engines typically run into the six-figures. For example, the average cost for Net Perceptions is $350,000 (Dragan 2001b). Thus, unless the traffic levels and usage patterns on a site warrant the use of this type of software, implementing it may be overkill.

Rules-based Personalization

Rules-based personalization systems allow a site to specify explicitly how the site should respond to a particular user based on a set of rules. This type of personalization is particularly appropriate for merchandising efforts, such as cross-sells, up-sells, and promotions. For example, a visitor seeking product information for a laptop, might also get suggestions for add-on items, such as an optical mouse or laptop carrying case. Or, when a visitor views the laptop category, the system could highlight products based on his past purchase history. This technique can be used to draw attention to more expensive laptops for users who have purchased high-end products in the past, while emphasizing lower-priced equipment for users whose past purchasing histories reflect budget consciousness.

In contrast to collaborative filtering, in which the content served to a user is based on recommendations inferred from the interests of like-minded users, rules-based personalization allows a site's business logic to be specified as a set of business rules that will be applied at run time to build pages. These rules are simple *if-then* statements. The *if* portion of the rule specifies the conditions under which the rule will fire, while the *then* portion specifies the action which should take place when the condition is satisfied. For instance, you may use the *then* portion of the rule to specify which content should be served in a given scenario. Suppose your current promotion set on your online retail site includes an offer of free shipping for goods in the electronics category. The rule logic for this rule might specify the following: *if category is "electronics," then serve offer for free shipping in electronics*. Your business logic need not arise only from your site's promotional schedules — you can use data mining technology to discover frequently purchased product sets, and use this knowledge to generate cross-selling opportunities.

Once you have defined your business logic as a set of rules, you can use them in the coded logic that builds the pages your site serves (Figure

5). A rules-based personalization architecture contains a rule base and a rule editor, in addition to the application server and content base.

The rule base serves as a centralized point for storage and retrieval of the rules, which may be used throughout a cluster of application servers on your site. Centralizing the rule repository provides two specific benefits. First, it mitigates the need to explicitly encode the rule logic in the page-building scripts. This reduces the work required to utilize the logic, and leads to the second benefit: consistency. Storing business rules in a single repository, rather than storing multiple versions of the same logic on the application servers, prevents inconsistency. The rule editor provides an interface to the rule base, allowing you to add, remove and modify rules as needed. Typically, the rule editor offers both interactive and batch (i.e., import and export) facilities for modifying the rule set.

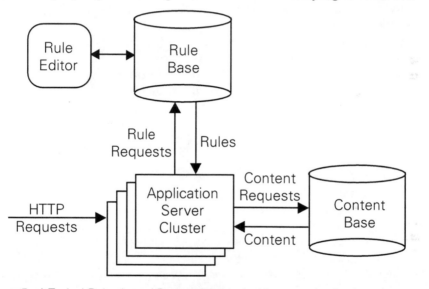

Figure 5. A Typical Rules-based Personalization Architecture. A rules-based personalization architecture includes a rule base and a rule editor. The rule base serves as a centralized repository for rules, while the rule editor provides an interface to the rule base.

Software for rules-based personalization falls into three basic categories: (a) software built into the application server; (b) optional proprietary modules on top of an application server; and (c) open toolkits, accessible from many other application servers.

In the first category, the personalization functionality is baked into the application server. For example, Broadvision's OneToOne application platform (Broadvision Inc.) tightly integrates its personalization technology into the architecture of the application server.

In the second category, the personalization technology is available as a proprietary option for a specific application server; you cannot mix and match personalization modules and application servers across vendors. BEA's WebLogic and IBM's WebSphere application servers fit into this category.

In the third category, personalization functionality is available as a toolkit, accessible from other application servers. ATG's Dynamo is an example of this type. Their personalization technology is non-proprietary; you can mix and match their personalization functionality not only with the Dynamo application server, but with other companies' application servers as well.

Rules-based personalization works well for sites that need to encode a large set of business logic, or need to manage large, complex promotional campaigns. For sites with limited needs in this arena, simple filtering techniques will likely suffice.

Like collaborative filtering technologies, rules-based personalization products are costly. Broadvision's average deal size is about $410,000 (Dragan 2001a). Costs for other rules-based personalization technologies are also in the six-figure range (Rosenberg 2001).

Potential Pitfalls of Personalization Technologies

While personalization technologies could enhance your Web site, you should be aware of their potential pitfalls.

Perhaps the greatest technical drawback to employing personalization on your Web site is that personalization technologies are usually very difficult to scale. Providing customized content for Web site visitors requires additional work (e.g., database queries, and creation and destruction of user profile objects) in the page generation process. It is not enough for the site to serve personalized pages — the site must also be able to serve these pages quickly to maintain an acceptable quality of service (QOS). As the number of concurrent visitors to a site increases, the server infrastructure may not be able to serve requests fast enough, thereby degrading QOS.

Organizations can address the performance and scalability issues associated with personalization technologies in several ways. One possible approach is to add resources (e.g., hardware, software) to the site infrastructure. This approach requires not only adding machines, but also purchasing additional software licenses, which can be costly, especially for enterprise software. Furthermore, there are significant costs to administer and maintain these additional resources. Due to these costs, this approach is actually very expensive and usually not a viable alternative in the long run.

A more promising approach is to employ some form of content caching. The basic idea behind content caching is to store content so that it can be used to serve future requests, thereby reducing redundant work where possible. Several content caching methods are available. Proxy-based caching solutions store and serve content outside the site infrastructure, thereby reducing the delays associated with content generation as well as other site infrastructure-related latencies, such as firewall processing delays. Most proxy caching solutions store full HTML pages (e.g., Dynamai from Persistence [Persistence Software Inc.] and ISA Server from Microsoft [Microsoft Corp. b]). However, highly personalized pages typically have limited reusability. For example, the Fiction category page displayed in Figure 2 will have a different **Personal Greeting** for each user, making each page instance unique. Furthermore, such page-level caching solutions must rely on the request URL to identify pages in cache. When pages are dynamically generated, different invocations of the same script, even with the same input parameters, are not guaranteed to produce the same page. Thus, proxy-based caching solutions may serve incorrect pages. When two different users request the *Fiction* category page in Figure 2, the request URL is the same (http://www.books.com/catalog.jsp?category =Fiction); however, the pages that are delivered to the users display different **Personal Greetings** (and possibly different **Recommended Products** as well).

In an attempt to address these issues, dynamic page assembly solutions have been developed, such as Akamai's Edge Suite (Akamai Technologies Inc.). These solutions use a template-based design for pages, where a template specifies the content and layout of a page using a set of markup tags. Each page is decomposed into a number of fragments, which are cached at a network cache and used to assemble the page when the page is requested. Referring back to the example page in Figure 2, each of the fragments (e.g., **Navigation Bar, Product Category Detail**) would be maintained as separate dynamic scripts (JSPs). The fragments that are generated by running these scripts are stored at a network cache and assembled on demand to produce a user deliverable Fiction category page.

One of the key drawbacks of this approach is that it requires that a site conform to the template-based design. In other words, a site is forced to use fixed page layouts. This is clearly a severe limitation for today's highly personalized sites, where page content and layout is usually determined at run-time.

Another problem with this approach is that it is not applicable in cases where pages have semantically interdependent fragments. For example, when a request for the *Fiction* category page (Figure 2) arrives, the script first queries the site's directory server and creates a user profile object, which is used to generate a **Personal Greeting**. Subsequently, the **Product Category Detail** fragment is created by querying the site product catalog database. Next, the script *reuses* the user profile object to generate the user's product recommendation set to produce the **Recommended Products** fragment. An important observation here is that the **Personal Greeting** and **Recommended Products** fragments are dependent on the same user profile object. If we try to decompose this page into fragments, the optimal decomposition is to have three fragments: **Personal Greeting, Product Category Detail,** and **Recommended Products**. However, decomposing in this way requires that both the **Personal Greeting** and **Recommended Products** fragments make the same call to the directory server to create the user profile object. Thus, in this case, using the dynamic page assembly approach actually results in additional work (repetition of the work required to create the user profile object) to generate the page.

In general, dynamic page assembly approaches are best suited for pages that have fixed layout and that can be easily decomposed into static, independent fragments.

Still another class of content caching solutions is back-end caching solutions, which are based on caching content at various layers within the site architecture. Back-end caching solutions address the limitations of proxy-based solutions in that they usually provide granular caching and they guarantee correctness of output. Database caching is a form of back-end caching. For instance, most application servers offer the ability to cache the results of database queries. Other solutions, such as TimesTen (TimesTen Performance Software 2001a) and Oracle 9i Database Cache (Oracle Corp. 2001) offer the ability to cache database tables in main memory. Database caching techniques can help reduce the database-related delays associated with dynamic content generation. Keep in mind, however, that there are many other types of delays associated with dynamic content generation.

For example, presentation layer tasks, such as formatting and content conversion (e.g., XML-to-HTML), contribute to content generation delays. *Presentation layer caching* solutions are designed to reduce these types of delays. Many application servers (e.g., WebLogic and iPlanet) offer this type of caching capability. These solutions require inserting tags into your dynamic scripts to identify the portions of code that generate cacheable output. Tags are simply APIs that communicate with a cache at run-time to retrieve and/or insert content.

Still other sources of delay are associated with dynamic content generation that neither database caching nor presentation layer caching mitigate: delays caused by the creation and destruction of objects and delays due to communication across multiple tiers. Object creation and destruction is costly due to the memory management overhead (e.g., garbage collection) it imposes. Cross-tier communication often results in significant delays. A common example of this type of delay is waiting for a connection to a DBMS. One type of solution that addresses these types of delays (as well as the other content generation delays) is PreLoader from Chutney Technologies (Chutney Technologies Inc.), which allows caching of arbitrary objects (e.g., HTML fragments, programmatic objects) at the back-end.

Most personalization solutions offer various types of caching. For example, ATG's Dynamo offers caching of HTML pages and EJBs. BroadVision offers numerous caching options, including caching of HTML pages, query results, and personalization rules. The various caching features these products provide can help reduce some of the delays associated with generating personalized pages. However, they also have drawbacks. For instance, the various caches run in the same process space as the application server and therefore, will often cause resource contention problems. Furthermore, these caching solutions do not address delays due to cross-tier communication.

As the foregoing discussion indicates, there are a number of solutions available to address performance and scalability problems associated with personalization technologies. If your site experiences such problems, then you should consider deploying one of these solutions. The best solution for your site depends upon many factors, such as the primary source of the delays and your budget. The above-mentioned solutions vary significantly in price. For instance, some caching solutions, such as presentation-layer caching, are built into the products, and thus have no cost. Proxy-based caching solutions are relatively inexpensive. For instance, ISA Server costs about $1500 per server (Microsoft Corp. c). Back-end caching solutions are typically more expensive. For instance, the TimesTen product costs between $20,000 and $240,000 (TimesTen Performance Software 2001b).

Another difficulty with implementing a personalization solution is being able to accurately measure the effectiveness of the solution. A commonly used approach is to perform an ROI analysis. This approach requires that the costs and benefits of the personalization solution be quantified. The precise costs and benefits used in an ROI analysis will depend upon the actual business. However, general frameworks exist that help analysts categorize the costs and benefits. For instance, the cost/benefit framework used by Peppers and Rogers Group (Eisenberg 2001) includes the following cost categories: *Technology* (e.g., hardware, software, and infrastructure), *Process* (e.g., customization and integration), and *Operations* (e.g., content and technology infrastructure maintenance). The benefits categories include *Increased Revenue* (e.g., higher cross-sell rates), *Increased Retention* (e.g., reduced customer attrition rates and higher conversion rates), and *Reduced Costs* (e.g., higher operating margin per customer).

It is useful to consider some of the effectiveness measures of certain well-known organizations that have implemented personalization solutions. Amazon.com, for example, primarily uses collaborative filtering to provide product recommendations. Amazon is reported to have increased conversion rates as a result: 78 percent of sales are from returning customers. Citigroup's online personalized banking has resulted in a 9 percent reduction in customer attrition (Eisenberg 2001).

Still another potential pitfall of personalization is the concern that it raises over customer privacy. The case involving DoubleClick in 1999 brought privacy concerns into a public forum (Mark and Schneberger 2001). With its acquisition of Abacus Direct, DoubleClick obtained access to personal customer information. As a result, it had the ability to merge personal information with online behavior. Internet privacy activists filed a formal complaint with the Federal Trade Commission (FTC) regarding DoubleClick's use of personal information. The FTC's inquiry into DoubleClick's ad serving practices caused DoubleClick to take several steps to rectify the situation. In particular, it established a rather aggressive privacy policy. Among other things, this policy disclosed DoubleClick's use of customer data and described the company's "Opt Out" policy, giving consumers the option not to receive ads that DoubleClick could deliver using their personal information.

Many other online companies have also established privacy policies, which they display on their Web sites. These policies typically disclose the details regarding customer data, including how the companies collect data, how they use it, and the extent to which they share it with third parties. There are also many industry efforts to protect consumer privacy. For instance, the Online Privacy Alliance[1] and the Electronic Privacy Information Center[2] both seek to protect online privacy. The Platform for Privacy Preferences Project (P3P)[3] is a privacy technology initiative of the World Wide Web Consortium (W3C) in conjunction with many industry partners. P3P is a privacy technology that will block access to Web sites or automatically notify the online user if a Web site's privacy statement is not in line with privacy preferences.

Online privacy is also becoming an active field of research. Researchers have conducted many studies to examine privacy attitudes and concerns, finding that consumers are privacy conscious and that they trust published privacy statements and seals (Ackerman, Cranor, and Reagle 1999, Westin 1996). In another study, (Spiekermann, Grossklags, and Berendt 2001) compared self-reported privacy preferences with actual disclosing behavior during an online shopping episode. This study indicates that while consumers state that they are privacy conscious, they often do not live up to these preferences, and will disclose personal information while they are shopping online.

---

[1] www.privacyalliance.org [2] www.epic.org [3] www.w3.org/P3P/

Final Thoughts

We offer the following guidelines for choosing the most appropriate personalization paradigm for your Web site: If ease of implementation and low cost are your primary objectives, simple filtering will likely meet your needs. On the other hand, if you wish to personalize your site content based on more detailed knowledge, such as customers' personal interests or past purchasing behavior, you will need to implement a more advanced scheme, such as collaborative filtering or rules-based filtering. Collaborative filtering is most appropriate if you want your site content to be personalized based on inferences about your customers' personal interests and your site has enough traffic to yield useful recommendations. Rules-based filtering is most appropriate if you want to personalize your site content based on explicitly coded business rules. Both collaborative filtering and rules-based filtering personalization schemes, however, require specialized and costly software.

We hope that these guidelines, along with other important considerations, such as performance and privacy concerns, will help you make the best choice for technologies to build and deploy a personalization solution for your Web site.

References

Ackerman, M. S., Cranor, L. F., and Reagle, J. 1999. Privacy in E-Commerce: Examining User Scenarios and Privacy Preferences, Proceedings of the ACM Conference on Electronic Commerce, 1-8.

Akamai Technologies Inc. EdgeSuite, http://www.akamai.com/html/en/sv/content_delivery.html.

Apache Software Foundation. Apache HTTP Server Project, http://httpd.apache.org

Art Technology Group. ATG Dynamo Product Overview, http://www.atg.com/en/products/overview.jhtml

BEA Systems Inc. BEA WebLogic Server, http://www.atg.com/en/products/overview.jhtml

Broadvision Inc. One-To-One Enterprise, http://www.braodvision.com

CAMWorld, Content Management Systems, http://www.camworld.com/cms/

Chutney Technologies Inc. PreLoader, http://www.chutneytech.com/products/

Colkin, E. 2001. Personalization Tools Dig Deeper, InternetWeek, 27 August 2001.

Dragan, R. V. 2001a. BroadVision Retail Commerce Suite, PC Magazine, 16 January 2001.

Dragan, R. V. 2001b. Net Perceptions for E-Commerce 6.0, PC Magazine, 16 January 2001.

Eisenberg, M. 2001. Calculating the ROI of Web-based eCRM Initiatives (Peppers and Rogers Group), presented at BEA eWorld Conference.

Hewlett-Packard Company. HP Total E-Server, http://www.hp.bluestone.com/products/total-e-server/

IBM Corp. WebSphere Application Server, http://www-4.ibm.com/software/webservers/appserv

IBM High Volume Web Site Team. 2000. Web Site Personalization (White Paper), http://www7b.boulder.ibm.com/wsdd/library/techarticles/hvws/personalize.html

Interwoven Corp. Interwoven TeamSite, http://www.interwoven.com/products/teamsite/

Kemp, T. 2001. Personalization Isn't A Product, InternetWeek, 31 May 2001.

Macromedia Inc. a. Macromedia Spectra, http://www.allaire.com/products/spectra/

Macromedia Inc. b. Macromedia Jrun Server, http://www.macromedia.com/software/jrun/

Macromedia Inc. c. Macromedia LikeMinds Personalization and Performance (White Paper), http://www.macromedia.com/software/likeminds/whitepapers

Mark, K., and S. Schneberger. 2001. DoubleClick Inc.: Gathering Customer Intelligence, Richard Ivey School of Business, University of Western Ontario.

Microsoft Corp. a. Internet Information Server, http://www.microsoft.com/iis/

Microsoft Corp. b. Internet Security and Acceleration Server, http://www.microsoft.com/isaserver/

Microsoft Corp. c. ISA Server Pricing and Licensing, http://www.microsoft.com/isaserver/howtobuy/pricing/

Net Perceptions. Personalization Manager for E-Commerce, http://www.netperceptions.com

Oracle Corp., 2001. Oracle 9i Application Server: Database Cache (White Paper), http://otn.oracle.com/products/ias/db_cache/db_cache_twp.pdf

Persistence Software Inc. Dynamai, http://www.persistence.com/products/dynamai/

Reichheld, F. F., and W. E. Sasser. 1990. Zero defections: Quality Comes To Services. Harvard Business Review 68:105-7.

Rosenberg, M. 2001. The Personalization Story, ITWorld, 11 May 2001.

Spiekermann, S., J. Grossklags, and B. Berendt. 2001. E-privacy in 2nd Generation E-Commerce: Privacy Preferences versus Actual Behavior, Proceedings of the ACM Conference on Electronic Commerce, 38-47.

Sun Microsystems Inc. iPlanet Application Server, http://www.iplanet.com/products/iplanet_application_se/home_2_1_1am.html

TimesTen Performance Software. 2001a. Architected for Real-Time Data Management: TimesTen's Core In-Memory Database Technology (White Paper), http://www.timesten.com/products/timesten/.

TimesTen Performance Software. 2001b. TimesTen 4.1 Hits the Network (Press Release), http://www.timesten.com/press/pr012901.html.

Vignette Corp. 2001a. Vignette Content Suite V6 (White Paper), http://www.vignette.com

Vignette Corp. 2001b. Vignette Sets New Standard in Enterprise Application Pricing (Press Release), http://www.vignette.com/CDA/Site/0,2097,1-1-30-72-407-3044,00.html

Westin, A. 1996. Harris-Equifax Consumer Privacy Survey, Atlanta, GA: Equifax, Inc.

9 Modeling and Personalization of Users

Eren Manavoglu, Research Assistant, School of Information
    Sciences and Technology, Penn State University

Lee Giles, David Reese Professor of IST, School of Information
    Sciences and Technology, Penn State University

Amanda Spink, Associate Professor, School of Information
    Sciences, University of Pittsburgh

James Z. Wang, PNC Technologies Career Development
    Professor, School of Information Sciences and Technology,
    Penn State University

Introduction

The Internet is becoming the common medium for providing information and arena of trade. To succeed in this market place, sellers must better serve customers by anticipating customers' needs and make the transaction process efficient and satisfactory for both the customers and themselves. The measurement for success depends on the products that sellers provide. For online magazines or newspapers success would be measured by the number of registered users they have. For online auction sites the number of registered users and the number of transactions they make would be measures of success.

For search engines and information providers it would be the number of queries they answer.

To adapt applications to the needs and preferences of different individuals, service providers must have some sort of knowledge about the individuals. To personalize the applications for users, the applications must first personalize their users. They must recognize the differences between individuals. A model of a user, a representation of all the properties of a user that may be relevant to his or her behavior in the system, can serve as the source of this knowledge.

Creating models of users depends on their willingness to give information about themselves and on their awareness of their own needs. People who visit real estate Web sites to find apartments for rent probably know what kinds of apartments they want to live in and are probably willing to state their preferences. They can build their own models by filling out a form or answering the questions of a software realtor agent. Most Web users, on the other hand, do not like giving information about themselves if they are not going to benefit immediately from doing so. A user who knows the title or the author of a research paper she's searching for probably would not want to waste time creating a personal profile. In this scenario a profile of the user is not necessary to provide the information sought after. However, a profile could be helpful for providing further services, such as notifying about the conferences or talks on the subjects the user is interested in, or new publications in those fields. In such cases, the system must construct the model of the user by inferring knowledge from the user's behavior. For this example, the search engine could use the author, title, and the keywords of the paper to determine user's research interests.

Users may change their interests over time. To reflect the true state of the individual's preferences the model of the user must be dynamic. The personalized software application must be capable of deriving information about users by monitoring their activities. Even if the system can capture a change in a user's behavior, it will interpret what the change means. Therefore uncertainty will always exist, and it has to be included in the model. The software systems use machine learning or decision-theoretic inference methods to represent it and decide under its presence.

Constructing and managing accurate and comprehensive models of users is of great importance for e-commerce applications (Peppers and Rogers 1993; Allen, Kania, and Yaeckel 1998). Personalized marketing depends on knowing customers, understanding their needs, and serving them individually. User modeling provides this necessary information, and makes it possible for sellers to predict their customers' future needs. Gathering this valuable information about consumers on the public Internet introduces serious privacy questions. The potential for improper use of private information could override any benefits of profiling users from the business standpoint.

Obtaining Models of Users

A model of a user can be created directly by that individual or can be induced by the system as it keeps track of the user's actions. From the designer's point of view explicit modeling by the user is easier to implement, because the user does most of the work, perhaps with some help from the system. However, users may lack the time, knowledge, or trust in the system to make the additional cognitive and physical effort required. For some applications, providing the necessary information requires no extra effort. In a tutoring system, for instance, the user's answers to the practice questions within the session will provide enough information to create a profile (Beaumont 1994).

When the system generates the model of the user from implicit information, users do not have to supply information directly and the system must infer what it needs. The history of the user's actions online is the main source for the system. Users' homepages (Muller 2000a, 2000b), favorite Web sites, and history files (Moukas and Maes 1998) are some sources implicit user-modeling systems rely on to generate initial models of individual users. Regardless of how they are generated, models of users must be capable of adapting to changes in users' interests and needs. The models of users based on implicit information can be constructed incrementally (Horvitz et al. 1998). Models created by their users can be updated either by the system or the users. Some systems use stereotype profiles (Rich 1989) as starting points and modify them to fit the actual users (Fink, Kabsa, and Nill 1997).

To recognize changes in users' preferences, the system must interpret their responses. Users are always welcome to give feedback and avoid the possibility of misinterpretation; however, most users will not provide explicit feedback unless they obtain some immediate benefit (Carroll and Rosson 1987). Software systems use the time users spend on a document (Moukas and Maes 1998; Horvitz et al. 1998), their history of actions (printing, saving, deleting documents) (Nichols 1997), their focus of attention and exploration of menus, their query strings (Horvitz et al. 1998), their navigation patterns (Mladenic 1998), and their repetitive actions to derive information about them.

Existing user modeling systems rely on various methods to acquire information about users. Based on Jameson's (2001) bibliography, user-adaptive systems are used for the following purposes: for helping individuals to find information (e.g., selecting documents of interest to the user, identifying relevant chat groups or communities, adapt Web navigation mode to user's knowledge); for personalizing information presentation (e.g., choosing appropriate format of text and diagrams, taking into account user's available working memory capacity, adapting health-education documents to individual patients); for recommending products or other objects (e.g., books, driving routes, vacation packages);

for helping users with routing tasks such as e-mail classification and driving user's car; for adapting an interface (e.g., adapting a hypermedia interface to user's disabilities); for providing online help (e.g., office assistant in Microsoft Office applications); for tutoring (e.g., choosing appropriate test questions); and for supporting collaboration (e.g., selecting appropriate collaborators).

Comparing the performance of the systems for modeling users is almost impossible without implementing and evaluating every algorithm. Chin (2001) claims that only one third of the papers on user modeling published by User Modeling and User Adapted Interaction (UMUAI) include some type of evaluation. Even if the papers include evaluation results, with no standard evaluation methods, we cannot compare the systems. In "Empirical evaluations of user models and user-adapted Systems," Chin (2001) proposes some common measures for evaluating user-modeling systems. We grouped examples of user-modeling systems by application domain and found that the effectiveness of the method used to model users might depend on the application incorporating the model. Systems for helping users with routine tasks, for providing online help, and for recommending products probably would not succeed in an explicit manner. On the other hand, systems for personalized information presentation and for tutoring individuals might rely on explicit methods.

User Information Inference Techniques

The validity of user-models depends on their ability to infer unobservable information about users from their observable actions. In addition to validity, the amount of input data required, the computational complexity, interpretability, and the ability to handle uncertainty are the main properties of inference techniques. The user-modeling literature so far mainly covers the application of three techniques: machine learning, logic programming, and decision-theoretic methods.

Machine Learning for Inference

A dictionary definition of learning includes phrases like "to gain knowledge, or understanding of, or skill in, by study, instruction, or experience" and "modification of a behavioral tendency by experience." Following this definition we can say that a learning system uses sample data to generate an updated basis for improved performance on subsequent data from the same source (Michie 1991). The nature of the inference problem, deriving information about users based on their observed online actions, has attracted the attention of researchers in the area of machine learning. Since the observed actions of a user

Learning Method	Reference	Purpose of application
Neural networks	(Gori, Maggini, and Martinelli 1997)	Help user to find information
	(Jennings and Higuchi 1993)	Recommend news articles
	(Paranagama, Burstein, and Arnott 1997)	Tailor information presentations
Rule learning	NewsDude (Billsus and Pazzani 1999)	Recommend news articles
	(Chiu and Webb 1998)	Help learning
	(Fleming and Cohen 1999)	Help user with routine tasks (e-mail classification)
	(Joerding 1999)	Tailor information presentation
	(Litman and Pan 2000)	Adapt an interface
	(Maes 1994)	Help user with routine tasks (e-mail classification)
	(Mitchell et al. 1998)	Help user with routine tasks (scheduling meetings)
Classification	MailCat (Segal and Kephart 1999)	Help user with routine tasks (e-mail classification)
	Syskill & Webert (Pazzani and Billsus 1997)	Recommend Web sites
Theory refinement	(Baffes and Mooney 1996)	Models student errors

Table 1. Examples of user modeling systems that use machine-learning techniques. The systems vary in purpose and in the learning algorithms they use. In the first column the learning algorithm is specified, the second column includes the reference to the applications, and in the third column the purpose of the application is given.

can provide the sample data necessary to train the system, standard machine-learning techniques can be used to predict the future behaviors and needs of users. Quite a few researchers have tried to exploit this idea (Table 1).

So far researchers find that machine learning is not the perfect method for user modeling, and that machine learning methods are of limited usefulness (Webb, Pazzani, and Billsus 2001).

Learning algorithms need a lot of input data for their training before they become reasonably accurate. They need more samples for training than the users of most applications would be willing to give.

However, if the new situations are similar to the training examples, some learning algorithms (e.g. nearest neighbor) can be quite accurate. Billsus and Pazzani (1999) use this property in NewsDude to recommend personalized news stories. Another approach to overcome the training problem is to start with an initial model and modify it, instead of starting from scratch (Baffes and Mooney 1996). In this case, the choice of the initial model determines the suitability of the user model.

The need for user input is problematic also because users must explicitly state which training samples they are interested in and which ones they are not. Thus, users are expected to perform additional tasks without any immediate benefit. In general, users do not want to provide this information. The solution might be to infer the labels of the training samples from users' behavior (Lieberman 1995), or to start with a small set of labeled samples and infer the labels of the rest of the samples (Kwok and Chan 1998).

Learning algorithms depend on the examples used for training to reflect the current interests of the user. However, the training set also retains information about the user's former interests. If they are to predict the true state of users' current preferences, learning algorithms should, somehow, learn to forget past experiences. Webb and Kuzmycz (1996) use weighted training sets for learning algorithms and put less weight on older observations to accomplish this. Klinkenberg and Renz (1998) propose the use of a dynamic time window, whose size determines the extent of the training data. Another approach is to use dual user models (Chiu and Webb 1998; Billsus and Pazzani 1999). With two user models, one to represent the user's long-term interests and the other to represent short-term interests, the problem is reduced to deciding when to use which model.

The conclusions derived with machine-learning techniques are usually not easy for users to interpret. Furthermore, there's no explicit explanation of the uncertainty represented. Users should be able to view their models and, if they are willing to do so, should be able to change them. Although machine learning remains applicable for user modeling, it will be impractical from the users' perspective as long as they cannot reason about the resulting models of themselves.

Logical Programming for Inference

Because it can represent users' beliefs precisely and make inferences based on those beliefs, logical programming is a candidate for deriving user models. Logical statements can represent users' complex beliefs. However, making assumptions based on users' beliefs requires background knowledge. To explain this problem Jameson (1995) uses the example of a sales representative trying to sell a car, C, to a user. The system might have the following beliefs: (1) the user knows the car, C, is a BMW and (2) German cars are well engineered. To conclude that the user knows that C is a well-engineered car, the system has to include the user's background knowledge of the fact that BMWs are German cars.

Examples of logic-based user-modeling systems (Pohl and Hohle 1997) assume that the user has the relevant background knowledge until proved otherwise. Evidence of a user's background knowledge is often not available (Jameson 1995). To handle this uncertainty, Pohl (1998) suggests the employment of a hierarchy among the assumption types and use uncertainty values to graduate assumptions. If a secondary assumption is derived from other assumptions, the uncertainty value of the new assumption could be computed from the values of its parents. Therefore, a change in the graduation value of an assumption depends on and affects the graduation values of the other assumptions. Thus, a change in the uncertainty of an assumption may also cause a change in the steps of an inference process. The use of an external mechanism to compute the conditional uncertainty values is also suggested.

Logic-based user-modeling systems require explicit input from the user to initialize the model. Furthermore, they require user feedback to verify the assumptions they make. During the evaluation of OySTER (Muller 2000a), an adaptive meta-search engine that uses inductive logic programming for user modeling, Muller found that the system needed about 20 to 25 feedback events (such as rating the relevancy of the search result with respect to all interest aspects) to learn a usable user model, and that the users did not want to provide them. Because of users' unwillingness to give feedback, the computational complexity required to reason about users' higher order beliefs, the need for an extra mechanism to handle uncertainty, logic is a nominee for user modeling only when it's used in conjunction with other approaches.

Decision-Theoretic Methods for Inference

Decision theory is built on the foundations of probability and utility. Probabilistic theory enables one to make uncertain statements explicitly. In fact, it has been demonstrated that the desirable properties for continuous measures of belief in the truth of a proposition logically imply that the measure of belief must satisfy the axioms of probability (Cox 1946; Horvitz, Breese, and Henrion 1988). Utility theory, on the other hand, introduces a set of principles for consistency among preferences and decisions. Thus, decision theory makes it possible to explore the alternative actions of a user and to compare their advantages and disadvantages from the user's point of view.

The common decision-theoretic method used in the user-modeling domain is Bayesian networks. Despite the name, Bayesian networks (also called belief networks) refers to any directed acyclic graphical model encoding probabilistic information that uses Bayes' theorem for inference. The nodes of a Bayesian network represent the random variables of the system, and the arcs represent the causal relationships between these random variables. Conditional probability tables specify this uncertain influence between the nodes. As an example, in a medical decision support system, two of the nodes could be "smoking" and "lung cancer." An arc from the smoking node to the lung cancer node would then indicate that smoking causes lung cancer. Given the causal relationship P(*smoking | lung cancer*), Bayes' theorem can be used to reason about the diagnostic relation, that is, P(*lung cancer | smoking*). This bidirectional nature of the Bayes' theorem allows Bayesian networks to reason about the user's actions.

A Bayesian network is specified by its structure and by the parameters of the conditional probability tables. It is possible to learn both of these properties from the training set. If the probability values for some of the nodes are not known, the learning task requires more effort. The values might not be known either because they are not measured in the training data or because it's not possible to measure some of the variables at all (the hidden variable case). If the structure of the network is unknown, however, learning the topology that fits the data best is very difficult (Table 2).

Bayesian networks have been applied to various user-modeling tasks. Heckerman and Horvitz (1998) use Bayesian networks to infer users' informational goals from free-text queries. They handcrafted the initial network with the help of experts; therefore, both the structure and the initial conditional probability values are known beforehand. Later Horvitz et al. (1998) used a Bayesian network to determine the type of assistance the users of Microsoft Office products needed. They again worked with experts to assess and construct Bayesian networks and to identify the classes of evidence to use for making inferences about users' problems. Albrecht, Zukerman, and Nicholson (1998) use dynamic Bayesian networks to predict a user's next action, next location, and current quest in a multi-user adventure game. Großmann-Hutter, Jameson, and Wittig (1999) investigate the learning of Bayesian networks with hidden variables where the users have changing resource limitations. Within the same domain, Wittig and Jameson (2000) consider the use of qualitative knowledge for learning about conditional probabilities. Unlike Horvitz et al. (1998), they modeled the experts' constraints in the overall system as state variables. Wittig (2001) also focuses on the structural part of the learning problem. The results of his work show that, in the case of a profile that has not been encountered

	Known Structure	Unknown Structure
Complete Data	Statistical parameter estimation (Statistical parameter fitting, Machine learning, Bayesian inference)	Discrete Optimization over structure (constraint based, score based)
Incomplete Data	Parametric optimization (Expectation maximization, gradient-based, maximum a posterior estimate, machine learning, Bayesian inference)	Combined (Structural expectation maximization)

Table 2. Bayesian network learning methods. The system can learn the Bayesian network from the training data. Experts of the application fields can build the structure of the network manually. Otherwise the system must also learn it from the data. The first column corresponds to the first case, and the second column corresponds to the latter. The training examples might sometimes contain unobserved parameters or missing data. The first row lists the methods used for complete data case, and the second row lists the methods for incomplete data.

among the profiles used for learning, the resulting structure's fit to the profile could be very poor. Nevertheless, results of this work also show that learning the structure of the Bayesian networks can indeed lead to better quality for the common profiles.

The use of Bayesian networks for user modeling so far has been restricted to users in general, instead of individual users. Therefore, unlike the machine-learning and logical-programming techniques, Bayesian networks have not been adapted to learning about particular users. Learned system must be able to adapt. The Bayesian network approach can be useful when information about individual users is limited, e.g., the first time they log onto the system. However, in some situations learning different Bayesian networks for each user may work better.

Computational complexity and the effort required to construct a suitable network structure with accurate probabilities are important issues about Bayesian networks. However, they are not insoluble problems. A possible solution is to use constraints and background knowledge (Großmann-Hutter, Jameson, and Wittig 1999; Wittig and Jameson 2000) together with the learning of Bayesian networks from data. The natural ability of Bayesian networks to handle uncertainty in user beliefs and interpretability distinguishes them from other candidate techniques for modeling users. "Why use Bayesian nets?"

(AUAI Testimonial) contains some experimental evidence supporting the use of Bayesian networks in areas of uncertainty.

Commercial User Modeling Systems

The electronic commerce community has recognized the possibility of turning Web surfers into customers through personalized marketing strategies. Modeling users in this user-targeted market place is very important. Software companies are advertising many systems for personalization on the Web, with different capabilities. Such commercial systems differ from academic user-modeling systems in their client-server architecture. Client-server based user-modeling systems have some important advantages over the embedded user-modeling components (Fink and Kobsa 2001).

- Firms can maintain user models in central repositories for use by more multiple applications simultaneously.
- Applications can use the information on users acquired by other applications.
- Firms can maintain the information about user groups, either static or dynamic, with little redundancy.
- They can use security and privacy tools to protect user models in the user-modeling servers.
- They can integrate complementary user information available across the enterprise with the user model in the server easily.

Commercial user-modeling systems must support some services in order to stay alive. For example, they must be able to compare the actions of different users. Some application domains may be unsuitable for reasoning about users' actions. Under such circumstances, the systems should be able to predict users' future actions based on the actions of similar users. Commercial systems must also support importing user-related information from outside. Most businesses already have customer and market data that should be integrated into the user-modeling system.

Most popular personalization tools as we wrote this chapter were Group Lens (Net Perceptions 2000), which predicts users' interests based on collaborative filtering techniques and explicit and implicit ratings by the user; LikeMinds (2000), which has a modular architecture and external database support; Personalization Server (Art Technology Group 2000), which uses defining rules to assign users to already defined groups of users; Frontmind (Manna), which relies on Bayesian networks for user modeling; and Open Sesame (Open Sesame 2000), based on defining a domain model and clustering.

User's Privacy

Privacy is an emerging issue in personalization of the Web. Commercial user-modeling systems should be able to support any company privacy policy that satisfies industry privacy norms and privacy legislation. User-model suppliers must come up with a privacy norm that satisfies e-business companies and at the same time protects individuals' rights to privacy. Whether to control the collection and distribution of user profiles, and how, are questions the Internet community and the governments should answer. Linking anonymous profiles with direct-marketing databases can yield more detailed personal information and even identify the anonymous Internet users. Is it ethical to provide information about individuals without their permission? Probably not, but ethics do not rule the Internet community; at least ethics did not stop DoubleClick from identifying physical locations of anonymous users and selling the information (Chiu 2000). Given the risk of abusing people's privacy and the potential repercussions, stronger actions should be taken to protect privacy.

Conclusion

Knowledge of users' current needs and goals, or even better, what they will need or want in the future, is invaluable information for many application domains, especially when users are potential customers. Although user modeling is not restricted to the Internet, the Internet's growing popularity as the new shopping center and knowledge base has caused an increase in interest in user modeling.

Another important playground for researchers working on user modeling researchers is the organizational networks for information flow within organizations, which are private environments, unlike the Internet. Organizations can use user modeling to manage their organizational memory, workflow, and internal communications. In such environments, users already have some kinds of profiles. They might have positional profiles related to their job and role profiles related to their roles in ongoing projects. These profiles are not exactly specific to individuals; a positional profile, for example, would be the same for the employees in the same position. However, organizations could also assemble personal models of their employees. They can build the initial personal models automatically from employee's curricula vitae or other personal information within their databases. They can use rule learning or logical programming to automatically extract information from these common records.

We also believe that by using several profiles for each individual, personalization application can obtain the advantages of the different user-modeling techniques, facilitating the adaptation of applications to the users' dynamic interest and simplifying the system's overall design.

Acknowledgements

We gratefully acknowledge support from a grant by Lockheed Martin.

References

Albrecht, D. W., I. Zukerman, and A. E. Nicholson. 1998. Bayesian models for keyhole plan recognition in an adventure game. User Modeling and User-Adapted Interaction 8(1-2): 5-47.

Allen, C., D. Kania, and B. Yaeckel. 1998. Internet World Guide to One-To-One Web Marketing. New York: John Wiley and Sons.

Art Technology Group. 2000. Dynamo Product Suite. http://www.atg.com/products/highlights

Association for Uncertainty in Artificial Intelligence (AUAI) Testimonial. Why Use Bayesian Nets. http://www.auai.org/BN-Testimonial.html

Baffes, P., and R. Mooney. 1996. Refinement-based student modeling and automated bug library construction. *Journal of Artificial Intelligence in Education* 7(1): 75-116.

Beaumont, I. 1994. User modeling in the interactive anatomy tutoring system ANATOM-tutor. User Modeling and User-Adapted Interaction, 4: 21-45.

Billsus, D., and M. J. Pazzani. 1999. A hybrid user model for news story classification. In J. Kay (Ed.), User Modeling: Proceedings of the Seventh International Conference, UM99. Vienna: Springer Wien New York. 99-108. http://www.ics.uci.edu/~pazzani/Publications/Publications.html

Carroll, J. M., and M. B. Rosson. 1987. Paradox of the active user, In J. M. Carroll (Ed.), Interfacing Thought: Cognitive Aspects of Human-Computer Interaction, Cambridge: MIT Press.

Chin, D. 2001. Empirical evaluations of user models and user-adapted Systems. User Modeling and User-Adapted Interaction 11(1/2): 181-194.

Chiu, Andrew S. 2000. The Ethics of Internet Privacy.

Chiu, B. C., and G. Webb. 1998. Using decision trees for agent modeling: Improving prediction performance. User Modeling and User-Adapted Interaction 8(1-2): 131-152.

Cox, R. 1946. Probability, frequency and reasonable expectation. American Journal of Physics 14: 1-13.

Fink, J., A. Kobsa, and A. Nill. 1997. Adaptable and adaptive information access for all users, including the disabled and the elderly. In A. Jameson, C. Paris, and C. Tasso (Eds.), User Modeling: Proceedings of the Sixth International Conference, UM97 Vienna: Springer Wien New York 171-173. http://www.cs.uni-sb.de/UM97/

Fink, J., and A. Kobsa. 2001. A review and analysis of commercial user modeling servers for personalization on the World Wide Web. User Modeling and User-Adapted Interaction, 10: 209-249.

Fleming, M. and R. Cohen 1999. User modeling in the design of interactive interface agents. In J. Kay (Ed.), UM99, User modeling: Proceedings of the Seventh International Conference Vienna: Springer Wien New York 67-76. http://www.cs.usask.ca/UM99/

Frontmind. http://www.mannainc.com

Gori, M., M. Maggini, and E. Martinelli. 1997. Web-browser access through voice input and page interest prediction. In A. Jameson, C. Paris, and C. Tasso (Eds.), User Modeling: Proceedings of the Sixth International Conference, UM97 Vienna: Springer Wien New York. 17-19. http://www.cs.uni-sb.de/UM97/

Großmann-Hutter, B., A. Jameson, and F. Wittig. 1999. Learning Bayesian networks with hidden variables for user-modeling. In J. Kay (Ed.), Proceedings of the IJCAI 99 Workshop "Learning About Users," Stockholm: Springer Wien New York. 29-34.

Heckerman, D., and E. Horvitz. 1998. Inferring informational goals from free-text queries: A Bayesian approach. In G. F. Cooper and S. Moral (Eds.), Uncertainty in Artificial Intelligence: Proceedings of the Fourteenth Conference. San Francisco: Morgan Kaufmann. 230-237. http://www2.sis.pitt.edu/~dsl/UAI/uai.html

Horvitz, E. J., J. S. Breese, and M. Henrion. 1988. Decision theory in expert systems and artificial intelligence. Journal of Approximate Reasoning, Special Issue on Uncertainty in Artificial Intelligence 2:247-302.

Horvitz, E., J. Breese, D. Heckerman, D. Hovel, and K. Rommelse. 1998. The Lumière project: Bayesian user modeling for inferring the goals and needs of software users. In G. F. Cooper and S. Moral (Eds.), Uncertainty in Artificial Intelligence: Proceedings of the Fourteenth Conference. San Francisco: Morgan Kaufmann. 256-265. http://www2.sis.pitt.edu/~dsl/UAI/uai.html

Jameson, A. 1995. Numerical uncertainty management in user and student modeling: An overview of systems and issues. User Modeling and User-Adapted Interaction 5(3-4): 193-251.

Jameson, A. 2001. Bibliography on user adaptive systems. http://dfki.de/~jameson/uas/index.htm

Jennings, A., and H. Higuchi. 1993. A user model neural network for a personal news service. User Modeling and User-Adapted Interaction 3(1): 1-25.

Joerding, T. 1999. Temporary user modeling for adaptive product presentation in the Web. In J. Kay (Ed.), User Modeling: Proceedings of the Seventh International Conference, UM99. Banff, Canada: Springer Wien New York. 333-334.

Klinkenberg, R., and I. Renz. 1998. Adaptive information filtering: learning in the presence of concept drift. In M. Sahami, M. Craven, T. Joachims and A. McCallum (Eds.), Learning for Text Categorization - Papers from the 1998 ICML/AAAI Workshop, Number WS-98-05. AAAI Press, Menlo Park, CA. 33-40.

Kobsa, A. 2000. Generic user modeling systems. User Modeling and User-Adapted Interaction. 11(1-2): 49-63.

Kwok, K., and M. Chan. 1998. Improving two-stage ad-hoc retrieval for short queries. Proceedings of the 21st Annual International ACM SIGIR Conference on Research and Development in Information Retrieval. Melbourne, Australia. 250-256.

Lieberman, H. 1995. Letizia: An agent that assists Web browsing. In C. S. Mellish (Ed.), Proceedings of the Fourteenth International Joint Conference on Artificial Intelligence, Montreal, Canada. San Mateo, CA: Morgan Kaufmann. 924-929.

LikeMinds. 2000. http://www.andromedia.com/products/likeminds/index.html

Litman, D., and S. Pan. 2000. Predicting and adapting to poor speech recognition in a spoken dialogue system. AAAI2000 Proceedings of the Seventeenth National Conference on Artificial Intelligence. San Antonio, Texas. 722-728.

Maes, P. 1994. Agents that reduce work and information overload. Communications of the ACM, 37(7): 30-40.

Michie, D. 1991. Methodologies for machine learning in data analysis and software. Computer Journal 34: 559-565

Mitchell, T., R. Caruana, D. Freitag, J. McDermott, and D. Zabowski. 1994. Experience with a learning personal assistant. Communications of the ACM 37(7): 81-91.

Mladenic, D. 1998. Machine Learning on Nonhomogeneous, Distributed Text Data, PhD thesis, Faculty for Computer and Information Science, Univ. of Ljubljana, Slovenia. http://cs.cmu.edu/~TextLearning/pww/PhD.html

Moukas, A., and P. Maes. 1998. Amalthaea: an evolving multi-agent information filtering and discovery systems for the WWW. Autonomous Agents and Multi-Agent Systems. 1: 59-88.

Muller, M. E. 2000a. OySTER: Web search as a playground for user modeling techniques. M. E. Muller, editor, Adaptivitat und Benutzermodellierung in interaktiven Softwaresystemen. Institut fur Semantische Information sverarbeitung, Universitat Osnabruck.

Muller, M. E. 2000b. Inductive Logic Programming for Learning User Models Proceedings of Fachgruppentreffen Maschinelles Lernen FGML-00, GMD-Report 114, GMD, Sankt Augustin.

Net Perceptions. 2000. http://www.netperceptions.com

Nichols, D. M. 1997. Implicit ratings and filtering. Proceedings of the 5th DELOS Workshop on Filtering and Collaborative Filtering, Budapest, Hungary: European Research Consortium for Informatics and Mathematics. 10-12. http://www.ercim.org/publication/ws-proceedings/DELOS5/index.html

Open Sesame. 2000. http://www.opensesame.com

Paranagama, P., F. Burstein, and D. Arnott. 1997. Modelling the personality of decision makers for active decision support. A. Jameson, C. Paris, and C. Tasso (Eds.), User Modeling: Proceedings of the Sixth International Conference, UM97. Vienna: Springer Wien New York. 79-81. http://www.cs.uni-sb.de/UM97/

Pazzani, M., and D. Billsus. 1997. Learning and revising user profiles: The identification of interesting Web sites. Machine Learning, 27: 313-331. http://www.ics.uci.edu/~pazzani/Publications/Publications.html

Peppers, D., and M. Rogers. 1993. The one to one future: Building relationships one customer at a time. New York (NY): Currency Doubleday.

Pohl,W. 1998. Logic-based representation and reasoning for user modeling shell systems. Department of Mathematics and Computer Science, University of Essen, Germany. Published with infix, Dissertations in Artificial Intelligence series.

Pohl, W., and J. Hohle. 1997. Mechanisms for flexible representation and use of knowledge in user modeling shell systems. In: A. Jameson, C. Paris, and C. Tasso (Eds.), User Modeling: Proceedings of the Sixth International Conference. Vienna: Springer Wien New York. 403-414.

Rich, E. 1989. Stereotypes and user modeling. In A. Kobsa and W. Wahlster (Eds.), User Models in Dialog Systems. Berlin: Springer-Verlag. 35-51.

Segal, R. B., and J. O. Kephart. 1999. MailCat: An intelligent assistant for organizing e-mail. Proceedings of the Third International Conference on Autonomous Agents, 276-282. http://www.research.ibm.com/swiftfile/

Webb, G. I., and M. Kuzmycz. 1996. Feature based modelling: A methodology for producing coherent, consistent, dynamically changing models of agents' competencies. User Modeling and User-Adapted Interaction 5(2): 117-150.

Webb, G. I., M. J. Pazzani, and D. Billsus. 2001. Machine learning for user modeling. User Modeling and User-Adapted Interaction 11(1-2): 19-29.

Wittig, F. 2001. Some issues in the learning of accurate, interpretable user models from sparse data. In R. Schafer, M. E. Muller, and S. A. Macskassy (Eds.), Proceedings of the UM2001 Workshop on "Machine Learning for User Modeling." Sonthofen. 11-21.

Wittig, F., and A. Jameson. 2000. Exploiting qualitative knowledge in the learning of conditional probabilities of Bayesian networks. In C. Boutilier and M. Goldszmidt (Eds.), Uncertainty in Artificial Intelligence: Proceedings of the Sixteenth Conference, UAI-2000. San Francisco: Morgan Kaufmann. 644-652.

10 Technological Aspects of Privacy and Security for Personalization

Ingemar J. Cox, Professor of Telecommunications, University
    College, London

David M. Pennock, Senior Research Scientist, Overture Services,
    Inc.

Eric J. Glover, Research Staff Member, NEC Research Institute

Introduction

The goal of personalization is to bring a sense of individualized attention and service to the often impersonal world of e-commerce. In general terms, personalization is the act of displaying different content on a Web site based on who is viewing it. While personalization offers potential benefits in terms of improved service for consumers and increased revenues for providers, there are potential conflicts of interest. Specifically, businesses must be careful to not collect so much personal information that consumers feel that their privacy, anonymity, or security has been breached. For businesses, the goal then is to encourage consumers to embrace personalization by providing sufficient benefits in terms of customization and individualized service while maintaining an adequate level of privacy, anonymity, and security.

The terms *privacy* and *security* are used in many contexts and defined in many ways. We define them as follows:

privacy Consumers' freedom from unauthorized intrusion into their personal information, e.g., his or her name, address, credit card, buying habits, browsing history, etc.

security The prevention of unauthorized access to a company's records.

While many businesses have used personalization technology successfully and beneficially, some businesses have "crossed the line" in the public's view. Perhaps the most notorious example is that of DoubleClick Inc. DoubleClick coordinates the placement of banner advertisements on hundreds of popular sites on the World Wide Web. By using cookies, a technology described in Section 2.3, DoubleClick is able to track a single user's online identity as he or she moves from Web site to Web site, although DoubleClick generally cannot connect the online identification to the user's real name. Around January 2000, DoubleClick purchased Abacus Direct, a large market research firm that owns millions of records of customer names and physical addresses, and announced plans to tie consumers' Internet identities to their real identities in order to improve ad targeting and cross marketing. The announcement provoked heated protests covered widely in the media, from consumer and privacy advocates, forcing DoubleClick to scale back its plan.[1]

In an example of a serious security breach, an estimated 350,000 credit card numbers were stolen by a hacker from online music store CD Universe around January 2000. When the hacker's attempt to blackmail CD Universe failed, he or she released some of the numbers on a publicly accessible Web page. [2]

---

[1]DoubleClick's current privacy policy (http://www.doubleclick.net/us/corporate/ privacy/privacy/default.asp?asp object 1=&) states that "DoubleClick does not use your name, address, email address, or phone number to deliver Internet ads," but does not explicitly rule out connecting online and offline identities for other purposes.

[2]Currently, CD Universe's statement of security (http://www.cduniverse.com/policy.asp? cart=112619673&style=music#sc) does not mention the theft. The statement says "The main concern of online shoppers is that their credit card information will somehow end up in the wrong hands, . . . It is actually safer to transmit your credit card info over the Internet than it is to use your credit card around town. . . . CD Universe uses world-class encryption and firewall technology to protect your personal and billing information including name, address and credit card details to ensure they can not be read as they travel over the Internet or accessed through our secure servers."

DoubleClick's situation was one example in which the perceived benefits of personalization did not outweigh consumers' perceived loss of privacy. The Web complicates the issue of maintaining privacy because (1) consumer information can be gathered without the consumer being aware of it, (2) e-commerce sites do not necessarily follow the same social contract expected by consumers, especially since privacy laws vary from country to country, and (3) the sharing and cross-referencing of consumer information across multiple databases offers/threatens unprecedented market targeting of consumers that some companies find hard to resist.

CD Universe's loss of credit card information was a security failure in which private and confidential information became public. While security is easier to define and understand than privacy, security may often be compromised by poor design of data storage systems or by design trade-offs made too much in favor of simplified user interaction.

At the core of personalization is consumer information. Before we can investigate security and privacy issues, we need a clear picture of what information is available and how it can be used or abused. In Section 2, we examine what information a business can gather implicitly from visitors to its Web site, including information built into the communication protocol of the Internet, and history information as users navigate a company's site. In Section 3 we cover potential inferences that can be made about a person by examining his or her behavior and comparing a particular user with other users. In Section 4, we discuss the privacy and security concerns that arise when companies collect, use, distribute, or sell such information. Section 4.1 focuses on the point of view of businesses, while Section 4.2 examines the viewpoints and responses of consumers. Section 5 summarizes the chapter, concluding with some thoughts about the future of personalization, privacy, and security.

2. Acquiring Personal Information

Businesses can acquire personal information in a variety of ways. In the most direct method, users knowingly disclose personal information to a Web site by, say, completing a questionnaire or filling in credit card information. Businesses that rely on explicit disclosure must still address privacy and security. However, in this section we consider how businesses acquire information through implicit disclosure—that is, by collecting information about user actions that naive consumers may be unaware that they are disclosing.

The information associated with an individual is potentially limitless. We restrict discussion to three main areas:

- Identification

  Obviously, personalization requires identifying the source of each request. Initial identification may be coarse, each user being assigned a unique identifier (e.g., user198). However, subsequent user actions (e.g., a credit card purchase) may allow the business to associate additional information such as a name and address with the unique identifier.

- Tracking

  If a business can accurately identify the source of each request, then it is straightforward to track a user as he or she navigates through a Web site. Usually, such tracking is restricted to a single Web site. However, in some circumstances, it is possible to track a user's path as he or she navigates from site to site. In addition, it is often possible to determine the user's geographic location or the company with which he or she is employed.

- History

  Identification also facilitates the creation of a history of a user's past actions (e.g., past purchases).

Clearly, identifying the source of a request is the key to personalization. In Section 2.1 we describe the basic communication protocol used for Web interaction and describe how this protocol can provide explicit and implicit information about a user. Section 2.2 then describes a more complicated yet more common communication arrangement in which communication between a client and server passes through a proxy. This raises additional privacy and security concerns. Section 2.3 then describes cookies, a mechanism for more accurately identifying users.

2.1. The http Protocol

In almost all communications between a customer and an e-commerce site, the customer uses a browser (e.g., Internet Explorer or Netscape Navigator). And almost all browsers communicate using the Hypertext Transfer Protocol, or http [7]. Other protocols, such as ftp, are employed less often and are beyond the scope of this chapter; however, note that these protocols can and do reveal personal information. Krishnamurty and Rexford [11] explain the http protocol in detail. We give a brief and simplified description indicating where personal information is provided, stored and accessed.

The http protocol is a message-based protocol that begins with a *request* and ends with a *response*. The request always originates from the *client* (usually the customer), while the response originates from the *origin server*. Intermediaries may also be involved, but, the simplest form of connection is between a client and an origin server, as illustrated in Figure 1.

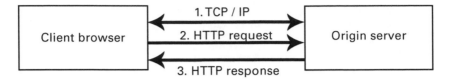

Figure 1. A simple client-server connection using the http protocol.

As a precursor to establishing an http connection, a Transport Control Protocol/Internet Protocol (TCP/IP) connection is created between the client and the server. The TCP/IP connection is the foundation for all Internet communications. A detailed description of this protocol can be found in [9]. For our purposes, it is sufficient to know that every computer connected to the Internet is assigned an identifying number called an Internet Protocol (IP) address,[3] and that this address is provided as part of the TCP/IP protocol. Although at any given time one computer has one unique IP address,[4] the same computer may have different IP addresses at different times; we discuss this issue further in Section 4.1.1.

Once the TCP/IP connection is established, the http protocol begins. In a typical request, the client seeks either to retrieve information (e.g., download a Web page), or to provide information (e.g., submit information from a form). A request from a client always includes

  • the type of request, and
  • a date field that provides the date and time of the request.

In addition, in many cases the request includes the following:

  • a Referer field provides the URL of the referring page, or the page the user just came from. For example, suppose that a user is browsing http://www.abc.com/ and clicks on a link to http://www.xyz.com/. Then the Referer field of the request sent to the server xyz.com contains "http://www.abc.com/," the URL of the referring page.

---

[3]IP addresses are typically represented as four individual numbers from 0 to 255 separated by dots (e.g.,10.253.0.79).
[4]Technically, it is possible at a given time for one machine to have multiple IP addresses or multiple machines to respond to one IP address, but these situations are not the norm.

- a From field provides the e-mail address of the user[5]
- an Authorization field can be used by the client to transmit such information as login and password, in order to access a secured resource

The response from the server may include

- a location field that is used to redirect a request to another site and
- a WWW-Authenticate field that is used to request authentication information from a user attempting to access secured information.

These are not complete lists of request and response fields. When the Referer or From fields are available, the Web server has access to considerable information.

Most information from every request is stored in the server's log. The server can analyse the log periodically to infer user preferences. This will be discussed further in Section 3. In Section 4, we describe how businesses can use information provided by the http and TCP/IP protocols (including the IP address) to identify and track users.

2.2. Proxies

The simplest and most direct form of communication is between a client and a server (Figure 1). More commonly, the connection between the client and server will include at least one proxy, as illustrated in Figure 2. A proxy will appear to the client as a server. Conversely, a proxy will appear to the server as a client. There are many reasons for introducing proxies into the communications channel. These include

- sharing access,
- caching responses,
- anonymizing clients,
- filtering requests, and
- monitoring network security and Web usage.

A proxy may be under the control of the client or the server or an independent third party. Moreover, there may be more than one proxy between the client and origin server. For example, the client may be running a proxy, the client's Internet Service Provider (ISP) may be running a proxy, and the origin server may be running a proxy.

---

[5]Note that most browsers do not by default include the user's email address in http requests; some do, however, in ftp requests.

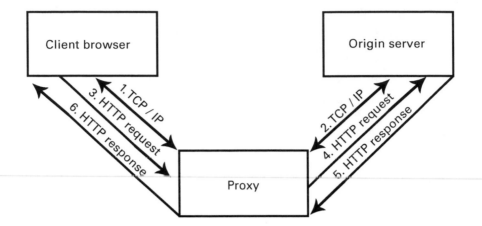

Figure 2. A client-server configuration with a proxy as an intermediary.

From the point of view of security, unless special precautions are taken (such as those described in Section 4), any Internet communication might be intercepted by a third party. The introduction of proxies simply means that more parties may have access to the communication. On the other hand, companies sometimes use proxies to aid security by controlling the flow of information between internal company networks and the external public Internet.

From the point of view of privacy, proxies can be helpful in ensuring anonymity, or some degree of anonymity, to the client. Certainly, the origin server can no longer rely on the IP address to identify the customer. Moreover, the proxy can be configured to strip out personal information contained in the Referer and From fields of the http request, prior to forwarding them to the origin server. Clearly, companies need additional means for identifying customers. One such method is the use of cookies.

2.3. Cookies

The basic http protocol is stateless or memoryless. That is, each http transaction (request and response) is independent of all previous transactions. As a result, servers ordinarily cannot distinguish between repeat visitors and first-time visitors. In many circumstances this is undesirable. For example, a fee-based Web service may prefer that registered clients do not have to retype their user ID's each time they return to the site. Cookies provide support for such customization by providing client state information that persists during sessions and possibly across multiple sessions.

A cookie is a text file that is stored on the client's local machine. Each cookie is associated with a particular domain (e.g., www.acme.com), and is (almost always) set by that domain's server during a client's visit. The information stored in the cookie is arbitrary and consists of attribute/value pairs (e.g., CUSTOMER=WILE E COYOTE).

When an origin server receives a request from a client, its http response may include one or more cookies. Figure 3 illustrates the process. Subsequent http requests from the client to that server will include this cookie, which may contain information identifying the consumer. Under normal operation, the server can access only the cookies that it created, not cookies created by other servers or any other information on the client's hard drive.

3. Drawing Inferences from User Actions

Businesses can achieve some degree of personalization based only on data obtained directly from the user. For example, a business could use a zip code to provide local weather forecasts or movie listings. Information about an individual's stock holdings can be used to provide portfolio tracking services. Past Web or news searches can be saved for later use. Personalized portals on sites like Yahoo.com and Excite.com work in this way.

Another level of personalization involves making *inferences* about the customer. The goal is to form an intelligent hypothesis about the customer's preferences or interests based on his or her past behavior and how that behavior compares with the behavior of other customers. For example, suppose that Pat purchases baby formula and diapers from a Web store. Because most people who purchase these items are parents, the site may conclude that Pat is likely to be a parent, even if she (or he) never explicitly said so. Then during Pat's next visit, the site may present advertisements for children's toys that sell well among parents. Automatic inference of this sort is also referred to as *machine learning* or *data mining* [10, 14]. Inferring attributes about a person may violate their sense of privacy, especially if those inferences are incorrect or are communicated to other companies without permission.

A *recommender system* is one technology aimed at automatically suggesting products of interest to consumers. There are three main types of recommender systems:

- *content filtering systems,*
- *collaborative filtering systems*, and
- *hybrid systems* that incorporate both technologies.

The three types can be distinguished according to the kind of information that they use to make recommendations. Content

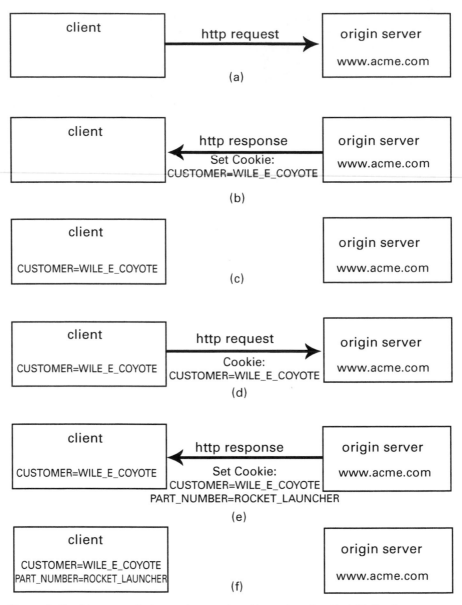

Figure 3. Cookie transmission and reception. Here, the client is initially shown
with no cookies (a). A request to the origin server at www.acme.com leads to a
response that includes the http field Set-Cookie (b) that instructs the client to store
the cookie (c). Subsequent http requests from the client to the origin server at
www.acme.com will include this cookie in the http Cookie field, (d). In this example,
the cookie contains information that identifies the consumer. This second request
to the server results in a response that updates the cookie, as illustrated in (e), in
which the order for PART NUMBER=ROCKET LAUNCHER is recorded. Once again,
this cookie is stored locally.

filtering systems match customer information with descriptive product information in order to recommend the most relevant products to the customer [15, 21, 22]. Collaborative filtering systems match customer information with *other* customers' information, in order to find products that people with similar tastes might recommend [4, 16, 20, 26]. Content filtering can be thought of as an attempt to mechanize the role of a librarian who interprets a customer's request and locates the most relevant information. Collaborative filtering can be thought of as an attempt to automate the word of mouth process of people recommending products to their friends.

If a site has enough users, collaborative systems tend to be simpler and to work better than content filters. Currently content filters rely on machine intelligence algorithms that do not perform as well as humans in many respects. Collaborative filters leverage human intelligence by matching people with other people, rather than matching people with products directly. In this way, the people in the system provide intelligence about what products are related, not the algorithms.

Still, purely collaborative systems can fail when little is known about a user, when a user has uncommon interests, or when a new item has no endorsements. Under these conditions, using content filtering technology on top of a collaborative system is often useful. Most evidence suggests that such hybrid systems using both types of information are more robust and provide better results than either technology alone [2, 5, 8, 19]. The design of hybrid systems is currently an area of active research, and researchers do not yet agree on the best way to combine the two methods.

A growing number of companies,[6] including Amazon.com, CDNow.com, Levis.com, and NetPerceptions.com,[7] employ or provide recommender system solutions [23]. Recommendation tools originally developed at Microsoft Research are now included with the Commerce Edition of Microsoft's SiteServer[8] and are currently in use at multiple sites.

Providing personalized recommendation on a Web site is one step toward a more comprehensive use of adaptive Web sites [17, 18] that adjust in more dramatic ways to accommodate individual users. For example, a university homepage may have completely different layouts according to whether the viewer is a student, a prospective student, a faculty member, or an unaffiliated visitor.

---

[6]The Web site http://www.cis.upenn.edu/~ungar/CF/ includes a list of such companies.

[7]Net Perceptions—a successful Internet startup offering personalization services—grew out of the University of Minnesota's GroupLens and MovieLens (http://movielens.umn.edu/) research projects.

[8]http://www.microsoft.com/siteserver

4. Privacy and Security Issues

Sections 2 and 3 provided a description of what personal information can be acquired or inferred, and how this information can be used to personalize a Web site. In this section, we discuss some of the privacy and security issues associated with personalization. In Section 4.1, we examine the issues from a business perspective; in Section 4.2, we take the consumer's point of view.

4.1. Business Perspective

A Web site may implicitly collect three kinds of consumer information: identity information, tracking information, and history information. Of course, a fourth type is information explicitly given by the consumer (e.g., his or her name, zip code, or credit card number). Of these four forms of information, identification is central—without it, all other information is useless. Moreover, once visitors can be reliably identified, it is straightforward to keep track of their navigation patterns, purchasing behavior, submitted information, and so forth.

What level of accuracy in the identification a business needs depends on the rights it is granting to the client. If, for example, it is using the information to customize a Web page with suggestions for additional purchases, then erroneous identification may lead only to a lost sale. Alternatively, if it is using the information to allow access to, say, stock trading from the user's account, then incorrect identification can result in a breach of security for the company and a loss of privacy for the falsely identified customer. The repercussions from such an error may be very serious.

We describe five different methods for identifying users—IP addresses, custom forms, cookies, simple authentication, and secure authentication—each with varying degrees of effectiveness and risk. We present them roughly in order of accuracy, ranging from the most course-grained to the most precise and verifiable.

4.1.1. IP Addresses for Identification

Every computer on the Internet has an associated IP address to which any messages (requests, responses) for that computer are sent. One advantage of using IP addresses for identification is that they are not easy to forge. If a user alters the IP address of his or her computer, then responses to requests for Web pages may simply never arrive. Another advantage is that no user actions are required: the IP infrastructure is already in place and will not change. The disadvantage is that an IP-address is a fairly coursegrained method of identification. This is because, over time, a particular IP address does not necessarily map to a single unique user. First, many dial-up services, including America Online, use dynamic IP addresses, assigning each user a random address each time they dial in. Second, proxies, used by most cable modem companies, for example, mask the true user's IP address, as discussed in Section 2.2. Third, if several people share a computer, they may all have the same IP address.

Although not always accurate, IP addresses can sometimes provide a lot of information about users. Some IP addresses are associated with specific companies or countries. For example, Microsoft Corporation owns a certain range of IP addresses and anyone connecting from one of these addresses can be identified as being associated with Microsoft. Sometimes the hostname associated with an IP address can specify the user's location—for example, a cable modem user could have the hostname host123.eastwindsor.nj.someisp.com, indicating that the user is connecting from a machine in East Windsor, New Jersey, USA.

Businesses should generally not use IP addresses for authentication when they require high accuracy (e.g., for online banking). However in many circumstances, using IP addresses for identification is valid. For example, some scientific journals grant online access to their articles only to paying institutions; the journals control access by accepting requests only from valid IP address ranges that are owned by those institutions.

4.1.2. Custom Forms and Passwords

Since IP addresses often cannot uniquely identify users, many businesses resort to more intrusive but more accurate means of authentication, including the use of custom Web forms. When a business needs a user's identity it asks the user to log in or provide a password. For example, some sites may ask for a password only before an important transaction and may combine the password with other fields. The forms allow for high levels of control and customization, but themselves do not have any persistence. With a form, the user can send a set of variables once. However, it is possible for a business to use the results of one post in future pages. One method is through using hidden variables (such as including an authentication string in all future user requests), a second is through cookies, discussed next in Section 4.1.3.

Most current systems that require explicit authentication, such as shopping or ecommerce sites, use some custom forms combined with cookies and secure Web servers for user identification.

4.1.3. Cookies

An alternative and more popular method for identifying users is through the use of cookies. This method is also one of the more widely discussed and controversial [3, 12, 27]. Cookies have the unique property that they are set by a Web server and are stored on a user's computer, and they can be sent back to the server as appropriate. Cookies are often not shown explicitly to the user, and can be set without any explicit user action (other than visiting a Web page). Cookies can be used for authentication because possession of the information indicates that the sending client has visited the site before. Cookies are usually associated with an individual user, but not always. Cookies can also have embedded expiration dates, allowing the server to control how long they persist.

For authentication, cookies are typically sent in response to an explicit user action, such as entering his or her password or user ID. For pseudonymous[9] connections, servers often set cookies that contain randomly assigned user IDs on the first visit. Although they never identify the actual users they may recognize repeat visits by the same users.

Although cookies have many advantages, businesses run a number of fundamental risks when they use them for positive authentication. First, although cookies are often hidden from users, they are stored on the user's computer and users may therefore edit, view, transfer, or delete them. Thus, businesses must take care to ensure the integrity of cookies. Second, because of the perceived threats of tracking or abuse, many users view cookies as dangerous and actively block them. Third, although cookies are stored on users' machines, shared machines or accounts may have shared cookies. For example people in a family who share one computer may have a single cookie file. A true multiuser operating system will permit multiple users to have their own sets of cookies, but unfortunately most versions of the Windows and Macintosh operating systems are not true multi-user and have a single shared set of cookies.[10] Fourth, servers send cookies in plain text (i.e. unencrypted), in response to users' Web requests, and users' computers store them in plain text.

When using cookies for authentication purposes, businesses find it simple to save the user's login and password in a cookie. Unfortunately this results in sending the user's private information (user name and password) in plain-text for each Web request, as well as risking compromise if the user's cookies are visible to any other users (such as through an unsecured backup). Typically cookies store a cryptographic hash that businesses can use to verify a password (or other information). Other protections can include storing encrypted or hashed versions of the

---

[9]As the term suggests, pseudonymous refers to the ability of users to identify themselves using pseudonyms, thereby concealing their true identity. The interested reader is directed to http://www.franken.de/users/tentacle/papers/search-privacy.txt.

[10]Mac OSX and Windows 2000 and XP are designed to be multi-user, but many users will treat them as single-user, using only one account for all users.

user's IP address, browser-type, or other information to help the business to verify that the user's cookie has not been modified or is not being used improperly. Many sites, such as Yahoo! Mail will ask for a user's password once per session, that is, each time the user restarts the the browser, or when many hours pass, as added protection.

4.1.4. Simple Authentication

Although custom forms and cookies are more prevalent (perhaps because of the flexibility they allow in designing the user interface), the http protocol itself does include simple means for authentication with a standard interface. A Web server indicates that a particular page requires authentication, and most browsers automatically pop up a window asking for a username and password.

Once entered, the password and username are automatically transmitted to the server for every page requiring authentication, typically an entire server or subdirectory. Although tied directly to the user, and relatively simple to add to several Web server configurations, this method has several drawbacks. First, the username and password are sent unencrypted,[11] so any "adversary" monitoring the network can easily recover both. Second, the user's computer does not store the user name and password when a user quits the browser. Some newer browsers may offer to save user authentication, but they do not do so by default. Of course, it is a matter of opinion whether this is an advantage or a disadvantage. Third, the method permits minimal control of the login interface. A Web site designer cannot customize what the user sees during the authentication process. Most sites prefer to use custom forms combined with cookies. However, when entire directories or servers need to control access, simple authentication is extremely easy to add.

4.1.5. Secure Authentication

One of the limitations of simple authentication, forms, and cookies is that they are all sent unencrypted across the Internet. A protocol called Secure Socket Layer (SSL) allows users to make encrypted connections toWeb servers. By sending cookies, forms and authentication encrypted over this channel the communicating parties reduce the chances that eavesdroppers will intercept anything intelligible [24].

In addition to encrypting data, SSL provides authentication of the Web site to the Web browser, ensuring that data is only sent to the intended recipient. Thus, someone cannot intercept a Web request to,

---

[11]The password is "encoded" using a simple transformation that is trivially reversible.

say, https://www.somewhere.com/.[12] This is because SSL ensures that the server claiming to be https://www.somewhere. com/ has a verifiable certificate given to them by a trusted third party (typicallyVerisign)—an imposter would fail the authentication process and be exposed. Typically, a failed authentication results in a visible warning to the user, allowing the user to abort the requested communication.[13]

If SSL is used properly, user data is sent encrypted (the level of encryption depends on the browser and the server). SSL allows a user to authenticate the business (but not the other way around). Most browsers display a lock icon to tell the user that the URL they are currently viewing is encrypted.

SSL does have risks. First, there are so-called semantic attacks where one site masquerades as another by, for example, replacing the letter "O" in https://www.somewhere.com/ with a number zero as in https://www.s0mewhere.com/. As long as the site obtains a valid certificate from Verisign, there is no obvious difference, and users browsing the site will see a secure lock icon.

A second disadvantage of SSL is the added computational cost to the Web server. A Web server can easily cache unencrypted pages. If users request the same Web page (say a static price list) many times, the actual server load will likely be small, allowing for hundreds or thousands of copies to be served from a single computer simultaneously. However, if the server must encrypt every page, then its performance may drop significantly. (The details of SSL that cause it to be computationally intensive are beyond the scope of this chapter.)

Most importantly, while the use of SSL means that a third party probably cannot intercept the data, it is no guarantee that the recipient server will use or store such data properly. Indeed, the weakest link in terms of security is often the people and computers at the recipient institution rather than the encryption technology [25].

4.2. Consumer Perspective

Degrees of privacy are largely subjective. Several options are available to users who want to take control of their information. A user's best protection is common sense. Explicit identification methods such as forms or basic authentication, require active entry by a user. A user wishing to prevent release of such information should simply not provide it. If a Web site requires information, such as a shipping address or an

---

[12]https denotes the use of the secure Web protocol SSL rather than the unencrypted http protocol.

[13]For a description of how SSL works, see http://developer.netscape.com/tech/security/ssl/howitworks.html.

e-mail address, a user should demand a secure connection. Even though a secure connection does not guarantee that the recipient of the data will protect it, it reduces the chance of interception, and at least the recipient is authenticated.[14]

4.2.1. P3P, Platform for Privacy Preferences

One way to satisfy the varied demands of consumers is to let them choose what forms of privacy are most important to them. The Platform for Privacy Preferences (P3P) offers a standard, machine-readable language that consumers can use to state their privacy preferences and that companies can use to state their privacy policies. Because the language is machine-readable, when a consumer visits a particular company's Web site, the consumer's browser can automatically detect whether the company's policy matches the user's preferences. If the policy and preferences don't match, the user's browser can warn the consumer about the policy or simply avoid interacting with the Web site. P3P requires companies to act in good faith in disclosing their privacy policies. P3P is becoming an industry standard; more information can be found on the Web at http://www.w3.org/P3P/.

4.2.2. IP Address and Proxies

Users can prevent businesses from using implicit methods for identifying users, such as IP address and cookies, and for revealing information about the user's browsing behavior such as the Referer field by using available software that allows them to control the release of information.

The IP address seen by a Web server is that of the machine making the request. In a typical situation the requesting machine is that of the user. One way users can mask their actual IP addresses is by using a proxy. As discussed in Section 2.2, a proxy acts as an intermediary, accepting requests from users and passing them along to their destination.

Many different proxy servers are available to users. First, most Internet Service Providers (ISPs) use some form of Web proxy. For example users surfing the Web through the AOL browser may utilize AOL's proxy—all AOL members appear to come from the same IP address. Second, users can purchase personal firewalls to operate between their home computers and their Internet connection. There are both external hardware and installable software versions of personal firewalls. Although a personal firewall uses the assigned IP address, it acts as an intermediary between

---

[14]There is always the risk of semantic attacks, such as a site replacing the letter O with a the number zero, however SSL does provide a signed certificate if the user wishes to check. See Section 4.1.5.

the rest of the Internet and the user's computer.[15] Third, many companies offer proxies to employee machines; in some cases they may block all non-proxy Web requests for security reasons. Fourth, many services on the Web, such as http://www.anonymizer.com/, provide anonymizing services. There are even proposed services that use proxies to allow both anonymity and personalization, by maintaining aliases on behalf of users [6].

A remote Web proxy, such as that used by an ISP or company, provides more than just a method to mask the requestor's IP address. In fact, this is often a secondary benefit, the primary reason for the proxy being to improve performance. A Web proxy can aggregate requests and provide caching services. If every employee of a company requests the same Web page within a short period of time, the proxy server will likely make only one request to the origin Web server.

Personal firewalls and proxies may also offer filtering services, such as blocking "inappropriate" content, or filtering out scripts or potentially dangerous programs (viruses, trojan horses, etc.). They can also be used to control fields in the http protocol including the Referer and Cookie fields.

4.2.3. Controlling Cookies

Cookies are unique with regard to Web identification methods in that they are set by the server and stored on the user's machine and so present unique privacy risks [3, 12, 27]. Although they are stored locally, most users are unaware when a cookie has been set and do not know how to control their cookies. Fortunately there are many tools to aid users in controlling what sites see cookies, who can set them, and how long they persist.

Some local proxies or personal firewalls (such as those described above) intercept Web requests (and responses) restricting what sites set or view cookies.

The recent demand for user privacy has caused several popular browsers to build in various levels of cookie control [13]. On Windows, users can set "Internet Options" to specify what different sites can do. For example, a user can specify that unknown Web sites cannot set persistent cookies (cookies that last after the user quits the browser). A user can also instruct that only user-specified "trusted sites" can set cookies or use scripts. The Internet options provide three different classes of sites; "trusted," "restricted," and "Internet." Each class can have its own options regarding cookie and other privacy related matters.

The Web browser Netscape has added an entire set of options specific to "Privacy & Security," allowing users to control cookies, images, forms,

---

[15]A software firewall resides on the user's machine and isolates requests between user applications and the Internet. Often personal firewalls are used to protect users from requests from the outside Internet from getting in.

stored passwords, and SSL. A user can specify different cookie options for each domain, allowing some and blocking others. Users can also integrate P3P into the cookie rules. For example, a user can specify that sites not having a privacy policy are not permitted to set cookies, or only sites that collect personal information with explicit consent may set cookies.

Since cookies are stored locally, as a last resort, a user can manually edit or delete cookies. Each browser stores its cookies in a different but documented location. Netscape allows users to view all of the set cookies through its privacy and security preferences menu.

5. Summary

A key requirement for personalization of Web sites is the correct identification of users. Businesses can identify users through a range of methods that are characterized by their reliability and accuracy. The http protocol supports an encrypted authentication requiring login and password over SSL, which is very secure. Unfortunately, users may find this procedure to be intrusive, especially if the purpose for visiting the Web site is simply to browse. Consequently, businesses often use less reliable identification methods that are less intrusive or completely unobtrusive. The appropriateness of these systems depends on (1) what implicit information is available to the server and (2) what the consequences of incorrect identification are.

A number of methods are available for identifying users, each with different advantages and disadvantages from a business perspective.

Consumers may often prefer personalized Web sites and may therefore be willing to disclose personal information. However, if the business subsequently uses this personal information in a manner that it did not disclosed to the consumer or that the consumer considers an inappropriate, then users' attitudes may quickly change from cooperative to uncooperative. In such circumstances, users can take a number of technological steps to enhance their anonymity and privacy. Even without clear legal protection of personal privacy, users can prevent information from being implicitly collected.

The relationship between a Web site and its users is fragile and businesses can easily damage that relationship through security or privacy infringements. Clearly, identification technologies have appropriate uses. However, the information businesses collect must remain secure and should not be disclosed to a third party without the explicit consent of the user. If businesses unhold this social agreement, both users and producers can benefit from Web-personalization services. If they break this social agreement, users may employ technological means to guarantee their privacy, even at the expense of personalization.

References

Ackerman, Mark S., Lorrie Faith Cranor, and Joseph Reagle. 1999. Privacy in ecommerce: Examining user scenarios and privacy preferences. In Proceedingsof the First ACM Conference on Electronic Commerce. ACM Press 1–8.

Basu, Chumki, Haym Hirsh, and William Cohen. 1998. Recommendation as classifi-cation: Using social and content-based information in recommendation. In Proceedings of the Fifteenth National Conference on Artificial Intelligence 714–720.

Berghel, Hal. 2001. Caustic cookies. Communications of the ACM, 44(5):19–22.

Breese, John S., David Heckerman, and Carl Kadie. 1998. Empirical analysis of predictive algorithms for collaborative filtering. In Proceedings of the Fourteenth Conference on Uncertainty in Artificial Intelligence 43–52.

Claypool, Mark, Anuja Gokhale, and Tim Miranda. 1999. Combining content-basedand collaborative filters in an online newspaper. In Proceedings of the ACM SIGIR Workshop on Recommender Systems—Implementation and Evaluation. ACM Press.

Gabber, Eran, Phillip B. Gibbons, Yossi Matias, and Alain Mayer. 1997. How to make personalized web browsing simple, secure, and anonymous. In Proceedings of the International Conference on Financial Cryptography. Springer-Verlag.

Gettys, J., J. Mogul, H. Frystyk, L. Masinter, P. Leach, and T. Berners-Lee. 1999. Hypertext Transfer Protocol—HTTP/1.1. Internet Request for Comments 2616, http://www.w3.org/Protocols/rfc2616/rfc2616.html.

Good, Nathaniel, J. Ben Schafer, Joseph A. Konstan, Al Borchers, Badrul M. Sarwar, Jonathan L. Herlocker, and John Riedl. 1999. Combining collaborative filtering with personal agents for better recommendations. In Proceedings of the Sixteenth National Conference on Artificial Intelligence 439–446.

Hall, E. A., and V. G. Cerf. 2000. Internet Core Protocols: the Definitive Guide. O'Reilly & Associates.

Hastie, T., R. Tibshirani, and J. H. Friedman. 2001. The Elements of Statistical Learning: Data Mining, Inference, and Prediction. Springer Verlag.

Krishnamurthy, B., and J. Rexford. 2001. Web Protocols and Practice. AddisonWesley,

Lin, Daniel, and Michael C. Loui. 1998. Taking the byte out of cookies: Privacy, consent, and the web. Computers and Society 28(2):39–51.

Millett, Lynette I., Batya Friedman, and Edward Felten. 2001. Cookies and web browser design: Toward realizing informed consent online. In Proceedings of the Conference on Human Factors in Computing Systems 46–52.

Mitchell, Tom M. Machine 1997. Learning. McGraw-Hill.

Mooney, Raymond J., and Loriene Roy. 2000. Content-based book recommending using learning for text categorization. In Proceedings of the Fifth ACM Conference on Digital Libraries, ACM Press 195–204.

Pennock, David M., Eric Horvitz, Steve Lawrence, and C. Lee Giles. 2000. Collaborative filtering by personality diagnosis: A hybrid memory- and model-based approach. In Proceedings of the Sixteenth Conference on Uncertainty in Artificial Intelligence 473–480.

Perkowitz, Mike, and Oren Etzioni. 1997. Adaptive web sites: An AI challenge. In Proceedings of the 15th International Joint Conference on Artificial Intelligence.

Perkowitz, Mike, and Oren Etzioni. 2000. Towards adaptive web sites: Conceptual framework and case study. Artificial Intelligence, 118(1–2): 245–275.

Popescul, Alexandrin, Lyle H. Ungar, David M. Pennock, and Steve Lawrence. 2001. Probabilistic models for unified collaborative and content-based recommendation in sparse-data environments. In Proceedings of the Seventeenth Conference on Uncertainty in Artificial Intelligence 437–444.

Resnick, Paul, Neophyts Iacovou, Mitesh Suchak, Peter Bergstrom, and John Riedl. 1994. GroupLens: An open architecture for collaborative filtering of netnews. In Proceedings of the ACM Conference on Computer Supported Cooperative Work, ACM Press 175–186.

Rosenstein, Mark, and Carol Lochbaum. 2000. Recommending from content: Preliminary results from an e-commerce experiment. In Proceedings of the Conference on Human Factors in Computing Systems.

Salton, G., and M. J. McGill. 1983. Introduction to Modern Information Retrieval. McGraw Hill.

Schafer, J. Ben, Joseph Konstan, and John Riedl. 1999. Recommender systems in ecommerce. In Proceedings of the ACM Conference on Electronic Commerce, ACM Press 158–166.

Schneier, Bruce. 1995. Applied Cryptography: Protocols, Algorithms, and Source Code in C, 2nd Edition. John Wiley and Sons.

Schneier, Bruce. 2000. Secrets and Lies: Digital Security in a Networked World. John Wiley and Sons.

Shardanand, Upendra, and Pattie Maes. 1995. Social information filtering: Algorithms for automating 'word of mouth.' In Proceedings of the Conference on Human Factors in Computing Systems 210–217.

Sit, Emil, and Kevin Fu. 2001. Web cookies: Not just a privacy risk. Communications of the ACM 44(9):120.

11 The Role of Privacy in the New Reality

Thomas Summerlin, Managing Consultant and Senior VP,

Touchstone Consulting Group

John W. Bagby, Professor of Business Law, School of Information

Sciences and Technology, Penn State University

The mass personalization of both products and marketing depends fundamentally on three conditions. First, there must be compelling reasons for sellers to invest in technologies that capture, analyze, and use private information. Clearly, a profitability advantage must be realized by sellers before they will invest in and maintain databases of private information. Second, the capture, analysis, and use of private information must be feasible. The products and services developed utilizing private information must be highly attractive to customers before they will freely divulge their private information. The compilation and storage costs of managing such data must be offset by the possible profits from utilizing private data.

Third, society must establish an effective balance between protecting private information and permitting access to data about individuals and their buying behaviors.

This chapter discusses this third requisite for successful mass personalization of products and marketing. We use the term personally identifiable information (PII) to indicate the object of privacy concerns. The Internet and other electronic technologies now permit the capture and collection of personal information enabling the mass storage, the association of pieces of information, and aggregation of large PII databases. The potential markets for products and services based on PII puts the privacy question in the spotlight.

A classic economic struggle is raised: sellers expand investment in new products and services while others try to protect the status quo and conserve traditional values. The use of PII can result in a grand societal rebalance between individual autonomy and the public interest.

Privacy is a Personal Challenge

The difficulties of protecting one's privacy begins at birth, and continues throughout a lifetime (and perhaps beyond). At best, an individual can attempt to control to some extent the accumulation and use of PII. The definition of privacy continues to change. As individuals try to preserve domain over personal information the government mandates disclosure of more and more information from citizens, and the commercial world is increasingly clever in eliciting private information from consumers. In both cases, the release of such information is characterized as serving the safety, benefit, and convenience of citizens and consumers.

As long as individuals consider privacy an issue and are concerned with maintaining the advantages of privacy, they will be required to take an active interest in how their information is used. Indeed many now argue that standards for protection of privacy have been inexorably altered by the political and social consequences of terrorism. The arguments and societal support for preserving privacy may have been overcome by the expediency to fight terrorism. This highlights a differentiation in the public thinking and debate regarding privacy in the context of national security versus the commercial marketplace. Though access and collection of private information by government agencies is increasing, the depth and regularity of privacy intrusions by government has not yet been fully realized. Ironically, increased public awareness over time of the dissemination of data from these new intrusions, the secondary uses and possible abuses, may ultimately result in limitations on the parameters of PII databases permitted by government.

Privacy as it pertains to personalization in commerce seems not to have been altered negatively by society's reaction to terrorism. While few citizens agree with the views articulated by Scott McNealy, a strong advocate of national ID cards and implanting children with PII chips at birth, many consumers believe they will soon be carrying and benefit from smart cards with biometric information and other commercial applications of PII.

Businesses have been pursuing privacy and personalization strategies for some time. For example, airlines define their service levels according to personal information and data. Consumers, post September 11, 2001, are perhaps more likely to demand greater use of PII to ensure their safety. Societal needs may be in opposition to individual needs to protect PII, but people in the U.S. and in many other nations believe they have the right to a safe society and wish to preserve a heretofore-safe standard of living.

But just as with government management of PII, key issues for consumers in the marketplace are: Who do you want to control your PII? Who is responsible for your PII's security? For what purpose is your PII used? A fundamental concept of information economics is that information wants to be free, that is once information, including PII, is known, it is unrecoverable. The public is recognizing that there are potential costs as well as benefits involved with PII ownership, control, economic exploitation, and misuse.

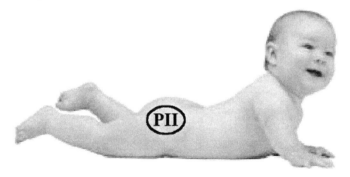

Can you afford privacy?

Many observers warn that a consequence of the commercialization of PII may be the creation of a narrow stratum of society which will be able to afford to maintain privacy.

Creating societal classes according to who and who cannot afford privacy would be dangerous. Right now, privacy has both personal and societal costs. Those who want to transact business, travel, or live anonymously are beginning to understand how expensive and inconvenient it can be to maintain their privacy.

We have reached a point at which the amount of PII detail a customer reveals defines the level of service a seller provides. Customer loyalty programs such as car rentals which provide expedited services exemplify this trend. Customers who are pre-screened, "cleared" based on a PII file are exempted from time consuming and inconvenient procedures. Luxury hotels have created a mystique by remembering who you are, what services you prefer, while creating an ambiance of both heightened security and enhanced personal privacy. Ironically, these market differentiators are enabled by PII databases, as well as by in house security surveillance programs. It makes us question what we mean by privacy!

What is IT Privacy?

Successful implementation of an IT mass personalization strategy requires an understanding privacy. Webster's Collegiate Dictionary defines privacy broadly:

> Privacy – The quality or condition of being private; withdrawal From company or public view; Seclusion, secrecy [told in strict Privacy], One's private life or personal affaires [invasion on one's Privacy]

Webster should probably place greater emphasis on the medium and context of privacy. The thesaurus reveals further nuances of privacy: "Solitude, Time alone, Space To yourself, Seclusion, Isolation, Retreat, Confidentiality." The contrast to privacy provides further insight; consider the antonym: Company. The definition is restricted almost entirely to the physical world. However, most invasions of privacy today take place in cyberspace. Identity theft, a predatory attack on privacy is usually based on data gathered in cyberspace. Identity theft makes it obvious that privacy rights must extend to cyberspace and the digital arena.

Individual Responsibility to Protect Privacy

Privacy can be protected in various ways. People who decide not to provide information increase the probability that they will be better able to protect their privacy. If an individual had an unrecorded birth, no personal relationships, and had not attended school, he or she would have a chance of being invisible. Is this what privacy means? Being so inconspicuous, undetectable as to be invisible. Not to most people. In fact, the cost of such anonymity to personal freedoms and quality of life in our society is enormous. Many citizens and consumers would likely share another definition of privacy — the right to live, act, move, and communicate without intrusion and without fear of interference, retribution, or predation.

Privacy can have negative connotations that imply secrecy, seclusion, disappearance, and lack of communication. A person living in total privacy could, in effect, be a threat to society: the lone man in the cabin might be the UNI-bomber. To what extent should privacy be a matter of personal choice? Being held in solitary confinement is not privacy, however, choosing to live outside the grid of society is an extreme form of privacy that may pose a threat to the security and well-being of the citizens.

Privacy also has an element of awareness. If you expect to be watched, your sense of privacy is less likely to be compromised. If personally indentifiable information is gathered, aggregated and processed into marketing profiles without your knowledge, has your privacy been violated even though you suffered no coercion? Most would say, "yes."

Privacy in the PII Supply Chain

We need to understand the PII supply chain, how information is gathered, analyzed, and used to determine the degree to which our privacy is invaded. How information is used, even the most generally available, such as a name, address, or phone number, influences an individual's sense of privacy. Confidentiality, a sharing of information within a distinct forum, can provide a level of comfort to the use of PII. Keeping information confidential is fundamental to maintaining privacy. But what are the standards, and who maintains them? Since we have different expectations regarding privacy, how can we set standards for securing confidentiality in our pursuit of privacy? The regulation of privacy by government and industry depends on a thorough understanding of the entire supply chain. Many questions are relevant. Who requested the information? Why? How was the information obtained? Where did the information come from? For what purpose was the information collected? What is the shelf life of the information? Who is in charge of managing the information collected over its life cycle? Who is in charge of ascertaining the accuracy of the information and of disposing of information when it becomes incorrect or useless?

PII Supply Chain

Collection-

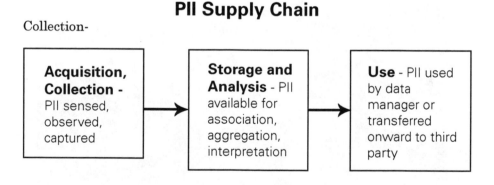

Figure 1. In the PII Supply Chain, personally identifiable information is collected, stored, analyzed, and utilized for product and market development.

Advocates of strong privacy protections may prefer to view the supply chain of Information as a chain of custody instead because that terminology clearly emphasizes responsibility. Granters and guarantors form links in the PII supply chain. Some use individuals' right to privacy and grant them the ability to protect privacy as a way to ensure consumers that their privacy is preserved and protected and to provide confidentiality. The legal right to privacy is an important tool for both subject individuals and PII users. In granting individuals privileges and asking for their preferences, the users ask individuals to give up personal information that is not already publicly available.

The Element of Trust in PII Acquisition

A key element that facilitates the acquisition, dissemination, and sharing of personal information is TRUST. An individual who trusts the entity seeking information is likely to surrender confidential PII. Gaining people's trust is the first step in acquiring information from them. People tend to trust some institutions, for example, the church, and not others, such as the IRS. Most individuals trust their parents, the longstanding close friends, and maybe their bartenders. People often extend their trust in an individual to the institution that person represents. This is the goal of personal relationships in sales. A sales representative may gain enough trust to gain access where her company cannot.

My Word Is My Bond?

To gain the trust of a community, a start-up company will hire someone well known in the community who is representative of its target audience. Such a person can open markets through personal contact. An established and trusted company, however, can hire people with less experience in the community at lower cost and leverage, instead, the company's relationship value based on its reputation. How does this relate to privacy? The interdependence of the firm and its employee, and their relationship with individuals in a community form the basis for many PII supply chains. Individuals should ask themselves, "Should I trust this firm with my personal information? Will my privacy be jeopardized by corporate negligence, incompetence, or even deliberate misrepresentation?"

The Importance of Self-Regulation in Earning Trust

The U.S. takes a much more laissez-faire approach than the EU to privacy regulation. The U.S. approach is consistent with longstanding values in the American psyche. Privacy is linked with liberty — an inalienable right. While their government is expected to serve as a guarantor of rights, Americans value most the freedom of individuals to make their own choices in life. This creates a commercial environment potentially favorable to building mass personalization markets. However, with a lack of government regulation, sellers must assure individuals that their privacy is protected in order to gain access to valuable PII. **Self-regulation** against the misuse of PII is critical to the success of mass personalization marketing.

Self-regulation involves an assortment of techniques that range from such passive forms as **netiquette** (unofficial, tacit expectations of courtesy, respect), to industry-wide standards enforced by trade associations, to market solutions such as third-party certification or **seal** programs offered by bbb-online and TRUSTe. Those firms that view customer loyalty as dependent of issues of privacy and trust will commit resources to self-regulation. For example, many Internet commerce companies appoint chief privacy officers (CPOs) to oversee privacy policies and to ensure consistent compliance. Under the safe-harbor agreement that the U.S. negotiated with the EU, U.S. firms doing business in EU nations MUST have effective, self-regulating privacy compliance programs. By regulating themselves, U.S. firms avoid stronger, EU-style approaches to privacy, and prevent their cross-border data flows being blocked at EU boundaries.

Privacy is the ultimate issue in information gathering and dissemination. Firms should discuss privacy within their organizations and industries, and make sure that all parties understand policies regarding PII. At its best responsible self-regulation should encourage industry-wide standards and practices as a matter of competitive advantage.

Who Owns PII?

PII processing raises many questions. Foremost is the question, who actually owns PII? In other words, who owns my privacy? As with tangible forms of property, and with intangible forms of property, ownership is not the only criterion. The right to control PII may override the right of ownership. Because of ownership and control issues, firms may have difficulty accumulating and analyzing enough information to develop personalization strategies.

Ownership Versus Control of PII

Some U.S. traditions and laws give individuals ownership of their PII. Federal laws in the U.S., such as the Privacy Act of 1974, reveal the difficulties in regulating the ownership, control, and use of PII. The Privacy Act regulates federal government agencies in the record-keeping and disclosure practices. The act has been modified several times; for example, in 1988 the "matching of data" between agencies became an issue. As is typical in legislation, the terminology leaves gray areas that protect the government when agencies fail to comply. The act concerns mainly "information maintained in a system of records." The act does not cover how information is gathered, whether federal agencies are entitled to information, and whether they are entitled to keep it. It also limits the information a citizen can request from the information any agency keeps with a "system of records." Therefore, the act apparently does not protect information unless it is held in a structured format, that is, unless it can be retrieved using a social security number, or name.

The act and its updates provide that "Each agency must establish procedures allowing individuals to see and copy records about themselves and amend that information which they can demonstrate as being incorrect." The federal agencies the act covers must publish notices describing their system of records, including their policies, practices, and systems for keeping personal data. The act attempts to prevent agencies from building and maintaining secret record systems. The agencies must make "every reasonable effort" to maintain accurate, relevant, timely, and complete individual records. They must keep records of "some" types of disclosure of PII. The act specifies rules governing the use and disclosure of PII and forbids the use of information collected for one purpose to be used for another purpose, in most cases, without the "notice or consent" of the subject individual. Finally, the act specifies legal remedies available to subject individuals. Noncompliance by federal employees may result in criminal penalties.

Accessibility May Be the Key Factor

The fact that the government has repeatedly established privacy laws to regulate the acquisition, maintenance, distribution, and control of private information signals that much of our PII is already in the public domain. For 30 years U.S. citizens fought to obtain the right to view government information (FOIA). Now we are fighting for control of our own information. The existence of information is not the issue; its **accessibility** is.

Protecting What You Create Versus Protection

Have you ever wondered why you can protect what you create but not what you are? Take a look at Figure 3:

Figure 3.

How long does it take you to recognize what Figure 3 represents? Not long! It is both an example of how recognizable characteristics work and of what is protectable legally. The United States protects the rights of Mickey's creator with many intellectual-property (IP) laws covering authors, creators' contracts, copyrights, trademarks, and unfair competition. Even a hint that one was using Mickey's image might cause Disney to sue. We have rights to our creative work, inventions, written words, and even our thoughts and deeds as valuable assets. However, our privacy and our PII, which we do not want to share with the public, is not similarly protected.

How can we obtain the same level of protection for information that we do not want used without our permission? Do we have to put everything in the public domain and then set laws around its use? Can we protect only that to which we ascribe individual value by placing it in the public domain and buying it back? Or can we get the same strong protections as Disney receives for Mickey Mouse?

Does Anyone Really Care? The Value of PII

The question is who cares? Scott McNealy, CEO of SunSystems, advises, "Privacy is dead, get over it!" On the other side of the argument, Jason Catlett, founder of Junkbusters, blasts the McNealy comment with: "That's like the CEO of General Motors saying, 'There is no safety; get over it!' We take the position that we *do* have an interest in our privacy. Therefore we must assess how we can control our PII, although that may endanger businesses implementing mass personalization.

Threatened by terrorism, we may be willing to relax laws preventing governmental use of our personal information. But does this mean we have lost interest in preventing outsider ownership and marketing of our PII. Forthright marketing strategists would certainly acknowledge that they do care about how others use our PII. Indeed, marketers are using PII to sell products. First, firms need PII to customize and personalize products, whether they are mass produced or individually tailored. Second, privacy policies, privacy seal programs, and mandatory privacy notices all tend to promote the seller's commitment to privacy.

Evidence That the Public Values PII

Earthlink, an ISP (Internet Service Provider), dramatizes the use of PII for unintended purposes in its advertisements using scenarios, as in the example:

> A woman sitting in a bar is chatting with a young man when he politely asks if he can call her sometime. She obligingly hands him her business card. Whereupon, another man sitting nearby asks him for the woman's card; then so does the bartender. As the woman sits befuddled and flustered, the first young man holds up the card and asks what its worth to others in the bar. They respond $5. An Earthlink voiceover asks, "Is this your expectation when you provide PII online?"

Researchers in a Georgetown University study found that 92.8 percent of Web sites collect PII. An Andersen-Vanderbilt study revealed that 95 percent of online citizens have significant concerns about the loss of PII. In a Federal Trade Commission study, 87 percent of the respondents said "they were somewhat concerned about threats to their privacy while online." A National Consumer League study showed that 70 percent of respondents were "uncomfortable with providing personal information to businesses online." Despite the level of concern in the U.S., it is Europe that is expanding its citizens' ownership and control over PII. The EU Private Data Directive provides subject individuals with stronger privacy rights than U.S. citizens enjoy. U.S. companies doing business in EU nations face difficulties in their compliance with EU privacy laws and data mining of PII databases.

Conflicts in survey data confuse policy making in the PII realm. For example, public reports in an April, 2000 survey conducted by the Personalization Consortium indicate that the public considers privacy issues important but perhaps not as important as benefits from sharing PII. The consortium obtained 45,000 Web users' opinions on personalization and online privacy and found that only small minorities were unwilling to provide PII if their online experiences improved. A majority found it convenient to have Web sites "remember" their PII (session cookies). Many expected clearly stated privacy policies but found the statements of companies' policies indecipherable.

People are saying that they are deeply concerned about losing their privacy, and yet, few, less than 15 percent, are unwilling to share personal information in exchange for better service. Is this because current service is so bad? Do companies intentionally provide poor service to those customers unwilling to share their PII? Are visitors to Web sites just lazy? Do businesses that work with customers to obtain information so they can deliver better service build trust?

Clearly, although people are willing to provide information, they do not expect businesses to invade their privacy, to share their PII with third parties, to expand selling opportunities to other firms, to assemble profiles, or to sell the information they provide for profit. Instead, consumers simply expect businesses they trust with their PII to enhance their own buying experience by better targeting its marketing or by providing customized products. Few Web users are willing to provide information to other Web marketers, but this is exactly where their information ends up.

In a sense, the U.S. federal government controls the ultimate marketing database because it assumes it has the right to obtain PII. It assumes it has because government entities provides citizens with the opportunity to participate in various activities, voting, driving, hunting, practicing various professions, and paying taxes. States have assumed they have the right to share PII they collected and to profit from it, for example, by selling driver's license information to marketers and third parties. However, Federal anti-stalking laws have prohibited states from providing collected data to others. By selling PII, states have violated the trust between citizens and government. In the private sector, individuals can refuse to participate but they have few rights to refuse information to government databases. In developing personalization strategies, what goals do businesses have? Where do these strategies conflict with individuals' rights to privacy?

What are the consequences when businesses violate the rights of individuals? In a case decided in the summer of 2001, a unit of Amazon.com, Alexa, was sued for repeatedly gathering, while continuously denying it, confidential information about users on its recommender site. A settlement was reached for $1.9 million in which each user could claim approximately $40 for the violation. The kicker was that to obtain the money, individuals had to provide their personal information, including their name, date of birth, mother's maiden name and social security number. In most cases, Alexa had not yet assembled all of this on its information database. The president of Alexa, Brewster Kahle, said, "The whole process is very curious" in describing the court's remedy.

Personalization, the Other Side of Privacy?

What is personalization? Mike Gotta, vice president and service director for Web and collaboration strategies at the META Group, defines personalization this way:

> "Personalization, profiling and privacy form the foundation of customer intelligence strategies that deliver relationship value by individualizing e-business interaction; balancing these elements is the foundation for customer trust, product and service innovation, and competitive differential."

Personalization in the digital age has been hailed as the next transformation in the delivery of mass customerization, improved customer service and of course, higher profits for those optimizing the strategy. Personalization is what people who live and shop in small towns encounter daily. Their grocers, doctors, hairdressers, and bartenders, all know everything they need to know to serve their customers. They also provide little to no assurance of privacy. Personalization was born out of a desire to improve customer service in a fragmented society. Personalization is an attempt to create communities and personal experience not inherent to mass marketing. Digital conversations have replaced personal interactions. Businesses need personal information to deliver exemplary service. In Internet commerce businesses need new, cost effective ways to harvest the information they need to provide service levels that will attract and retain customers by targeting their preferences. Through personalization, businesses can infer or invisibly obtain information. In traditional economies, merchants obtained information about their customers without their explicit consent or active participation. In the online environment, privacy regulations may require businesses to obtain individuals' consent and perhaps even to repeatedly review the PII-sharing relationship.

The bygone world in which customers gave businesses implicit permission to use whatever PII they come by to conduct commerce has evolved in a world in which businesses must actively seek permission to use PII and individuals must deliberately grant it. In a small town, someone who wanted to know what meat you preferred would just ask the butcher, and no one would see this as threatening your privacy. Tolerance of such information gathering dwindles as intrusions increase and the gatherers become strangers, as when someone searches credit card transactions to determine individuals' buying habits. Even today, some people feel strongly that transaction history is the property of the buyer as well as the seller, and should be controlled by the buyer. People expect the seller to use such information to conduct its business efficiently and for accounting purposes and nothing more. In the small town scenario, neither buyer nor seller expected such information to be collected and sold to some third party to enhance its opportunities.

This concept of the commercial transaction is similar to most peoples' ideas about conversations. In conducting face-to-face conversations, the people involved do not imply that they permit someone to record that conversation for future purposes. Someone might paraphrase a speaker's general views and try to quote some highly provocative comment. However, those conducting the conversation do not envision verbatim publication and general availability. Certainly, this understanding lies at the heart of laws prohibiting surreptitious taping of conversations. While digital dissemination of conversations may not be constrained under these laws, other rules are developing for the online environment. No rules seem to govern digital communications, and those trying to pry into our habits are realistically without constraint. They can track our keystrokes and our very move with the object of personalizing our online experiences.

In an eye-popping decision in May 2001, the Supreme Court furthered the uncertainty about the direction of digital communications with the context of the First Amendment. In *Bartnicki and Kane v. Vopper* (also known as Williams et al.) the justices decided that illegally intercepted electronic transmissions could, in certain instances, be made public without consequence to those making the communications public. The implication that transmitted communications do not have the same weight as face-to-face communications raises privacy issues. It is understandable that potential users of PII press for the resolution of privacy versus personalization questions; they clearly have the most to gain from weak privacy protections.

The Role of Privacy Law

Society's views on legal protections of privacy can be inferred from the sectoral approach taken in the U.S. The primary areas in which legal protections of privacy rights has been created in recent years are health information, financial information, and targeting children. The HIPPA legislation (the Health Insurance Portability Accountability Act) was initially proposed to establish individuals' right to see their own health care information and to instill standards to control health providers' exchange of personal information. In a compromise, the Congress passed the legislation allowing health care providers to exchange information within the health-care industry, and hence they can market to you based on an opt-out approach. To put this in perspective, let us say your bartender knows you are depressed, he calls a pharmaceutical company to obtain Prozac to sell to you.

Despite peoples' wish to control the use of their PII, a Harris Interactive study showed that

- 75 percent of adults wish there were more customized and personalized products and services,
- 70 percent say they stay loyal to companies that make an effort to get to know their needs, and
- 70 percent say they are willing to pay a premium for a personal approach.

What do we really want? We want to be treated well, and if it takes communication and exchange of information, we are willing to participate. But, we expect the information we provide to be used only for the express purpose for which we supplied it.

Since a 1973 privacy study sponsored by the U.S. Department of Health Education and Welfare, the Fair Information Practice Principles have been applied broadly, as part of regulatory agencies' privacy policies, in the implementation of new privacy regulations, and in the tough EU privacy laws.

Fair Information Practice Principles

The Fair Information Practice Principles concern:

1. Notice and Awareness,
2. Choice and Consent,
3. Access and Participation,
4. Integrity and Security, and
5. Enforcement and Redress.

The Privacy Quadrant

We have discussed issues pertaining to the collection and use of PII as well as, questions of rights and control of this information. But the issues of who, what, where, when and how can easily be eclipsed by the WHY? Why is this information being gathered?

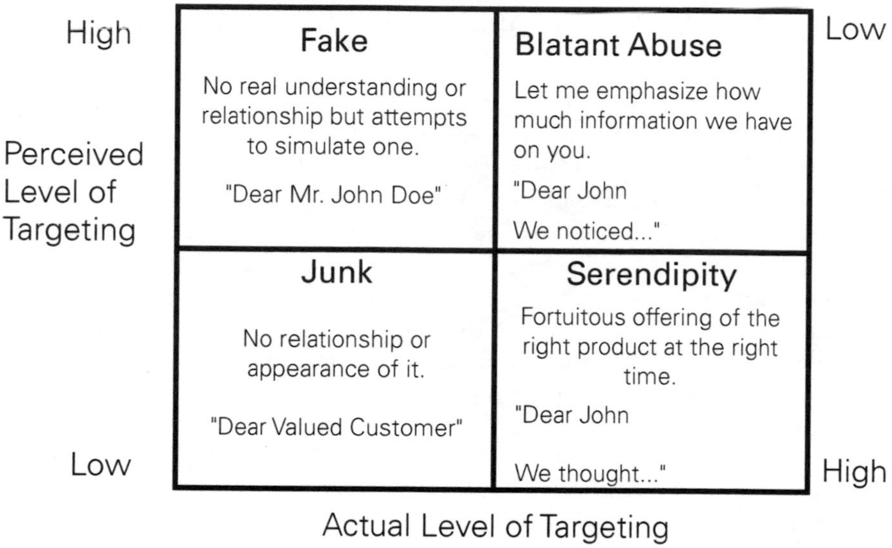

	High			Low
	Fake	**Blatant Abuse**		
Perceived Level of Targeting	No real understanding or relationship but attempts to simulate one. "Dear Mr. John Doe"	Let me emphasize how much information we have on you. "Dear John We noticed..."		
	Junk	**Serendipity**		
	No relationship or appearance of it. "Dear Valued Customer"	Fortuitous offering of the right product at the right time. "Dear John We thought..."		
	Low			High

Actual Level of Targeting

Figure 4. Gartner's Privacy Quadrant

The Privacy Quadrant provides a snapshot as to the ways to obtain information. The method of attainment often speaks to the "why" of the acquisition. In simple Web-related practices methods vary, these being the most used:

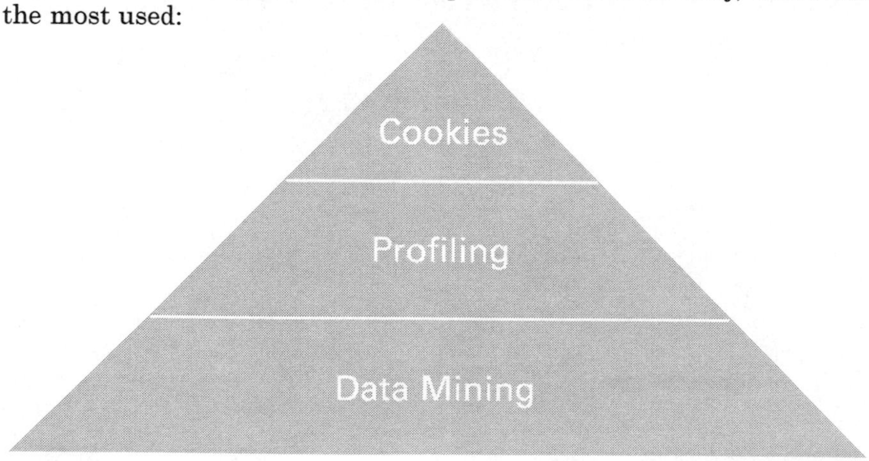

Figure 5.

Other sections of this book have provided more details about these tools, but suffice it to say, personalization is a business tool. Personalization is yet one more way, perhaps an effective way when combined with other schemes, to better serve the customer, deliver more focused products and services and increase revenue to the supplier.

Opting-In Versus Opting-Out

A central focus of the Fair Information Practice Principles is the opportunity for choice, that is that individuals agree to share PII only with full understanding of the use the collector will make of it. Individuals generally choose by (1) consciously deciding to participate, that is, by **opting-in** or, (2) consciously deciding not to participate, by **opting-out**. EU law generally requires an opt-in procedure, but the opt-out approach has taken hold in the U.S., both in such laws as the Gramm/Leach/Bliley (G/L/B) financial modernization regulations and in self-regulatory privacy policies for businesses. Individuals are assumed to have opted-in unless they opt-out in person, in writing, verbally, or over the phone by a touch-tone signal, or online by clicking responses on a menu, or by sending an e-mail message. Additional opting methods will likely be developed in the future as constrained by communication technology, laws, or regulations.

Europeans' experience with totalitarian regimes has caused them to highly value their privacy, and they therefore insist on the opt-in approach. With an opt-in approach, the database of PII grows only as a result of consumers receiving value in exchange for their PII. They need to do nothing to protect their privacy. A data collector has no right to collect or use any individual's PII until he or she grants permission.

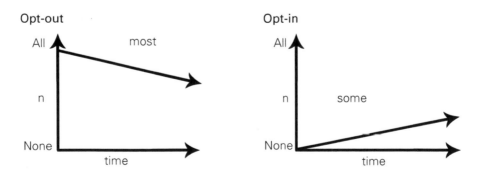

Figure 6. Comparing Opt-out with Opt-in

Comparing Opt-Out with Opt-in

In the U.S., the PII-data-management industry prefers the opt-out approach. The database is large at the outset and declines only slowly because subject individuals must act to withdraw their consent. Further, the opting procedure is controlled by the data manager. Making a choice can be facilitated, but data managers are more likely to do this for choosing the opt-in approach. Instead, as already well documented in the first wave of G/L/B privacy notices during 2001, when data managers control the opting procedure, it is likely to be ambiguous, difficult, even bewildering. The data managers' interests lie in discouraging individuals from opting out.

Privacy and Mass Customization and Mass Personalization

"Mass" anything and personalization or customization seem, at first glance, to be mutually exclusive. In reality, efficiency (profitability) comes from extensive use of customization and personalization. Mass customization is the delivery of highly specific, custom if you will, mass-produced products. An example of an easy way to customize a product is monogramming a hat or a shirt. An example of a more difficult way to customize a product is to tailor a car or a computer specifically to a customer's preferences. Customization requires the active participation of the customer, personalization, however, requires only the collection and aggregation of preexisting information — data collected online about buying habits or collected through loyalty programs. Personalization, even when based on custom content about preferences collected on a Web

site usually does not depend on the cooperation, or even the knowledge, of the customers. Almost always, companies use personalization to entice customers with offerings that suit their profiled interests.

The problem is that mass personalization is basically a broadcast approach, not much different from mass marketing although marketers hope it is far narrower. In their mass-personalization attempts, marketers make assumptions based on what information they have. These assumptions determine the advertisements they direct to individual   customers. When the efficacy of online advertising is measured by objective means, marketers flourish or perish according to the quality of their assumptions, analysis, and recommendations. Mass personalization is taking place in an environment of mass distribution where marketers have the opportunity to readily gather information about individuals or groups.

Before the digital era, few could have envisioned that so much information would become available for commercial use. As the debate on privacy versus personalization continues, the marketplace will seek more productive ways of using the information we gather and how to more efficiently deliver it to meet demand. John McCarthy at Forrester Research commented that consumer concerns about privacy cost online businesses at least $15 billion annually. With such a financial impact, the pressures to invade the privacy of individuals will increase.

About the Contributors

Nirmal Pal is the Executive Director of the eBusiness Research Center (eBRC) at the Pennsylvania State University. He assumed this role in February 2000. Under his leadership, eBRC is now considered a preeminent research center in this country. eBRC has established a network of world-renowned scholars and many of their research papers are available on line at the eBRC web site. Nirmal is sought after by the media for his expert opinion for many e-business and related topics. He has given talks on e-business in many conferences both at national and international levels. eBRC published a book in 2001 called Pushing the Digital Frontier, which was rated by the Choice magazine as one of the two best academic titles of 2001. Before joining the University, he was Director, IBM Global Services Consulting Group, White Plains, NY. As one of the leaders of IBM's e-business consulting activities, he was responsible for business development in this space, as well as development of supporting analytics, methods, tools and other intellectual assets for this new area of consulting and services. He had been a member of IBM Consulting Group's management team since its inception in 1991 that helped grow the business for this unit to over one billion US dollars and over 5000 consultants, in just seven years. He has degrees from Polytechnic University of New York: Master of Science (Computer Science): 1984 and Jadavpur University, Calcutta, India: Bachelor of Electrical Engineering: 1961.

Arvind Rangaswamy is the Jonas H. Anchel Professor of Marketing at Penn State, where he is also co-founder and Research Director of the eBusiness Research Center. He received a PhD in marketing from Northwestern University, an MBA from the Indian Institute of Management, Calcutta, and a B.Tech from the Indian Institute of Technology, Madras. Before joining Penn State, he was a faculty member at the J.L. Kellogg Graduate School of Management, Northwestern University, and at the Wharton School, University of Pennsylvania. He is actively engaged in research to develop concepts, methods and models to improve the efficiency and effectiveness of marketing using information technologies, including such topics as marketing modeling, online customer behavior and online negotiations. He is internationally recognized for his research on these topics. He has numerous publications in such leading journals as Marketing Science, Journal of Marketing Research, Management Science, Journal of Marketing, International Journal of Research in Marketing, Marketing Letters, Psychometrika, Multivariate Behavioral Research, and Journal of Economics and Statistics. He is Area Editor for Marketing Science and serves on the editorial boards of The Journal of Interactive Marketing, International Journal of Intelligent Systems in Accounting, Finance, and Management, Journal of Service Research, and the Journal of Business-to-Business Marketing. Recently, he co-authored a successful book titled, Marketing Engineering: Computer-Assisted Marketing Analysis and Planning, now in its second edition. Prof. Rangaswamy is a Fellow of the IC2 Institute (www.icc.org), an IBM Faculty Partner (2000-01), and the Chair of the e-Business Section of The Institute for Operations Research and the Management Sciences (INFORMS). He has consulted for a number of companies including Marriott, Xerox, IBM, Kodak, Nokia, PPG Industries, AT&T, TVS (India), Bristol-Myers Squibb, Walker Digital, Peapod, and Syngenta.

John Adcox has developed strategies using both new and traditional media to create memorable experiences — and tell stories with impact. His creative work makes people sit up, take notice, and say wow. He is presently a consultant and freelance creative director, writer, and information architect. Most recently, John was Chief Creative Officer at Talisman Creative, and Vice President/Regional Director of the Digital Media Group at Caribiner International. There, he served as a strategist creative director, and team leader on projects for a number of major clients, including BMC Software, IBM, Nortel, BellSouth, Clarus, 3M, Glaxo Wellcome, Home Depot, and several others. John has also worked as a communication strategy consultant/information architect for Southern Company, Lucent Technologies, Travelers Group, MindSpring, Glue Communications, New World Marketing and more. He even designed CD-ROM games for Turner Interactive. Previously, he was Executive Producer and Creative Director at Cadmus Interactive, where he designed and produced interactive solutions for Lucent Technologies, AT&T, MCI, Holiday Inn, BellSouth, Delta Air Lines, NBC, IBM, Coca-Cola, First Union Bank, Cox Communications, Scientific Atlanta and several others. A former radio host and Astronomy teacher, John has also written and designed collateral materials, newspaper and magazine articles, press releases, video scripts, a play, and a soon-to-be-published book on content strategy for new media and a novel. He has won Invision and Show South Creative Gold Awards.

John Bagby's areas of expertise integrate cyber law, securities regulations, regulatory process, and business organizations. He has completed funded research projects in liability risk management, and technology transfer. He teaches regulatory process, business organizations, securities regulation, and intellectual property. He joined the School of Information Sciences and Technology after 18 years with Penn State's Smeal College of Business Administration, where he was a professor of business law. He is codirector of the Institute for Information Policy. Bagby's legal practice experience involved clerkships for a Multi-national oil company and with a Wall Street law firm in matters of securities regulation, regulatory and commercial law. He conducted post-graduate MBA work at New York University.

Anant Balakrishnan is Professor of Management Science and Information Systems and holds the McCombs Endowed Chair in Business at the University of Texas at Austin. He has previously held faculty appointments in the business schools at MIT, Penn State, and Purdue. Mr. Balakrishnan received his Ph.D. from MIT; he holds an undergraduate degree in Electronics engineering from Indian Institute of Technology and

MBA from Indian Institute of Management. Dr. Balakrishnan's research and teaching interests include operations and supply chain management, management science, and telecommunications. His research focuses on modeling and solving decision and planning problems in supply chain management and telecommunications. Dr. Balakrishnan has worked closely with several manufacturing and service firms, and published in leading journals such as Management Science, Networks, Operations Research, Information Systems Research, Transportation Science, Manufacturing & Service Operations Management, and Mathematical Programming. Professor Balakrishnan serves on the editorial boards of several journals. His professional awards include the Zannetos Prize for research, and the Salgo-Noren award for teaching. He was Vice-President of Subdivisions for INFORMS (Institute for Operations Research and the Management Sciences).

Judy Cavalieri, Vice President Emerging Products, leads AT&T Wireless' Emerging Productlines including GoPhone and Prepaid Services. She has accountability for developing new products and offers and driving the overall profitability of these products that enable AT&T Wireless to serve the next quartile of customers entering the wireless category. Cavalieri previously was the Product Manager for AT&T Direct Services and was instrumental in growing that product line to be over $1 billion dollars annually for AT&T. She also served as a Director of Business Marketing for AT&T Wireless Services where she led the successful introduction of AT&T Wireless Corporate Digital Advantage program, which is now the flagship business offer for Enterprise customers. Beginning her telecommunications career nearly 15 years ago as a Marketing Manager at AT&T, Cavalieri subsequently held positions in Sales, AT&T Labs, Customer Care, Product Management and International. She ultimately served as International Marketing Director leading AT&T Consumers International business, which generated more than $2 billion in annual revenues. In January 2001, Ms. Cavalieri moved from AT&T to AT&T Wireless to become Sr. Director of its eBusiness program. In 18 months, she led the eBusiness program from 1M to 3M online customer service customers and winning an award as one of InfoWorlds Top 100 Innovative Firms. Ms. Cavalieri earned a Bachelors of Science degree from Rutgers University and an M.B.A. from Rutgers Graduate School of Management.

Ingemar J. Cox was a member of the Technical Staff at AT&T Bell Labs at Murray Hill from 1984 until 1989 where his research interests were focused on mobile robots. In 1989 he joined NEC Research Institute in Princeton, NJ as a senior research scientist in the computer science division. At NEC, his research shifted to problems in computer vision and he was responsible for creating the computer vision group at NECI. He has worked on problems to do with stereo and motion correspondence and multimedia issues of image database retrieval and watermarking. In 1999, he was awarded the IEEE Signal Processing Society Best Paper Award (Image and Multidimensional Signal Processing Area) for a paper he co-authored on watermarking. From 1997-1999, he served as Chief Technical Officer of Signafy, Inc, a subsidiary of NEC responsible for the commercialization of watermarking. In 1999, he returned to NEC Research Institute as a research Fellow. He is a senior member of the IEEE and on the editorial board of the Int. Journal of Autonomous Robots and Pattern Analysis and Applications Journal. He is co-author of a book entitled "Digital Watermarking" and the co-editor of two books, `Autonomous Robots Vehicles' and `Partitioning Data Sets: With Applications to Psychology, Computer Vision and Target Tracking'. Dr. Cox received his B.Sc. from University College London and Ph.D. from Oxford University.

Anindya Datta is the CEO and founder of a venture-backed software company called Chutney Technologies, and is regarded as an industry authority on Web infrastructure issues. As a renowned "thought leader", Anindya is frequently invited to speak at industry events. Recently, he delivered presentations at Supercomm 2001, Networld+Interop Fall 2001, and the SunTrust Internet Acceleration Conference. A substantial contributor to several innovations, Anindya holds numerous patents for a variety of data management and Internet technologies. He has also worked on broadcast technologies for mobile users and the access security of subscription-based broadcast information services. In addition to his leadership of Chutney, Anindya is an Associate Professor at The Georgia Institute of Technology and Founder of the iXL Center for Electronic Commerce. Previously, he was an Assistant Professor at the University of Arizona, after finishing his doctoral studies at the University of Maryland, College Park. Anindya's undergraduate education was completed at the Indian Institute of Technology, Kharagpur. His primary research interests lie in studying technologies that have the potential to significantly impact the automated processing of organizational information. He has published over 50 papers in prestigious refereed journals such as ACM Transactions on Database Systems, IEEE Transactions on Knowledge and Data Engineering, INFORMS Journal of Computing, and the VLDB Journal, and in reputed conferences such as ACM SIGMOD, and VLDB. He has also chaired as well as served on the program committees of reputed international conferences and workshops.

Mary Donato is Vice President of the Global TeleWeb Channel for Dun & Bradstreet. Previously, she held a similar position at Xerox Corporation. Global TeleWeb utilizes professional sales representatives to cover the market using a blend of telephony and Web enabled technologies in a Contact Center environment. Prior to this role, Mary was VP of Industry and Marketplace Transformation for Xerox's North American Solutions Group. She led the North American transition of Xerox into an industry focused marketing organization. From 1996 to 1999, Mary was VP of Worldwide Marketing for Xerox Business Services with annual worldwide revenues in excess of $3 billion. XBS provides document and facilities management services to more than 5,200 companies in 40 countries. Prior to XBS, Mary was the Director of Integrated Marketing for Xerox Canada creating and implementing marketing strategies. She spent 4 years in Minnesota as District Manager where she consistently led the team with double-digit revenue and profit growth while increasing levels of customer and employee satisfaction. From 1987 to 1990, she was Sales Operations Manager for the Central Region living in Chicago and started her career with Xerox in Columbus, Ohio. Mary earned a Bachelor's of Arts degree in Psychology with Honors from Ohio State University with a minor in Business Communications. She is a member of the Penn State University eBRC (Electronic Business Research Center) Advisory Board, leads the Marketing Council of the American Management Association.

C. Lee Giles is the David Reese Professor of Information Sciences and Technology, Professor of Computer Science and Engineering, and Associate Director of Research at the eBusiness Research Center at Penn State University, University Park, PA. Currently, he is a consulting research scientist in Computer Science at NEC Research Institute, Princeton, NJ; and adjunct Professor in Computer and Information Science at the University of Pennsylvania. His research interests are in web and Internet computing, computational models of e-business, intelligent information processing and agents, and fundamental models of intelligent systems. He is a Fellow of the IEEE and a member of AAAI, ACM, and AAAS. His previous positions include that of program manager for the Air Force Office of Scientific Research. His graduate degrees are from the University of Michigan and University of Arizona.

Eric Glover is a research staff member at NEC Laboratories America in Princeton, NJ. He received his PhD in Computer Science Engineering from the University of Michigan, Ann Arbor, in the summer of 2001. His research interests include extending search beyond simple keywords, and focusing on issues related to multiple data sources and multiple user needs. Research interests also include web mining, data discovery, and classification.

Gerald Häubl is the Banister Professor of Electronic Commerce and Associate Professor of Marketing at the University of Alberta's School of Business. He is also the founding director of the Institute for Online Consumer Studies (iocs.org). His primary areas of expertise are consumer behavior in electronic shopping environments, human-computer interaction, consumer decision-making, persuasion, preference construction, the formation of value judgments, and bidding behavior in auctions. The Marketing Science Institute, the Social Sciences and Humanities Research Council of Canada, the Austrian National Science Foundation, and various corporations have funded Professor Häubl's research. He is the recipient of several research-related awards and prizes, including the 2000 Petro-Canada Young Innovator Award.

Terry Madonia began her AT&T career in 1982 as a Market Research Manager in the Market Research Service Center. From 1985 – 1995 she held positions in Marketing for AT&T Consumer Services including: Consumer Long Distance, Calling Card and Operator Services, and International Consumer Services. From 1995 – 1996 she held a corporate Strategy and Planning position for AT&T Corporate Headquarters. In 1996, Terry moved to AT&T Business Services where she was Marketing Director Wireless Offers. In 1999, Terry became the Chief of Staff for the office of the President of Consumer Services Group. Following that assignment, Terry became the Vice President for International Consumer Marketing where she had P&L responsibility for AT&T's International Consumer business worldwide. Her latest assignment is with AT&T Wireless Services, where she is the Vice President for Business Marketing and E-Business. Terry has her Bachelor of Arts in Psychology from Lafayette College in Easton, Pennsylvania and her MBA in Marketing from Seton Hall University in South Orange, New Jersey.

Eren Manavoglu is a Research Assistant in School of Information Sciences and Technology, The Pennsylvania State University. She received her B.S. (1999) degree in control and computer engineering from Istanbul Technical University. She is currently working on her M.S. thesis in Computer Science and Engineering Department at The Pennsylvania State University. Her research interests include intelligent information processing and novel applications of machine learning and AI in Web computing, information extraction, and personalized information retrieval.

Alan L. Montgomery is Associate Professor of marketing at the Graduate School of Industrial Administration, Carnegie Mellon University. His fields of interest include electronic commerce, micro marketing, pricing, and data mining. Some current research projects include the design of shopbots, customization of pricing strategies to micro-markets, automated approaches to the analysis of marketing data, new methodologies for estimating consumer price sensitivity, using radio airplay to forecast album sales, and forecasting time series using non-linear models. Dr. Montgomery's research on electronic commerce has focused on how to extract value from a Web user's session history. Specifically he has modeled browsing behavior across web sites and through time, and is currently working on predicting purchase behavior using clickstream data. An important finding to date shows that previous usage history is the best predictor of current behavior. Dr. Montgomery's research has appeared in a variety of publications including Advances in Econometrics, IEEE Computer, Interfaces, Journal of Marketing Research, Journal of the American Statistical Association, Marketing Science, Case Studies in Bayesian Statistics, and Computational Statistics & Data Analysis. He holds Ph.D. and M.B.A. degrees in Marketing and Statistics from the University of Chicago and a B.S. degree in Economics from the University of Illinois at Chicago.

Kyle B. Murray is an interdisciplinary PhD student in Business and Psychology at the University of Alberta. His research focuses on consumer judgment and decision making, with an emphasis on how consumers make choices in electronic environments. Murray's work in this area has been published in the Journal of Consumer Psychology, Communications of the Association for Computing Machinery, and Advances in Consumer Research. As an educator in the field of electronic marketing Murray has taught undergraduate, MBA and executive level courses in e-commerce. He has also been active as a consultant for a variety of organizations in fields as diverse as oil and gas, manufacturing, financial services, retailing, and not-for-profit enterprises. Murray acknowledges the support provided by the Province of Alberta Graduate Fellowship and the Institute for Online Consumer Studies, as well as the Social Sciences and Humanities Research Council of Canada through its Initiative on the New Economy Research Alliances Program (SSHRC 538-2002-1013) and its Doctoral Fellowship Program.

David M. Pennock is a Senior Research Scientist at Overture Sciences, Inc. Prior to joining Overture, he held a similar position at the NEC Research Institute in Princeton, New Jersey, and an Adjunct Assistant Professor at Pennsylvania State University. Dr. Pennock's areas of interest include electronic commerce, recommender systems, the World Wide Web, and decision theory. He has published numerous articles in peer-reviewed journals and conferences, including a Finalist for Best Student Paper. Dr. Pennock has patented a method for providing accurate personalized recommendations to customers. He interned at Microsoft

Research in 1998. Dr. Pennock has a Ph.D. in Computer Science from the University of Michigan, an M.S. in Computer Science from Duke University, and a B.S. in Physics from Duke University.

Kirk Rothrock is the President of Intracorp, a subsidiary of CIGNA Corporation. Intracorp is the nation's largest medical case management firm, utilizing clinical resources, medical research and technology to improve medical outcomes in workers' compensation, disability and healthcare programs. The company pioneered the concept of medical management over 30 years ago, and today counts more than 20,000 organizations among its customers. During his tenure, Intracorp has been recognized as an industry leader in leveraging technology and, specifically, the Internet to speed critical medical information flow, improve decision making, and ensure quality regarding appropriate treatment protocols for sick and injured patients. A fifteen-year healthcare veteran, Rothrock has held leadership positions at Humana, Employers Health Insurance, and Blue Cross & Blue Shield. Rothrock earned his bachelor's degree in education and master's degree in business administration from the Pennsylvania State University.

Venkatesh (Venky) Shankar is the Ralph J. Tyser Fellow and a Professor of Marketing and Entrepreneurship at the Robert H. Smith School of Business, University of Maryland. His areas of specialization are e-Business, Competitive Strategy, Entrepreneurship, International Marketing, Supply Chain Management, and Bioinformatics. He has a Ph.D. in marketing from the Kellogg Graduate School of Management, Northwestern University and has won research awards from American Marketing Association (AMA), Center for International Business Research and Education, the Government of Canada, IBM, and the Marketing Science Institute. His research has been published in the Journal of Marketing Research, Marketing Science, Marketing Letters, and the Journal of Retailing, Wall Street Journal, Financial Times, Chief Executive and Executive Excellence. He is winner of the 2001 IBM Faculty Partnership Award, the 1999 Paul Green Award, and the 2000 Don Lehman Award. He is an associate editor of Management Science and is also on the editorial boards of Marketing Science, International Journal of Research in Marketing, Journal of Retailing and the Journal of the Academy of Marketing Science. He is a two-time recipient of the Krowe Award for Outstanding Teaching at the Smith School of Business. He is a member of CNN's international business expert panel and has made several appearances on CNN, C-SPAN, and Voice of America. He is on several advisory boards, including IBM's e-Business Academic Advisory Committee, European e-Business Center, ESSEC, France, and Ingenium Corporation and is a Fellow of the e-Business Research Center at Pennsylvania State University.

Amanda Spink is an Associate Professor at the School of Information Sciences at the University of Pittsburgh. She has a B.A. (Australian National University); Graduate Diploma of Librarianship (University of New South Wales); M.B.A. (Fordham University), and a Ph.D. in Information Science (Rutgers University). Dr. Spink's research focuses on theoretical and applied studies of human information behavior and interactive information retrieval (IR), including Web and digital libraries studies. The National Science Foundation, Andrew R. Mellon Foundation, NEC, IBM, Excite, FAST and Lockheed Martin have sponsored her research. She has published over 180 journal articles and conference papers, with many in the Journal of the American Society for Information Science and Technology, Information Processing and Management, Interacting with Computers, IEEE Computer, and Internet Research, the ASIST and ISIC Conferences.

Kannan Srinivasan is H.J. Heinz II Professor of Management, Marketing and Information Systems at Carnegie Mellon University. Prior to earning his Ph.D. at the University of California at Los Angeles, Kannan worked as a product manager at Procter & Gamble. His recent research interests include dynamic Internet data analysis, dynamic pricing, Marketing/Information Systems interface, Impact of Electronic Data Interchange, New Business Models for E-Commerce. He has extensively published in leading journals. He was a member of the steering committee that launched the first full-time Master of Science in Electronic Commerce program, a joint initiative by the business and computer science schools at Carnegie Mellon. Kannan was nominated for the Leland Bach Teaching Award in 1991, 1993, 1995 and 1996. He has also taught at the graduate schools of business at The University of Chicago and Stanford University. He has worked on numerous consulting projects and executive teaching engagements with firms such as General Motors, Asea-Brown Boveri, Kodak, Chrysler, Fujitsu, IBM, Calgon Carbon, Kraft Foods, IKEA, Management Science Associates, McKinsey &Co., Pricewaterhouse Coopers, and United Technologies. He actively works with Internet startups. He serves on the board/ advisory board of these companies as well as advisory board of a venture capital firm. He is also Director of the Center for E-Business Innovation (eBI) at Carnegie Mellon University. In collaboration with eBI, Pricewaterhouse Coopers has developed a comprehensive tool (known as emm@) to assess the e-business maturity of firms.

Tony Summerlin is managing consultant and Senior Vice President of the Touchstone Consulting Group. Before joining Touchstone, he was vice-president of e-Business at Unisys Corporation. He brings a proven talent for identifying and implementing e-business strategies and a knack for spotting and exploiting new markets. Before joining Unisys, Tony held a number of executive positions in marketing and management, helping companies transform their businesses, develop innovative products, and dramatically increase sales and profitability. As president of Provenance Systems, a fledgling Canadian e-records management company, Tony conceived an Internet-based records management system recognized as a breakthrough paradigm by leading technical consultants. While Tony was vice president of sales and marketing for USI, a $100 million product and solution provider, he developed the "e.State" methodology for value-added services – the first consultative tool capable of defining existing e-business/e-commerce capabilities and delivering a roadmap for improvement. From 1995 to 1997, Tony was executive vice president and president Europe/Asia/ Australasia Division for London-based LAVA Systems. Tony has also held senior executive positions, including director of corporate development for emerging technologies, Omni International; senior vice president/managing director, Washington Capital Markets; and senior vice president and managing director, Mercantile Bank and Trust/F&M Bank. Tony earned a masters degree in business administration from Loyola College in Baltimore and a Bachelor of Arts degree in Latin American studies and journalism from the University of North Carolina, Chapel Hill.

Helen Thomas is an Assistant Professor of Management Information Systems at Carnegie Mellon University. Her research interests include data management in e-commerce and decision support databases. Helen is also a co-founder and V.P. of Research for Chutney Technologies, a software company that develops solutions to improve the scalability and performance of enterprise web applications. Helen is a technical expert in the area of decision support databases. She has considerable experience in the design and development of commercial data warehousing/OLAP solutions and has served as the lead on several commercial projects. Prior to her contributions to the database technologies on which Chutney is based, Helen played a major role in the design, development and implementation of STORM, a scientific data warehousing application for the USDA Southwest Watershed Research Center. She also led a project to develop data mining models to predict customer churn for the telecom industry. Helen has significant consulting experience, including several years working with American Management Systems. She has published articles in well-known information systems journals, such as Information Systems Research and Decision Support Systems. Helen received her Ph.D. from Georgia Tech. She also received an M.S.E. degree in Operations Research and Industrial Engineering from the University of Texas at Austin, and a B.S. degree in Decision and Information Sciences from the University of Maryland at College Park.

Valerie Trifts is a Ph.D. candidate in Marketing at the University of Alberta. She received her B.B.A. from the University of Prince Edward Island and her M.B.A. from Saint Mary's University. She is currently a lecturer in Marketing at Dalhousie University, teaching Consumer Behavior, Marketing Research, and Internet Marketing at both the undergraduate and graduate level. Her work has been published in Marketing Science and the Journal of Consumer Psychology, and she has presented papers at Association for Consumer Research and Marketing Science conferences. Her research interests include electronic commerce, interactive decision aids, and trust in online shopping environments.

Debra VanderMeer holds a Ph.D. in Computer Science from the Georgia Institute of Technology. Her research interests include performance and scalability improvement in e-commerce systems, with particular emphasis on data-intensive systems and personalization, as well as the design of mobile data access systems. She is currently the Director of Technical Services for Chutney Technologies, a software company that develops solutions to improve the scalability and performance of enterprise web applications. Debra has considerable experience in the design and development of commercial software systems. Prior to commencing her doctoral studies, she worked for Tandem Computers on the development of public key infrastructure software. She has published articles in well-known computer science journals, such as ACM Transactions on Database Systems, IEEE Transactions on Knowledge and Data Engineering, and the VLDB Journal. Debra received an M.S. degree from the University of Arizona, and a B.S. degree from Georgetown University.

James Z. Wang, holder of the endowed PNC Technologies Career Development Professorship, is an assistant professor of the School of Information Sciences at The Pennsylvania State University. He is also the Vice Director of the Intelligent Information Systems Laboratory and an Associate Research Fellow of the e-Business Research Center. He received a Summa Cum Laude Bachelor's degree in Mathematics and Computer Science from University of Minnesota (1994), an M.S. in Mathematics and an M.S. in Computer Science, both from Stanford University (1997), and a Ph.D. degree in Medical Information Sciences from Stanford University's Biomedical Informatics and Database groups (2000). His research interests include semantics-sensitive image retrieval, biomedical informatics, learning-based linguistic indexing of images/image classification, art image retrieval, and computer vision. His monograph Integrated Region-based Image Retrieval has been published by Kluwer Academic Publishers and included in the Kluwer Series on Information Retrieval. He is the author or coauthor of more than 40 journal articles, book chapters, and refereed conference papers.

The SIMPLIcity system he coauthored has been sought after and obtained by researchers from more than 50 institutions. He has served as a Program Committee Vice Chair for the 12th International World Wide Web Conference and as a reviewer for 30+ scientific journals and many conferences. He has been invited to serve on government panels including the EU/DELOS-US/NSF Working Group on Digital Imagery for Significant Cultural and Historical Materials and National Academies Panel on Tools and Strategies for Protecting Kids from Pornography and Their Applicability to Other Inappropriate Internet Content.

Bruce Weinberg is a leading authority on the online consumer experience. His research is focused on issues that pertain to a variety of online consumer experiences, including m-commerce and u-commerce, e.g., his 24/7/360° concept. His research on what he calls Exchange Spaces looks at places where buyers and sellers come together, such as online auction environments, and analyzes them from a marketing and customer satisfaction perspective. Weinberg has developed the first course in the world that is focused exclusively on exploring and understanding the online consumer experience. His research and teaching have been featured or covered in books and media such as The Wall Street Journal, MSNBC, Business 2.0 and NPR. Inc. Magazine dubbed him The Netty Professor and Ericsson selected him as one of their On People for the year 2000. In his Internet Shopping 24/7 Project he immersed himself in studying online shopping as a participant observer by retail shopping exclusively online for one year. Weinberg has conducted research or consulting, and made keynote presentations or participated in special events with many fortune 500 companies and significant associations. He earned his PhD at the MIT Sloan School of Management and BA in Computer Science/Mathematics at Boston University. Weinberg has received awards for both teaching and research -- e.g., in 1997, he received the MSI/H. Paul Root Award from the American Marketing Association for the "most significant contribution to the advancement of marketing practice" for the paper "Premarket Forecasting of Really-New Products" published in the Journal of Marketing. His publications have appeared in journals such as the Journal of Marketing, Journal of Marketing Research, Journal of Interactive Marketing, Marketing Science Institute and Advances in Consumer Research.

Mike Wittenstein has 18 years of successful experience with theory & ideas as well as with practice & profit. Most recently, as a leading consultant and "e-visionary" for IBM's management consulting practice, Mike identified early-stage opportunities for the company and its clients and built two consulting practices. Experience Architecture (the design and implementation of customer-centric business strategies) and

Adaptive Marketing (1:1 marketing as whole business strategy) were his latest efforts and are what brought him to our attention as a contributor to this book. Prior to IBM, Mike led Galileo, an award-winning interactive agency, as its CEO, launched two software start-ups, and consulted on and supported sales force automation software. A frequent speaker and writer, Mike is a Phi Beta Kappa graduate of the University of Florida and earned an MBA in International Management from Thunderbird. He also represented the US in exchange programs to Brazil and the former Soviet Union; as a result he is fluent in English, Portuguese, Spanish, and Russian.

Index

ISBN 141201121-3